T0366005

BUDDY PAYS
ATTENTION

A COLLECTION OF PERSONAL ESSAYS

JOSEPH N. MUZIO

Order this book online at www.trafford.com
or email orders@trafford.com

Most Trafford titles are also available at major online book retailers.

Print information available on the last page.

ISBN: 978-1-6987-1191-1 (sc)
ISBN: 978-1-6987-1192-8 (e)

Library of Congress Control Number: 2022908560

Trafford rev. 06/25/2022

 www.trafford.com

North America & international
toll-free: 844-688-6899 (USA & Canada)
fax: 812 355 4082

PROLOGUE AND ACKNOWLEDGEMENTS

"THE essay is the most direct form of expression. An essayist is a writer and describer." Edward Hoagland's memoir, <u>Compass Points: How I Lived.</u>

After retiring and then moving to Rockport, Massachusetts after living in Leonia, New Jersey for almost 46 years, there was new time to observe, think, reflect, analyze and write. This was the first time since early childhood my life was not being governed by the clock or by required schedules. No long car trips to and from the college in Brooklyn; no classes to prepare and teach; no meetings to attend; no reports to submit; and certainly no occupational appointments, evaluations, or other professional obligations and commitments. Adaptations had to be made; new ways of spending this unencumbered time had to be identified.

Let me offer clarifying explanation regarding my recent interest in personal writing, which includes the completed memoir about my parents <u>Buddy Remembers – Then and Now</u> and this <u>Buddy Pays Attention – A Collection of Personal Essays</u>. I began seriously practicing the discipline and habits of memoir and personal writing. One has to be dedicated and focused. One doesn't just write only when you're in the mood. Even on days I don't have much to write about, I still habitually write. My pattern is to get up early in the morning, and look at the beauty and silence of a new day.

There's peace and quiet in the morning. A person can write anywhere. From the standpoints of time, location, history and beauty, Rockport, Massachusetts is an exceptionally fine milieu in which to write.

The writing of personal essays is an engaging, absorbing and serious descriptive process. Essentially, it is a mental discourse with one's self. The reader is encouraged to at least try it and decide if you like it. Besides writing essays, you can keep a journal or diary of thoughts, feelings and activities (even your remembered dreams), they can provide a more permanent gathering of a person's journey. My simple suggestion is to write about subjects or matters that are directly familiar to you and those you are concerned about.

Writing personal essays, poetry, song lyrics, books and the spoken words are well beyond the more transient, hurried electronic transmissions so prevalent in today's accelerating society. Despite the many advantages and privileges of engaging electronic advances, information storage approaches, and the ability to modify what one has written, I still prefer the words-on-paper format. A belated thanks to my loving attentive mother who gave me a portable Royal Typewriter and taught me how to type when I was 12 years old.

Writing is a major component of those unique human traits, along with art, music and language. All of them encompass at least some reasons humans transcend other life forms in our evolutionary development. To put one's thoughts into the written, observable, recorded, more permanent format is a complex and sometimes mysterious process. It is a creative human experience that requires discipline, thought and effort. Writers struggle with critical analytical decisions as to which words and sentences clearly and accurately convey their thought processes. Sometimes this can be simple and other times it can be exhausting; there are times it requires major revisions, other times few. And yet there are doubts as to how these decisions pan out. Has the writer done what he/she set out to do? When is the writing finished?

We do not escape our past and those influential forces from our childhood coupled with our subsequent experiences in life. They are still with us, in our memories and feelings. There are references to this author's childhood and earlier years of deep involvement in the Roman Catholic Church; years as a United States Marine Corps Officer and their impact; and his having spent almost 50 years in the education/ research profession. All of these experiences and others have had direct bearing on my thinking processes, behavior, development, and beliefs along with more recent reflective writing interests. All of these factors contribute to the template or writing process.

Each essay in this personal collection can stand on its own; there is no singular overriding theme to them, at least not to me. If you think you can decipher one, please contact me and let me know what it is. In many, I present related questions. Why are there long-standing troubles and issues that seem to go on forever without resolutions? Are there plausible answers? What explains the personal actions carried out or ignored?

Various topics unfolding in our society and culture are disconcerting; others are more troublesome tragic ones; and others have been in existence seemingly forever. The history and untoward repercussions of assassinations of our leaders; the civil-rights actions still existing; riots in our cities; the environmental movements during the 1960s and 1970s and more recently; the Viet Nam disaster; economic disruptions, unresolved social and environmental issues; and global public health and contagion disease issues, along with chronic widespread poverty and inequality are integral to understanding our nation's issues and the world beyond our country.

No doubt similar and even more tragic issues have existed throughout human history and diverse civilizations. Such subjects require careful and open analysis, and must be given thoughtful treatments if we want to understand the dynamics taking place across our society and in our personal lives. You might not agree with what I've written, the approaches and emphasis, even the opinions and various interpretations. That's perfectly OK. What would life be if we all simply agreed on everything and somehow believed everything was all right? How dull and erroneous this would be. In a democratic society, we can believe and express conflicting thoughts and perspectives without having to hate others, or becoming irrational, bitter and cruel. We might benefit if there was more civility, more respect, more comity and new found kindness for others we differ with. We need to calm down and despite our disagreements, differences and prejudices, pay more attention to one another.

More of the earlier essays are shorter than those written later on. Perhaps the subject itself or those serious developing thoughts caused this. The <u>titles</u> of these personal essays often indicate the specific subjects. There is an essay about <u>Jackie Robinson</u>, the great ballplayer I saw at Ebbet's Field in Brooklyn. Two essays are about the subject of <u>Italian Americans: Pervasive Misrepresentation of Italian-Americans</u> and <u>Being An Italian-American - The Battle Goes On</u>. Some essays were originally written primarily for <u>Family and Friends</u> and have been revised. Subjects such as <u>College Fraternities, and on Rape and Sexual Harassment</u> and <u>The</u>

Slaughtering of Children are ongoing provocative matters. There's a Eulogy about a special dear friend; and another about another friend who committed suicide. The essay on Violence, along with others about life experiences that are expressions of serious concern; sometimes they focus on our country and individuals. Some essays in this collection are about members of our family and friends and involve the entwining of our lives.

There are even essays that focus on broader ethical/moral issues of large institutions and individuals. For example, the behavior of the high level Volkswagen Corporation executives in major illegal clandestine practices and their intended cover up regarding the diesel engines in millions of purchased vehicles. Several essays focus on Donald Trump's noted behavior. In my opinion, before and throughout his presidency, he exhibited deceitful political machinations and used destructive approaches to our nation's internal and external problems. He specializes in lying and hurting others. Portions of the Remembrances: Vietnam War Memorial Visit essay were written more than 20 years ago, and were expanded to include further thoughts on issues about war and killings. As for the essay Attention Must Be Paid, which is about Arthur Miller's play Death of a Salesman, it's the source of the personal essays collection's title. We all need to pay attention.

Over the years I've noticed how some friends and others, including college students would comment on those things they were reluctant to do, are afraid of, or would dislike doing. That list is pretty straightforward and can include: Making a formal speech in public; preparing an important writing assignment with a specific deadline date; or being near a snake, a spider, seeing a rat, or even observing someone with a physical injury pain and discomfort. There are undoubtedly many other similar situations. When such events do present themselves, that person typically expresses avoidance, an irrational fear or possible phobia and then blurts out their reason do doing so.

Such irrational mental/physical strictures can control a wider variety of lifetime experiences and potentially positive opportunities. They prevent us from reaching out for newer ones because of fear, and this can become a stifling pattern of avoidance and denial. It was either Ralph Waldo Emerson or Henry David Thoreau, I'm not sure which one of America's first home grown philosophers, might have warned how at death, such restrictive, irrational denial patterns can result in a life unlived.

A special thanks, long-term deep appreciation and admiration to my partner in life, Lois Grant Muzio. <u>These essays are dedicated to her.</u> Lois carefully read many of these essays in their earlier stages. She provides rational and positive reasons to pursue writing; offered suggestions and questions to help to make them clearer and better organized. Sometimes she was influential; occasionally for better or worse, I choose to disregard them.

Another vital thanks to my long-time dear friend and former colleague Sheldon Friedland. From early on, Shelly guided the electronic process so these essays could be posted on the web site <u>www.joemuzio.com</u> he designed and maintained. Over these years, his advice, patience and commitment are most appreciated. He provided graphics, instructions and humor. Without his involvement it is unlikely the progress made to date would have occurred.

Thanks to our sons Frank, Edward and Matthew who read these essays early on. Each offered thoughtful comments. A special thanks to our granddaughter Mia Frank Muzio, who patiently formatted these essays so they could be properly designed for printing. To our long-time dear friend, Thomas E. Ford, who read many of the essays and sent detailed written comments about each of them. And to Nicole Pagano, a dear family friend, who provided astute suggestions telephonically from Berkeley, California.

Finally, a special thanks to the Trafford Publishing team and staff for their guidance and our relationship, especially Eve Ardell, Josh Laluna and Fresno Factor for their support and competence throughout the arduous preparatory process.

It is noteworthy these selected topics and written statements along with any errors in them are solely my responsibilities and no one else's.

If you do read any of these personal essays and would like to communicate with me about them, it would be appreciated if you do. Thank you. Best wishes. Go well.

DEDICATED TO LOIS GRANT MUZIO

With love and admiration, she encourages and helps throughout my long journey and our lives.

GADFLY, n. 1. Any of various bloodsucking flies, esp. of the family Tabinidae (Tab-a-ni-day) to bit to annoy livestock and other animals (they include the horseflies. 2) One that acts as a constructive provocative stimulus. 3) One habitually engaged in provocative criticism of existing institutions.

(Provided by dear friends Diane and Tom Ford on the author's 80th birthday, June 4, 2012.)

TIGER WOODS

A SHORT time ago, the world-famous and perhaps the finest golfer ever, Tiger Woods had a car accident with his Escalade. But, it turned out to be much more. Besides the wrecked vehicle, some facial cuts, and a journey to a local hospital in Florida, suddenly and almost inexplicably, his world came down around him, his wife, his children and those who adore him. What happened?

While it's still unclear the correlation between the vehicle being damaged, windows broken by his wife with a golf club, and the police investigating and confirming no alcohol, a lot of new information rapidly unfolded. Apparently, Tiger had some relationships with other women besides his wife; at least eight women have come forward to broadcast their "kissing and telling." (There may be more, and not all of the announced 8 have been verified.)

America's media and those in Europe and elsewhere have been telling the world. There's talk of Tiger's many sponsors withdrawing; he's also withdrawn indefinitely from all golfing events; and he's announced to the world he needs private time to work on himself, his marriage and his relationship with his two children. He's publicly confirmed his "infidelities" and his fallibility, as he seeks forgiveness.

With this background, the underlying issue is: Why is America so fascinated with Tiger's behavior? Does it have anything to do with his incredible golfing abilities? Is it because he is on his way to being a billionaire? Is it because he's black (by definition) and the alleged partners are exclusively white? Are women's groups upset with his behavior because of the what it represents? How is his behavior remarkably unique in the powerful world of celebrity, money, and opportunity? Did any of us expect Tiger to be our "moral compass," our "spiritual leader?" Why do so many concern themselves about him? In the ultimate scheme of things, what did his behavior matter?

Within a reasonable time, Tiger will join the ranks of those whose behavior will be conveniently forgotten. He will be replaced by some other equally surprising transitory gossip. Right now, we're engaged in two wars. We are in the midst of the worst economic situation since the Great Depression, caused by greed, corruptions, arrogance, and ineffective regulations. More Americans are on food stamps than ever before. Millions are unemployed. Our nation's infrastructure is crumbling. Yet, there is inordinate concern and focus on Tiger Woods, his marriage, and where he and others choose to sleep together. Can anyone clearly and distinctly explain this preoccupation with Tiger? Or others in similar circumstances? Why?

2009

∞

ON LANGUAGE

L ANGUAGE is constantly changing. How words are put together, their meaning, the frequency with which these words are used, these and other factors undergo changes in daily and long-term contexts. Sometimes, there is even confusion, how one person expresses a word or thought can have a totally different interpretation to another person. In a conversation or in writing, language can be given a different perception, resulting in the person questioning saying "What did you mean by that?" as he/she seeks clarification. There's no doubt that language is dynamic.

Lately, I have been paying close attention to how people express themselves, to financial spokespersons explaining what has been occurring, to news and sports television commentators, and to the rest of us in general conversations as we move through our lives. For example, when someone asks a question of another person, why does the other person respond by repeating the same question? Or when you ask someone serving food or drink in a restaurant for water, why does the server automatically say "no problem?" Why would this have been a "problem" in the first place? And on that same restaurant topic, why does the server frequently refer to a mixed group as "guys" even though the majority of the group might be women? I've wondered what the reaction would be if it were a group of men and no women or only one and the server called to them "girls" or "gals" or some other inappropriate term? How about this: Right after you've chosen a particular item off of the menu, the server blurts out "good choice!" How does the server know this? Did he/she already eat that menu item? Were all the items on the menu "good choices?" Maybe it was a "good choice" for them, but not necessarily for you. What knowledge is available about your eating preferences and taste buds?

Here are some other things concerning language usage: Why are more and more speakers doubling the word "very" or "really" to modify a verb? Does this modification make it more "very" or "real?" How about the frequency of the word "actually" when someone is describing something, does this give it greater credence? Of course, there is far more use of the words "awesome" and "amazing" being used to describe rather ordinary events or situations, even viewing scenery or a new item just purchased. Everything about us is definitely "awesome" or "amazing." And if it isn't either of these, then it's just "cool," another overused term to fill space in conversation.

There are other strange things going on in word usage. The other day when I was talking to someone about a particular topic, he responded by saying "My bad." When I initially didn't understand, he repeated this and told me it meant he'd made a mistake; it was sort of a verbal shorthand acknowledging fallibility. Then I asked him why he just didn't say he'd made a mistake, and he had a puzzled look on his face. Maybe the more frequent use of texting and hurried communications is making us more tolerant of more abrupt language. There are all sorts of single-letters and abbreviations being used in texting, some of them only known to the users. Nevertheless, they are all forms of modified language usage, newer methods to rapidly communicate, and to get our verbal points across to others as we strive for greater clarity and understanding. Perhaps, eventually, we might devolve into just grunting or nodding to one another, and then we can start all over again.

2009

PRESIDENT OBAMA'S POLL RATINGS

A BOUT 13 months ago, our country's voters selected Barrack Obama to be its next president. He had a popular vote of more than 10 million over Senator John McCain. Spirits were high; there was more enthusiasm and optimism that we would have a new, refreshing, articulate, smart leader.

His administration was barely in office when it inherited a barrage of economic, military, and social issues. Almost immediately new efforts were undertaken, some of them as radical as those needed in the last Great Depression to hold the country and in some ways the global economy together. Some are beginning to work, others are still uncertain, and some of the issues still remain with us, especially the stress of unemployment by large numbers of our citizens. Many people are hurting, although banking and financial institutions appear to be recovering rather nicely for themselves and their high-ranking employees.

So, after incredibly high public ratings, President Obama's ratings have dropped considerably. Of course how such polls are taken, who are the respondents, and the possibility of underlying motives in those doing the polls, all of this is uncertain. What's interesting to me is we now evaluate our leaders the way we do TV programs, celebrities, movies and other activities in our society. Does a lowered rating for President Obama indicate he's doing the right or wrong things? What about the Senators and the Congressmen and women, are they doing the wrong or right things? Does the polling process give us any valid indication as to what is taking place in our entire nation of 306 million people, and the world's economy which is directly connected to our own conditions here at home? Did we seriously believe any one person and his administration could easily correct and modify what has been going on in our country for almost 20 or so years?

Please! Let's make an effort to think more clearly. Complicated issues, whether personal or institutional ones are not easily effectively solved. The existing economic chaos and its effects on so many will not be resolved with any magic wand. If they could be easily handled, then that would border on being a miracle, and miracles happen rarely, if ever.

Maybe we could all benefit if we stay as fully informed as possible, if we remain calm, cool, and collected, if we make sure our views on issues are not simply emotional reactions, and if put combined pressures on ALL of our elected officials to make sure they are carrying out their responsibilities in a comprehensive and sensitive manner. Polls are nothing but rushed opinions through fragmented and bias views.

2009

BERNIE MADOFF

THE other night after showering, getting in between clean bed sheets, pulling up the blankets and reading a book, my mind aimlessly wandered to another person. Suddenly, I was thinking about Bernie Madoff, now in a North Carolina Federal prison. According to a newspaper article, his cell mate is a 22 year old convicted drug dealer. Madoff received 150 year sentence; and he's in his mid 70s. His wife Ruth is supposedly getting an apartment near the prison so she can regularly visit her incarcerated husband.

What was I thinking about? Was Bernie Madoff mad? For the rest of his days he shares a minimal cell with another convicted felon; he wears prison garb instead of having a most elaborate wardrobe of suits and leisure clothes; each day he washes, urinates and defecates in public; his meals are routine, minimal prison chow; and rather than penthouses with expensive beautiful art objects, yachts and his home in Montauk he functions within a most depressing and dull, regimented confined existence, surrounded by equally dysfunctional persons.

His visits with his wife, his children and grandchildren will be under tight, observed controls. He befriended and scammed so many; he ruined friends, institutions, even those who believed in him, and inevitably himself. He joins the infamous, almost endless list of great financial wizards that have become the legacies of 20th century greed, corruption and evil. Bernie went up the ladder of dishonest materialistic success and he tumbled down in ultimate disgrace and failure. What a ride he has had.

I thought about how when the lights go out in his prison cell at night, does his mind ever wander about his life's outcome? Does he reflect about all of the people he financially destroyed? Does he ever hold his head in his hands and say "What have I done?" Does he chat with his 22-year-old cell bunkmate and advise him as to how he could live a better, more productive and decent life? What does he think about, if anything? How could he have become such a distorted selfish organism? Will he ever be a case study in graduate business programs or in ethics courses?

Addendum:

Madoff's wife Ruth divorced him; one son died of cancer; the other committed suicide.

2010

FOOD ALLERGIES

T ODAY in the media there was an announcement about how a new method is being used by some families to cope with their children's food allergies. Certainly this is a terribly serious topic; some children's food allergies are so severe they can have an immediate and devastating biological reaction, including death itself. But, let's examine the solution just presented today and you evaluate whether or not this does the trick.

Recently, selected dogs are being trained to sniff out a variety of food products capable of causing an allergic reaction in a child. The cost of this intense training is about $1500. Once the dog is fully prepared, he/she goes into the classroom of the child early in the school day and checks it out for these potentially dangerous food products. In addition, when that family goes out to restaurants or other places where food will be ordered and eaten, the dog accompanies the family. Then, before there is any consumption, the dog goes into action and will determine via the keen sense of smell if the food will have an ill-effect on what the dog's been trained to identify.

Are all children with food allergies going to have a trained dog to prevent an allergic reaction, and who's going to pay for such a method? Or will only those children whose parents can afford such protection going to receive it, thereby letting the rest of the population continues to suffer, possibly even die?

Without getting into a lengthy discussion about the sheer logistics and pre-occupation of this dog-sniffing method, nor the issue about the value of any child to be so protected from the possibility of an allergic reaction to certain food substances, isn't anyone going to raise the question as to how beneficial and necessary such efforts are? Can't a problem solving society come up with more effective methods to prevent a harmful reaction at home, at schools, in restaurants, and just about any other place?

It seems to me there must be a better and more cost effective way to help those in need. Essentially, children's lives are being trusted to the reliability and training of dogs. Dogs are highly effective at border crossings and airports to alert the authorities to drug trafficking, but now to use them for potentially allergic food products seems well beyond reasonable practices. And, we haven't even dealt with the possibility of a child being allergic to dogs! What next?

2010

SEXUAL ASSAULTS OF CHILDREN BY ROMAN CATHOLIC CLERGY

WHEN I was a child and attending school, I went to St. Ephrem's in Bay Ridge, Brooklyn. I received my First Holy Communion and Confirmation there, and went to school there for several years. I believed in God, the Church, the priests and nuns, and the differences between heaven, purgatory and hell, along with right from wrong. When I sinned I went to confession, did my penance, and felt relieved that my sins were forgiven. Periodically, there were novenas, special commitments throughout the year, and with a couple of my buddies I would attend these. There were even some times I went to Communion twice on Sundays because I thought this was a deeper commitment to God. No doubt this was highly irregular, but I didn't tell anybody and never thought it was a sin or wrong. I prayed for my family, for others, for doing the right things and thought God was watching and helping me.

I loved the nuns and priests. My primary contact was with the nuns. They taught us, corrected us, sometimes punished us, and then they complimented us and expressed love and encouragement, too. When the nuns were giving us religious instruction and a priest walked in on us, we obediently stood up and greeted the priest. Life seemed so simple and patterned, and in many ways quite peaceful.

What happened? In the past few weeks, no, much more than that, in the past few years there have been almost endless disclosures about priests having molested young boys. There are also priests revealing sexual relationships with single and married women, some fathering children, and even occasional cases of priests living luxurious lives on funds unknowingly provided by parishioners. And none of this includes those documented priests who left the church and married.

The Catholic Church in the United States has already paid out some 2 billion dollars to settle some of the many claims brought forth by now adults, those who have come forward to verify their being molested by priests. In fairness to the Catholic Church, there are other respected organizations and institutions whose members interact with children, and they too have unknown numbers of molestation of children. Recently, the Boy Scouts of America along with individuals involved in coaching children in sports have been identified. Child molestation is hardly unique to Catholic clergy.

For a while it was thought by some these revelations were evidence of a unique American Catholic Church problem, or purely isolated incidents. But, similar incidents have occurred in Ireland, Germany, Austria, Italy, and other countries. We simply do not know the breadth and depth of such violations and probably never will be able to in the long history of such behavior, maybe decades, possibly hundreds of years. We can surmise it is far greater than one might have imagined, or ever admitted to by church officials. Nor do we have any measurement of those lives permanently destroyed by such sexual abuses. Who knows what long-range impacts there have been on the abused?

There are significant legal and moral issues encompassing these sexual abuses of children by Catholic priests:

What do practicing Roman Catholics believe needs to be done so that the church and those practicing their faith/belief are respected. What can be done?

Is the celibacy commitment the underlying force promoting such abuses/

What role has Pope Benedict XVI played prior to his becoming pope and since then in this matter?

Is the Roman Catholic Church above the laws of the various countries where the abuses have occurred so that those committing violations are excluded from prosecution and/or removal from their religious responsibilities for their behavior?

What purposes are served by the Vatican officials suggesting recent media revelations are merely "petty gossip," or similar to the persecution of the Jews by the Nazis?

What individual and collective forces were involved so that these abuses have been ignored, denied and kept clandestine; and thereby allowed to continue for so long?

What can be done regarding such sexual abuses of children?

2010

WAR IS HELL

O N May 19th <u>The New York Times</u> (pages A12-13) are presented the facial photographs, ages and hometowns of American casualties in Afghanistan since late July 2008. Operation Enduring Freedom, a euphemistic term, enunciates our involvement in Afghanistan since 2001. About 1002 American servicemen and servicewomen have died in this operation, this war. These pictures are from a variety of sources and they are arranged alphabetically. The Times has done similar photographic presentations since America's involvement in Iraq and Afghanistan, and after the tragedy of September 11, 2001. Carefully, I looked at each of the deceased faces, all of them. A few only have the notation "photograph not available," just showing instead their names and location.

What do these two full pages tell us? First off, try counting to 1000, slowly, not the hurried way we did when we were kids and playing hide and seek and would rush or slur our numbers. A thousand-count is a lot of dead bodies. Some are in their late teen years; most in their early twenties and thirties; and fewer are older than that. Lately, more have been dying at earlier ages, often shortly out of boot camp training, and usually from what are called enemy "homemade bombs," improvised explosive devices, I.E.D.s.

They are Americans from all over the country; a mixture of military branches, with the majority from the United States Army and the Marine Corps. Some are smiling, others have more serious expressions. They seem so alive. They all volunteered to serve our country, yet it seems unlikely they thought about dying, at least not publicly. Many come from across the country, believing in the causes they choose to fight.

Although the branches of service are not identified with each person, those from the United States Marine Corps are more easily recognized because the enlisted Marines are typically in their dress white covers (caps) that go with their dress blues uniforms; the distinct USMC collars are sometimes visible in the photographs. They're gotten by those who've successfully completed boot camp at Parris Island or the Marine Corps Recruit Depot (San Diego). Those wearing the unique berets of their United States Army units can also be identified. The rest have fatigue caps, battle helmets or no covers at all.

The faces and names give these human beings a closer, more personal direct identity. Normally, we don't see pictures like this. We tend to forget those who have been dying for us, unless you're a member of the family or a friend of the dead. Then you experience the grief and confusion, remembering the lost living that might have been. The rest of us move along in some state of amnesia. This Iraq-Afghanistan war is seldom before us. It's far away; somewhere in remote places most know little about, and seem to care even less.

Dreams lost, futures gone, potentials never given a chance to evolve and flourish. Not even being able to have those experiences that are mistakes and from which something can be learned. Lives lost. We keep finding reasons to send our youth off to yield their lives. They are gone.

Perhaps the next time any of us complains about some inconvenience, some seemingly significant disruption or disappointment, some whining about a particular irritation, maybe there will also be a fleeting thought about those who are no longer alive because our nation's leaders sent them off to war and they did not come back or if they did they are spiritually or physically maimed from their military experiences.

Addendum reference:

American Empire, A Global History, A. G. Hopkins, Princeton University Press, 2018.

2010

CHANGING CHAINS

L ATELY, my mind inexplicably wandered to the topic of objects that have been kept around my neck since I was a little boy. This triggered all sorts of remembrances and associations covering a lot of years.

Some people wear objects that are simply decorations; some are symbols of one's religion such as a Christian cross or Jewish Star of David; or a locket with photos of dear ones, a good luck charm or a person's first name. There are the words of "love" objects manifesting affection worn long after the celebrated Valentine's Days when they were first given. Sometimes they're just the word "love" itself expressed in gold or diamonds. There was a brief period when small figures, "angels" were on chains and positioned around a person's neck. These objects can be noticed, admired, discussed, even wondered about by others. In certain ways they reaffirm the wearer's identity, importance to another, how we strive to be unique or perhaps to make some sort of statement about our beliefs and ourselves. They help to define the wearer's life, making them special.

Then, there are other kinds of objects you can tie around your neck. Once securely around your neck, it's almost part of your person; you always know where it is; and it's quickly within one's grasp. By carrying objects this way makes them readily available, they're certainly less likely to get lost or misplaced. You don't need to shove them in pockets in your clothing; and if you put something in the pocket of a jacket or coat and take it off, you might forget it or leave it down somewhere

So, what are some of the historical objects showing up in my mental wanderings as I pulled them up from those crevices of my mind from so long ago? First of all, from early on when I was a little boy and a devout Roman Catholic, I used to have a sterling silver Immaculate Conception medal on a sterling silver chain around my neck. How did I know it was sterling, maybe even valuable? Well, if you carefully examined the bottom of this medal, it was stamped so; and also, my parents told me this. There was much detail in the figure carved on the medal, sometimes I would look at it. The chain never seemed to break no matter what sort of horseplay or sport activity. It was extremely well made, and I wore it all the time.

Such medals and chains are typically given to children by close relatives. In some cultures they're as common as having female babies ears pierced for wearing earrings. There are even adults who wear them, too. They are seen today on some athletes, although they've gotten much more elaborate, showy, larger, and undoubtedly more expensive as they contain diamonds and other precious stones. Mine was given to me by my parents, my godmother, or I think a nun at St. Ephrem's Elementary School in Bay Ridge gave one to me for being a good speller in a class contest. I remember wearing one throughout most of college and certainly for some of the time when I was in the United States Marine Corps. I still have this medal from childhood, long after I stopped wearing it and being a devout Catholic. It's in a small wooden box with other items. When in the Marine Corps, I also wore something else around my neck, but I'm getting ahead of myself, and this isn't unusual for me.

Later on, instead of the religious medal and chain, I wore a scapular, which for the unknowing can easily be confused with the term "scapula." They sound much the same but are totally different. The scapula, we have two of these anatomical structures, are somewhat thin, flat triangular and irregular shaped bones on the outer parts of our upper backs. They work with other bones and muscles at the shoulder joint with the humerus, the upper bone of the arm, and also the clavicle or collarbone. The scapula helps us to carry out a wide range of shoulder and arm movements.

As for the scapular itself, the dictionary tells us this is some sort of badge of membership, worn over one's shoulders. That's not exactly what I mean. The scapular is made of soft cloth, it's about the size of a large Air Mail stamp from the old days when the stamps were much larger than now, and it is wafer thin. It's usually worn under one's shirt or underwear, and rests comfortably against the chest. It hangs around one's neck by a thin, sort of shoelace cotton fabric, but softer and flatter. The message on this large stamp size fabric is a picture of a particular religious person, a saint, with a brief message on it. The one I used to wear around my neck would remind me in the small print on it that if I died while wearing it, I was assured of heaven, salvation and God, or similar religious contractual commitment. Sometimes, if you wore it long enough, it took on a slight odor from your body, but not necessarily offensive because the cloth portion was rather small.

Strange, I still have one in the same wooden box housing my long ago Immaculate Conception medal. Yolanda Murphy, a dear friend gave it to me many years ago; she's another fallen away Catholic. After Yolanda gave it to me, and although I had long fallen away or been shoved out the church door, I wore it off and on, although not lately, or in a long time. It's highly unlikely she wears a scapular but I've never asked her. She lives in Oregon, used to live in Leonia, and lately her health hasn't been too good. We haven't seen her in years but once in a while we chat on the phone.

Another religious article I wore during my early teen-age years was a set of rosary beads. This might surprise a lot of people. A rosary is much heavier and bulkier than the almost weightless scapular or a medal on a chain. I did this again when I eventually served in the Marine Corps, then only for a short period of time. But during the teen years, it was part of my continuing commitment to being a serious Catholic, and it gave me much comfort. It was similar to the same reason when I was a young boy I used to attend two masses on Sundays to receive Holy Communion twice, believing such a double involvement with this Holy Sacrament. I thought by receiving Christ twice, I was a better person, doubly so. Nobody told me to do this. More devout Catholics have reminded me this was totally inappropriate, although I do not know why, then or now.

One time when I was playing sandlot football for a semi-pro football, The Sunnyside Robins in Jackson Heights, Queens, before that field became the massive Elmhurst General Hospital, and was involved in a major pile-up of bodies, the rosary beads broke. Apparently the repetitively thin metal twists connecting the spaced beads in their rows of Hail Marys and Our Fathers wasn't especially strong.

21

The strain and force of the twisted bodies crashing together caused them to snap into smaller, uneven disassembled clusters of beads. Maybe someone from the opposing team grabbed at my neck and accidentally caught his fingers under a portion of the rosary. Somehow, these broken clusters slipped past my T-shirt under the Sunnyside Robins' uniform jersey and got caught at the waist of my Kelly green, matching football pants. Later on, during the half-time break or after the game I had to discretely drop my football pants behind some make shift benches and seek those various sections of the rosary out of there. I even checked inside my protective-cup jock to make sure I had located all of the bead sections or possibly a single bead or two. It was one of the last times I wore my rosary beads, excluding that brief time in the Marine Corps.

I no longer have a set of rosary beads, but I do have almost half a set. Many years later, a dear friend who's a practicing, committed Catholic and I were sitting and talking; she suddenly took out her beads and pulled them apart, and gave me half. My half also has the crucifix on it. I thanked her and we did not say anything more. A while ago I noticed the word "Italy" imprinted on my portion. This half-set of rosary beads joins my childhood Immaculate Conception medal and the scapular in the same small wooden box. Why I continue to keep these items is a complex issue, with dimensions I'm not sure I can present or understand. They may very well be part of the mystery of my having once been a Catholic. Obviously they remain significant to me, otherwise why keep them?

Besides having worn religious articles around my neck during different times in my life, there were other times in childhood when I was required to wear an object for identification or utilitarian purposes. One time when my parents, mostly my mother, thought it would be a good idea for my sister and I to go away to summer camp to Mrs. Stuyver's camp in Goshen, New York. That place seemed so far away. We were both young, and separated into girls' and boys' groups, only meeting when we had fruit juice snacks and meals together. We had to wear a tag with our names and addresses until others knew who we were, especially the camp counselors. Nobody told us why this was important or needed, but eventually after the first week or so, they disappeared. We also had our names sewn into all of our articles of clothing and blankets, that was another camp regulation.

Later on in childhood, two more items were worn around my neck, usually on a piece of thin string or a shoelace, which over time became worn and somewhat dirty. I wouldn't put these objects on the Immaculate Conception sterling silver chain I was wearing. That seemed to violate the sanctity of the medal it was attached. When my mother began working full time during World War II, she assigned a key to my sister Maria and another to me for the apartment door. We were instructed to never lose it, never leave it around, and never let anybody have it.

Periodically, my mother reminded us of these rules. With the key, we would be able to come home from school for lunch, drop off our schoolbooks after school and change our clothes before going out to play, and use the bathroom if we had to do so. But, and this was repeatedly said, there could be no friends in the apartment unless there was an authorized adult present, and only for a few minutes even then.

Sometimes in cold weather, you could feel the key's coldness against your body until the key was warmed against it. Once in a while, I would lose the key. Without telling my mother or father, I would have to have a friend boost me up to the fire escape ladder safely removed from the street and climb up to the metal landing and go in through the kitchen window. In those days, we never locked windows. Shortly afterwards and having resolved the immediate problem, I would borrow my sister's and go to the local hardware store and have another key made, tie it on a measured length of cord or a shoelace and I was back in a safe zone. My sister would say nothing about this to my mother.

The other object was more specifically related to seasonal activity; it was a metal skate key. It was OK to have the skate key on the same piece of string as the house key; after all, both were not religious articles and their purposes allowed them to be mingled. For all skaters, a skate key was a mandatory piece of equipment. You'd have to know the metal skates were entirely separate from any shoe structures, not like these days when the skate and the supportive shoe are one unit.

Having a readily available skate key to make any needed adjustments, even doing repairs on one's skates was quite important. It saved time and kept you in the flow of the skating activity of hockey, or just skating all over the neighborhood. This key was multipurpose, it could be used to lengthen or shorten the entire skate frame, skates served several members of a family in those days; or tighten the metal clamps around your shoes; and one had to do this carefully so as not to significantly mark the leather shoes or damage the soles of the shoes you kept on after school.

After all, sneakers were usually a rarity in those days, you had one pair, and sneakers didn't hold well at all when the clamps were tightened because there was no border or lip on them for the clamps to be pushed into. With sneakers, you'd keep having the skates come right off. And, if for some reason one of the four ball-bearing metal wheels was eventually worn down, the skate key could loosen the nut and that wheel could easily be replaced. Sometimes, sort of for security, you would carry one wheel in your pocket; just the way a bicyclist carries a flattened down, folded extra tire on long trips. The skate key could feel cold against your body, too, on those fall or early spring days, but like the key, it warmed up against you.

During World War II, all school children in New York City were required to wear a somewhat yellowish or faded white plastic identification badge around their necks, I forget what the chain was composed, it might have been strong cloth. Some teachers periodically checked to see that you wore it. If you weren't, depending on the teacher, there was some sort of punishment for not having it on, a note home, staying in after school, something supposedly done to bring about any further foolish forgetfulness. Excuses were not accepted; after all we were at war. There were teachers who did such inspections just before we had the supposedly unannounced air raid drills in the school, but such checking was a telltale clue to get ready.

Shortly after loud bells sounded throughout the school signaling a drill for a bombing attack, we hurriedly dove and scrambled under the wooden desks and tables to be protected from shattering glass and flying objects if the bombs from the enemy planes landed in or near the schools. These desks and chairs were quickly arranged distal to the large window sections in our classrooms. No one bothered to ask how being under desks and chairs would save us from the massive German and Japanese bombs right near us. That didn't matter; we still sat huddled, heads down, in almost fetal positions until the "all clear" was sounded. Talking was not permitted, so you just stared at the various markings under the desks, the stale secured pieces of gum fixed there, occasional ink stains that somehow had seeped through the desks, wondering if you would live or die, or ever see your parents again. These off white with blue black lettering badges with personal identity information about us were worn during the school year until the end of World War II. Most of us removed them during summer vacations and holidays. Once the war was over, I'm not sure whether they were recollected or just thrown away.

In sort of an interval summary, the reader has to appreciate the religious medal and chain, the camp ID badge, the house and skate keys on the rope, and the World War II ID on its chain; some of these could be and usually were worn simultaneously because they had overlapping periods of necessity. For smaller children, any combination of these gave a slight bulge in the middle of the chest area; nothing so pronounced that anybody said anything, and not enough to be painful or inconvenient. And who would dare complain, anyway? It all seemed to work without discussion or concern.

Later on, maybe in high school or possibly in college, there was the possibility of another object being worn around one's neck. It was the high school or college ring of the person you were dating, and was a sign of being taken, possibly owned by the giver, or amongst some deluded possessive givers. This was quite serious. It was a visual insignia, a public badge you belonged to the person who owned that ring. It was usually worn on a chain and visible, outside the sweater or shirt so all could see it. Usually, the boy gave the ring, but there were occasions when the boy would wear a girl's smaller size and less obvious ring he'd received from her. It gave the wearer pride, an affirmation of worthiness; and also a public warning to others to possibly keep away from that person, hands off.

Naturally, there were many occasions when suddenly that ring was gone, no longer worn by the original recipient, it had been returned, the relationship had dissolved and its disappearance indicated a significant social shift. But, a different one might in due course replace it; or the original one eventually appeared around someone else's neck or again on the same person who'd yielded it at an earlier time.

For a while I thought there was some sort of connection between being female cheerleaders and having one of those rings around their necks. Every cheerleader I observed seemed to be taken. Surprisingly, I was too shy to do anything like this. It seemed far too serious for me and implied a commitment I was incapable of then. Besides, I was into studying and playing sports and neither of these activities could have been successful while giving one's ring away. This ring exchange activity was well beyond any abilities or thoughts I had.

After college, I joined the United States Marine Corps. Although I was giving serious thought to no longer being a practicing Catholic, I found there were some aspects of the Marine Corps that reminded me of my early Catholic training. From the day I entered, was sworn in, received my full uniforms and other equipment that had to be guarded with my life, at least according to the drill instructor in charge of my life, there was now another object around my neck. It was a flat, slightly notched on one end identification tag, usually called one's "dog tags." I guess we put such tags on dogs, thus the name, but I cannot verify this is so. There were two identical ones, and probably one was supposed to be kept in reserve in case you lost one, but I wore both of them, as did everybody else I knew. They were on a metal, utilitarian chain, a series of tiny balls strung together; similar to the old style kind that one pulls to turn on a light, except much longer. These tags had your name, rank, serial number, and the initials of your religious preference if you wanted it. Mine was imprinted "RC," for Roman Catholic, or just a "C," I'm not quite sure right now. Occasionally, there were a few of my buddies that didn't provide any preference.

You might be wondering what the notch on the ID tag was for. Nobody ever told me, but at least several times I heard some of my buddies talk about it. Supposedly, if by chance you were killed in combat, and your dog tag was still around your neck, that is, you weren't blown all over the place into unidentifiable pieces, then that dog tag was taken from your neck and wedged in between your teeth. The notch made it easier to secure the tag in your mouth until your body was moved to some other location for further identification and processing; that's when your body was sent to the Graves Identification Unit.

Recently, I went up in the attic, where there are several USMC-green wooden foot lockers containing my remaining military gear, uniforms, books, emblems, but I didn't find my dog tags. The light up in the attic was disconnected because the attic fan runs on the same line during the summer, and I couldn't see everything in the boxes. Perhaps another day.

As an adult and after leaving the Marine Corps, there are other times things had to be worn around my neck. While attending schools, or working in certain places like a hospital, and long before more recent obsessive concerns with security systems and identity clearances, we were required to wear a photograph ID on a cloth necklace. The picture wasn't a very good one, and the information with the picture verified your identity, the badge allowed you to move freely within the institution. Usually, it was within a protective plastic cover with a clip on it and not easily readable, just in case you wanted to convert the location from around your neck to a laboratory coat or jacket you were wearing. It always seemed easier to put it around the neck in one unit, less likely to get lost that way. It helped you avoid going to the security office if it were lost and having to go through the third degree by a zealous clerk as to where was it, where did you lose it, when did you last see it types of questions. A lost badge meant explanations along with a penalty fee, unless you could talk sweet talk your way out of this. We weren't working or studying at the Pentagon or for the CIA, but it sure felt like that if you lost the badge. I know this. In all the time I did wear such an ID badge not once did a security guard or anyone else ask to look at to verify my identity or right to be where I was in the facility.

Now, you ask, "Do you still wear anything around your neck, now that you are no longer a child, in school, in the military or working?" Well, yes and no, first the "no." Over the years, I have never worn a decorative piece of jewelry around my neck. Gold or silver chains have never interested me, even though many men choose to wear them, and that includes those wearing religious articles. You might have noticed the number of adult professional and college athletes having such decorations, some for good luck superstitious purposes and others because they are gifts from those important to them, their loved ones. But I didn't.

Reluctantly, I now come to my "yes" response. Whenever I travel using some air transportation, especially when we've gone overseas, I wear a flat nylon bag round my neck; it contains my passport and some currency of the country where we're going. The nylon string is similar to the type mentioned earlier when I wore a religious scapular as a child. But, instead of wearing this inside my clothing, it's kept outside, totally visible and hanging from my neck. It seems to some rather strange. How do I know this? People look at it, some stare. But it's easily accessible when I have to produce identification. Lois, my wife and the person I travel with most finds my doing this "silly," but I continue to do it. In some ways it's become a joke between us. Somehow, it vaguely reminds me of the immigrants that came to our country, my mother and her family were some of them and so too many of my father's family, who when they arrived at Ellis Island in New York had certain tags hanging around their necks as they were catalogued and shuffled to various lines by uncaring and sometimes unkind immigration officers.

As I've gotten older, reading glasses were needed. They probably were needed long before I got them, but I choose not to get around to getting them, so this was put off. For a long time I used those cheaper glasses usually bought in drug stores. Well, these reading glasses seem to walk off on their own, they disappear from tables, desks, restaurant tables, moving to distant locations and never available again. It's as if they were thrown off in space and defying gravity never return. Despite intensive searches, they don't show up, not even in the narrow spaces between the car seats or in the pockets of jackets used months ago, or behind the armoire on which they were last placed.

Why don't the manufacturers put a small alarm device in the frames, similar to those that help you find your lost car or house keys? Then, one's mind starts racing, giving cause and effect relationships to such recent, continual loses. Perhaps this is the onset of something far more serious. What's going to happen down the road if these events keep occurring? These thoughts subside when I find out people of all ages misplace, lose or can't remember the location of their car keys, a phone number written down, even their eyeglasses. And, if there is some slippage, how come I have the full capacity to write statements such as this one, to read and to think clearly, and to express my thoughts to others? This is the ongoing conflict between short and long term memory.

Recently, as I was getting the third or fourth replacement pair in the past year, I recommended to the optician some sort of signaling device should be implanted in the glasses. That way, you'd find them right away; the technology is readily available. We both laughed and realized neither he nor others involved in the expensive and profit making replacement process would have as many jobs to do as they do.

After many pairs of glasses "disappearing," once again I have something new around my neck. It's a cloth leash, this is my term, and it attaches to the arms of the eyeglasses. A dear friend of mine has repeatedly reminded me to use such a leash, and even gave me a couple. It looks strange having the leash protruding from the back of my neck or caught in the collar of my shirt when the glasses are in place. Sometimes particles collect on the inboard eyeglass surfaces if I'm eating something crumbly, or perhaps a drop of liquid, when the glasses just hang in front of me on my chest. It works for me and sure saves money in replacing eyeglasses. Incidentally, if you do need one these eyeglasses' leashes, you can get it in just about any store. They come in all sorts of colors and fabrics, even metal, more decorated and expensive ones. Some are fashion statements, just like the frames of glasses or other necklace jewelry can be integrated into one's décor and persona.

I suspect at some point down the road, someone will suggest it would be helpful if I get one those "Life Alert" signal devices and put it around my neck. Then, if and when I fall down, I can easily push the device and say into it, "Help, I've fallen and I can't get up!!!" This will be the ultimate concluding chain around my neck.

2010

WHAT RULES AND PROCEDURES
ARE IN EFFECT IN AMERICA???

I T is extremely difficult to keep up with all that's going on in our country and beyond. Maybe it's an impossible task. And yet, every so often something catches our individual and collective attention. Certainly, the millions of gallons of oil spilling into the Gulf of Mexico, the oceanic destruction and the lack of environmental resolution after two months have captured our attention. It should, unless we're in a coma. Less significant issues slip by. Yet, they too call out for some kind of minimal comment and analysis.

For example, there's a major Chinese supermarket in Flushing, Queens, New York that has a unique, probably unconstitutional and illegal approach to coping with store thefts and the ancient practice of shoplifting. A comprehensive article with photographs about this store and its rather nasty procedures appeared earlier this week in July 22, 2010 The New York Times.

With about 30 surveillance cameras operating all the time, shoppers are under constant observation. This is called "surveillance." The store owners believe this method assists them in curtailing incidents of shoplifting. Let's pursue this further.

When a person is observed in shoplifting, or perhaps thought to be doing so, through internal communications taking place in the store, that individual is confronted by security employees, has their identification taken away, questioned and then subjected to this Chinese food store's justice: Right off, if the person denies or refuses any punishment, their photographs are posted on the wall in a large format. If they do acknowledge they were stealing, they will be forced to pay a penalty fine of $400. (That's right.) The store's operators maintain it's their right to do so because the police, if called do little about the issue and only "hold" that person for 24 hours before releasing them. The threat of involving the police is obviously an inexplicably effective stimulus for patrons to pay up.

Surprisingly, to at least me according to the article, most of the shoplifters pay up. They use credit cards or pay the $400 in cash. Some even leave the store and return with the money in hand. How come? What would possess anyone to pay this coerced and outrageous amount for simply several dollars worth of groceries? What mental developmental processes and cultural forces have promoted such compliant behavior to accept this activity? Also, do the insensitive owners of this Chinese food store report their illicitly obtained fees to the IRS as "earnings" or do they bury this amount? They cheat the customers and might be cheating the government.

My only conclusions are these, although I am receptive to other possibilities that are more enlightening:

1) People pay this $400 because they are either afraid or culturally conditioned to such procedures. If they are fearful, it must be because they are hiding something of a more serious nature, far beyond the $400 imposed penalty.

2) They are ignorant of their rights in our democracy: the presumption of innocence; right to be formally charged; opportunity for legal representation; and the entire system of due process long established in our country.

3) They have a great deal of disposable money to throw away.

4) They do not want to be involved with any law enforcement agencies because they are here illegally or have committed other crimes.

5) They understand such a punitive system because they were subjected to it in their home country and have already given up rights, they are conditioned to it. They have no choice, or don't think they do.

Beyond all of these, some other final questions: Why would anyone bother to willingly shop in such an abusive and dehumanizing environment? Will this practice and other similar ones expand in America? Have we gone mad? Are we so willing to give up our individual rights?

2010

NEIL YOUNG

A WEEK or so before my 78th birthday we were watching Charlie Rose, who does all sorts of interviews on public television. He was interviewing an older man, probably in his 60s, someone not familiar to me. His name is Neil Young, a Canadian guitarist/composer. This man seemed a little uneasy, tapping on the table and changing body positions as he was responding to Rose's questions and comments. He'd had a brain aneurysm; he said his recovery changed him, but wasn't specific. His expansive comments gave strong indications he knew a great deal about popular music's more recent history. He described the creative process he experiences, and how songs spontaneously come to him; he rushes off from wherever he is to capture them before they escape from his consciousness. Neil Young has written hundreds of songs before, during and after the 1960s and 1970s.

Within the interview, a few fragments of Neil Young's songs were played. It was mentioned how at one time he was a member of Crosby, Stills, Nash and Young. There was a vague memory of this quartet. I made a connection about that

Young with this same Neil Young, and mentioned to Lois how one of these days I was going get one of his discs.

The night of my birthday Lois handed me a nicely wrapped package. It was heavier that what I thought a package that size should be. What was it? The gift was an attractive, decorated box of 8 discs, more than 150 songs written by Young, his musical archives from the early 1960s through early 1970s: Topanga, Riverboat, Massey Hall, Fillmore East and North Country. The next morning I rushed to put 6 of those discs in the car player, replacing the Junior Mance Trio, George Shearing, Roy Orbison and Pavarotti. The remaining Young discs would be phased in.

The words of these songs are poetry, evoking different visual, emotional and thoughtful activities. Some are reminiscent of youth; others are spiritual; and many are Young's lamentations about lost loves and dreams, drugs, aging, loneliness, separation, nature and life's journey. The music and words are powerful, unique and intimate, and written by a musical genius. He captures a portion of America's cultural guts. Some are directly related to what was going on in our country at that time.

As for the 1960s and 1970s in the United States, there was disruption, violence and ongoing national strife. A lot of it is long forgotten or pushed aside. An unpopular and confused Vietnam War was on, with anti-war protests, public draft card burnings and thousands of body bags of our young servicemen coming home, as well as more thousands of maimed men. Some dodged the draft by fleeing to Canada, and/or abruptly becoming conscientious objectors. Others randomly went off to war in their place. There were peace marches and civil rights marches in major cities, resulting in violence and riots. Police dogs, fire hoses, charging horses and arrests were used to combat the protesting citizens. Progressive civil rights legislation desegregated schools and other public places. There were forces battling to keep them "separate and equal." (They were separate but never equal.) National leaders were serially assassinated: John Kennedy, Martin Luther King, Robert F. Kennedy, Malcolm X, George Lincoln Rockwell; Medgar Evers.

At Kent State College in Ohio, National Guard members fired on and killed 4 students and injured others. In Mississippi, civil rights activists Chaney, Goodman and Schwerner were slaughtered, each shot once through the heart after being stopped for a supposed traffic violation.

The Civil Rights Act of 1964 began to prevent further discrimination against women in the workplace; NOW and other women's organizations were promoting women's rights and equality. Still there were groups negatively reacting to such legislation. The President of the United States (Richard Nixon) was caught deceiving and lying to us. Eventually he had to resign; he waved to us, smiling and disgraced from his departing Marine helicopter.

And America's love affair with illegal drug use was underway. We were experiencing the early damages, crime and deaths resulting from heroin and LSD; some drugs were supposedly going to release inhibited creativity in music, poetry, writing, inner discovery and personal freedom. We could be more alive.

The country was coming apart on many fronts. We were a toxic nation. Some of us thought or hoped someday it might come back together again anew. Or it might explode beyond any repair and peace into a totally unknown state. During these upheaval years, there were many fine, socially sensitive songsters out there questioning what was going on. They were writing influential, powerful music: Pete Seeger, Joan Baez, James Taylor, Linda Ronstadt, Buffy Sainte-Marie, Willie Nelson, and Judy Collins are some that I listened to and we went to see. And Crosby, Stills, Nash and Young, too, the group I'd forgotten about.

I almost went back into the United States Marine Corps in the early 1960s. The USMC sent me a formal letter inviting me to active duty. Lois was unalterably opposed to my going back. She reminded me of our children. To demonstrate the seriousness of her opposition, she announced she'd picket (with our children) at whatever Marine Corps base I was stationed carrying a protest sign. She was quite convincing; no much more, she was outright adamant. As a Marine Captain Infantry officer with training in Explosives Ordnance Disposal (EOD), the USMC would use me in Vietnam. There's a strong probability I might have returned in a body bag.

In an e-mail to our youngest son Matthew, I told him of the birthday gift of Neil Young's songs. He was surprised I didn't know him. One of Young's songs reminds Matthew of his life and mine, it's called "Old Man." Matthew liked this song when he was 24 years old and traveling across America. He's now 45. There are at least two versions of it on these Young discs. One of the lines in the song is "Look at my life I'm a lot like you were." The first time I heard it, I cried. Years ago Matthew introduced me to Sade and Nina Simone. Now, he thinks I'm ready for Van Morrison, too.

After listening to these discs for the past several weeks as I'm driving, I've memorized many of the words; sometimes I accompany Neil Young. Thank you, Lois. Neil Young is a newer buddy late in life, and he's with me for the rest of the ride. Life moves inexorably along.

2010

MULTITASKING – NEW, OLD OR WHAT?

T HE English language is dynamic and evolving. Words, how they are put together, and their context can have widespread meanings. Sometimes a term used for a long time abruptly takes on a new meaning. This doesn't mean there was anything inappropriate with its original use; just that it has fresher dimensions more relevant to now; and thus it appears more frequently in speech and writing.

Another possibility is this same word simultaneously can have different meanings and uses. Naturally, how an individual internalizes and then responds to its usage can have bearing on its meaning. One individual's interpretation can be remarkably different from another, perhaps even contributing to confusion between a speaker and a listener, or a writer and a reader.

The term "multitasking" is a clear example of such language transformation. It might be helpful if we heed Socrates; "Define your terms." Obviously, "Multitasking" is "The performance of multiple tasks at one time." There's no clear definition of exactly how many concomitant activities constitute "multitasking." At least two or three seems reasonable, maybe even a few more. (This word doesn't even appear in earlier editions of Roget's International Thesaurus or Webster's International Dictionary.)

In recent years, the term "multitasking" frequently appears, so much so it has become a cliché. It seems to have originated in computer parlance, where a single microprocessor handles a concurrence of several tasks in a seemingly simultaneous way. It's also used in other media, but particularly when humans are describing their activities. Now, it has taken on a life of its own, as if synonymous with making things happen. Some research suggests "multitasking" is a myth, with the brain and mind handling essentially one subject at a time while giving the impression of doing several activities together or sequentially.

"Multitasking" implies some sort of explanation for handling or coping with more than a single matter at a time; it can be offered to indicate exaggerated workplace accomplishments; and to justify a person's continued employment during difficult economic times. Some people mention "multitasking" while chatting in a restaurant; others use it when working out at an athletic club; and when friends bump into each other and refer to their comparative "multitasking."

"Multitasking" can involve extensive use of technological communication devices of all sorts: Twitter, Face book, You-tube, e-mails, cell phones, and virtual games. Sometimes "multitasking is occurring when a person handles a bunch of unrelated tasks, perhaps talking to one person while texting a second person, fingering their iPhone or iPod, at the same time while driving their car or SUV! All of this can be going on while the driver could be petting a small animal on his/her lap, or even reading a newspaper or book while moving slowly through traffic, and yes, applying make-up or shaving with an electric shaver!

"Multitasking" also serves as a possible excuse after disappointing another person or letting them down in a totally unrelated matter. "Sorry I'm so late, there were so many tasks or things I was doing at the same time; you know how that is" Another example: "Between driving the kids to soccer practice, shopping, going to the gym, planning dinner, and of course working, I'm multitasking all the time."

Is "multitasking" a unique part of our more modern lives, as if some <u>de novo</u> human enterprise? Do we see ourselves as especially productive and activated human forms carrying out more and more roles? Does recent "multitasking" make us any more creative for resolving individual and group problems? Is it possible "multitasking" is in reality an inefficient, non-beneficial activity blocking clearer thinking? Or are we just keeping busy, as in Neil Young's words "we rush ahead to save our time?"

Perhaps we could put aside any preoccupation with our supposed "multitasking." Then, there would be time for quiet contemplation about nature and the stars, and even for occasional introspection and reflection.

2010

THREE SISTERS IN ROCKPORT

W E'VE been living in Rockport, Massachusetts for two and a half years, having moved here in May 2008 after living in Leonia, New Jersey for almost 46 years. It's a beautiful New England coastal town with older traditions, behaviors and expectations.

Rockport is on an island that's part of the Cape Ann peninsula protruding into the Atlantic Ocean, surrounded on three sides by ocean; it's 4 miles north of Gloucester, America's oldest fishing port. Cape Ann is also called the "other Cape." In contrast with the more popular Cape Cod south of Boston it has less traffic, crowds, business and beaches. I do hope Cape Ann stays this way. By train, Rockport is about an hour north of Boston; the train follows the coastline to its final stop, Rockport.

Throughout the town the ocean and its coastline can be seen, along with the ocean smell and the winds from it. Sometimes when I look out on the ocean, I am reminded of Aaron Copeland's "Billy the Kid" opera, particularly the "open prairie" portion with its limitless sounds, rhythms and feelings, just like the ocean. Although I have no instruments to measure the validity of this, the air in this entire area seems forever clean and crisp, whatever the season.

Historically, Rockport was known for shipbuilding, fishing, high-quality granite from its many quarries, and as a resort and artist colony. Today, some lobstermen and many artists are still active. There are no more shipbuilding or quarry activities. This place and its residents make a strong argument for "small is beautiful" concept. Living is easier in Rockport primarily because life is simpler, with far fewer daily activities or disruptions.

Whatever stereotypes there might be about New Englanders, we haven't witnessed them. Maybe because of our relative newness here, our impressions are that people are calmer, more courteous, openly friendly and less pretentious. They move about more slowly and seem more relaxed; spend time chatting with one another; and wave to each other when passing in cars. Workers coming to your house show up on time; their prices are fair and the work is well-done. Some stay and talk and become your friends, too. Recently, an attractive British-style tea room opened not far from us; it offers a calm and peaceful spirit to the area. It's quiet here. Seldom are car horns or sirens sounded. t.

There is concern and sensitivity for the environment by most of the residents; many individuals are involved in the community and in their own independent activities; there is much effort to insure this community remains attractive, uncluttered and esthetically pleasant. Also, there is a respect for nature that is certainly evident throughout Rockport.

Older homes and public buildings, some 200-300 years old, are preserved and restored; many of them are cedar shingled or with older wood planking, often accompanied by old, weather-worn uneven stone and wooden fences. Rotten wood is replaced only with newer wood, there's virtually no aluminum siding on town buildings, at least I haven't seen any. The red cedar shingles are usually left untreated or unpainted; eventually with time and New England weather they turn smoky worn gray, even an occasionally darkened brown-black. Our home's shingles are painted cottage red. A lot of homes are painted traditional white. Sometimes the front doors of homes are vivid, eye-catching reds or blues or purples. Other buildings are well maintained and painted with diverse soothing earth-tone colors typically seen throughout New England. Wherever you look, structures are clearly old and settled, yet fixed and preserved for tomorrow and beyond. If it's old or needs repair it gets taken care of; restoration and salvaging are common, intrinsic concepts in Rockport.

Years ago the stone quarries were busy and operating. Today, these quarries, their sheltered harbors and their massive granite formations remain throughout the town and along its coastline. Maybe that's why the town's name is Rockport. The cut stone from the quarries was hauled to the coastline, loaded on barges and moved to building sites of the East Coast's major cities. Now, silent and no longer active, they're naturally filled with fresh water flowing from above and below; in the summer residents can swim in a couple of them. A few of the quarries are protected to provide Rockport's fresh drinking water.

Besides the quarries keeping us in touch with the past, there are frequent remnants of granite that are visible and used throughout the town: well-constructed granite walls and street curbs, granite columns outside of houses, along with granite pathways, patios and steps. Many homes have granite fireplaces in them. Also, there are boundary stone walls on most properties and barns from yesterday are still in use. The textures and plantings in fields change with the seasons. Sometimes when I'm walking or driving and it's late in the afternoon on a clear, sunny day, these fields take on a soft, quiet, golden glow. All about are gardens, and then more gardens, with natural and cultivated plantings. There's a community garden organization made up of perhaps 150 or so women (and a few men) meeting, planning, tending and financing some 15 public gardens disbursed throughout Rockport. The town looks forever attractive.

Rockport has regularly scheduled Town Meetings at which the town's business and financial items are openly discussed; all attending residents have the right to stand up and speak to the issue; and then the public voting decides the outcome. This can be time consuming and drawn out, even occasionally boring, more so when the speakers are less focused. Supposedly "Robert's Rules of Order" are in effect, but one would never know this. By some standards it's an outwardly inefficient process. Yet it's the essence of democratic practices because citizens are actively engaged in determining public issues affecting them.

The town operates a highly organized environmentally sound transfer station; most residents continue to call it "the dump." (There is no local public garbage and trash collection.) Its primary purpose is to prevent further violations to nature and the planet. It is where the town's citizens separate, recycle and reuse waste products and goods. When you go there you can't help but believe you're at some sort of precision factory/depot, with everyone actively engaged in work. Neighbors meet there and chat while delivering and separating paper, plastic, metal and garbage, sharing old clothes, books, building materials, and other unwanted articles. Commercial and building contractors must abide by the same rules and regulations. Even the brought-in garden and landscaping wastes are decomposing into massive compost piles available for community use. At the station, flocks of seagulls scatter and patiently (sometimes not) await their turns to scavenge for edibles through those massive garbage/waste containers before they're hauled away to a recycling plant for further salvaging treatment and disposal.

All of this is evidence of a seemingly endless battle between our human consumption and accumulation of products and materials, and then methodically and effectively making them less damaging to the planet and us. By regularly going to the transfer station citizens are habitually sensitized in their personal and collective lives to actively support such programs to protect this delicate and messy planet.

Since being here we've noticed all sorts of wild animals moving about on our property. Over the seasons, we've observed a few domesticated cats that have been wandering for so long they might not be domesticated any longer. Our recent inventory includes: coyotes (frequently and openly observed, and this is unusual), deer, rabbits, groundhogs, foxes, voles, woodchucks, chipmunks, the elusive fisher cat (neither a cat nor does it eat fish, and we have a photo of one), occasional snakes, salamanders, field mice, many different butterflies, bees and other insects. The coyotes are especially beautiful to watch. On occasion they move across our property with stealth, minding their own business, trotting quickly and seeking no confrontation or notice. It can be just a couple of thin-legged adults; other times a female following or leading a pair of her young offspring. Some nights, for long periods of time, the coyotes yap and bark in solo or group communications. These are wild, haunting sounds.

A few other comments about coyotes: Recently research confirmed coyotes seen in the Northeast contain wolf DNA. Because of this, wildlife researchers prefer to call them "coywolves," thereby indicating their hybrid genetics and perhaps giving them the benefit of the protective status wolves have. Contrary to prevalent rumors, coyotes are typically harmless and seldom have any interest in humans or our domesticated pets. It's difficult to know how many coyotes are in any area, including within urban areas. If you think there are just a few, there may be many more elusively avoiding any contact.

Beyond all of these animals are countless varieties of birds, some dropping in regularly, such as various finches, hummingbirds, chickadees and the ever-present crows, starlings and sparrows; others, often hundreds or more e stop by to rest and feed while on their long established migratory routes. Often there are clusters of hawks soaring on updrafts over open fields as they seek prey below. The surrounding estuaries and wetlands are brimming with permanent and seasonal water fowl. Frequent trips to our bird identification books confirm such diversity. Near to the ocean, we see seagulls moving towards it or away from the coastline in their quest for food and/or shelter. And, within several hundred yards of our home are various breeds of horses stabled and maintained by Rockport residents.

In addition to this rough inventory, there are several groups of wild turkeys which visit our property. Usually the hens or females are accompanied by a larger, multi-colored tom or male. There can be as many as 5-8 turkeys in a group. They look alike, with the toms or males much larger and multi-colored. With more study and observation, each can be identified by certain unique physical characteristics. They are remarkably different from the turkeys most of us think about; those penned close together being readied on turkey farms for those holiday feasts.

· After studying them, and even though I've studied animal anatomy, I came to the realization their heads, excluding their large eye structures, and their brains are extremely small. Comparatively minute is a better term. They have thin, gangly limbs. But the rest of them, their bulky feathered bodies are quite large, almost seeming to be too large for their legs. Their dark blue-gray feathers help camouflage them in the woods where they typically live. Hanging from beneath their chins and over their beaks are varying-colored, thin long growth structures.

For more than a year or so just three turkey hens, without any other hens or toms, habitually move slowly up and down the two-way, two-lane road between Gloucester and Rockport. They're seen throughout the seasons. During the daytime, they move freely all over the south Rockport realm; and at night, they probably sleep in lower branches of trees for safety. In case you didn't know this, turkeys do fly! But not very far!

I decided to name them the "Three Sisters." They are always together, these same three. They seem oblivious to any potential danger from ongoing traffic, which is especially heavy during the morning, and late afternoons when commuters and workers are hurrying about; and more so during the summertime with increased tourist travel. No, more than that. Regardless of traffic, they just mosey along right along the road. They move about at a rambling pace, as if the roads belong to them.

No driver wants to have a collision with the meandering "Three Sisters." After all, they are long-established community members known to most local residents. They belong to Rockport. Sometimes while disregarding traffic, they jam up the road. Vehicles in both directions abruptly slow down or stop; some flash their lights warning other approaching vehicles and patiently wait until the "Three Sisters" move off the road to lawns and gardens to scratch and forage for food. If somehow a driver decides to impatiently "honk" a car horn to move them along, the "Three Sisters" quickly respond by making repetitive "gobble gobble" sounds, almost in a unison protest chorus.

Once in a while, a passing, totally surprised tourist stops to avoid hitting them, will open the car door and take a hurried photo of the "Three Sisters." They bear some resemblance to those on safari trying to quickly capture photos of wild animals to take home for showing. But, if the "Three Sisters" notice that person, they embark on an immediate frontal assault. This photographer then leaps back into the car to avoid the trio's combined attack. The hens have an almost innate desire to come along and peck at the sides of slowing-down cars and trucks, and occasionally to join forces and do the same to bicyclists, joggers and walkers. Then, they move much more hurriedly, sometimes running along together. Turkeys running seem awkward on their thin spindly legs, but they can move rapidly.

There's an older man, one of our neighbors who's lived in Rockport a long time. Each early morning he walks along South Street, carrying a walking stick made of dark wood with a heavy scrolled silver handle. Sometimes he carries a small plastic bag of grain or corn and feeds them. Some residents told me this is not a good idea, but he does it anyway. The "Three Sisters" appear to wait for him. They reflexively react when seeing him. The turkeys and this man seem to have an unspoken paradoxical relationship: in case the "Three Sisters" confuse him for an interloper on their land instead of a food source, he has his walking stick to gently swing at them as they move ever closer. Other times, they keep a lookout for him while he spreads feed for them and they gingerly move towards it. The other day I spoke with him and he mentioned they hadn't been around for a couple of days and he seemed concerned.

Most days, "Three Sisters" await the US Post Office delivery truck on South Street. When the mailman steps out to put mail in roadside boxes, the "Three Sisters" quickly move towards him. This almost game-like ritual is an expected event carried out by the turkeys and the mailman. One mailman, however has refused to deliver in this area because of these aggressive turkeys. Our granddaughter Mia claims they used to chase her every day for years when she got off the school bus. Her sprinting abilities vastly improved, and if necessary, she would swing her school knapsack at them during the ongoing chase. She's off at college now, but remembers well her daily after-school encounters with them.

Is there some lesson to learn from all of this more relaxed and tolerated co-habitation taking place in Rockport? Only that it's possible for humans to co-exist with other animals rather than pursuing the belief that other animals need to be destroyed in order to "cleanse" it for our exclusive use. How did this happen in Rockport, where people remain sensitive and caring? They value the past, along with all animals, including the wandering "Three Sisters," wherever they roam.

Does all of this have anything to do with how long Rockport has been a settled and spirited community, where for hundreds of years New Englanders have been living here amidst other animals? Is Rockport a unique cultural sanctuary somehow surviving within our more chaotic, stressful, hurried society? Perhaps eventually humans will learn to be as tolerant of other humans, too.

Addendum Reference:

Half – Earth, Our Planet's Fight for Life. Edward O. Wilson, Liveright Publishing, New York, 2016.

2010

PREJUDICE

A FEW weeks ago, Lois and I had traveled to Washington D.C., Roanoke Virginia, and Southport, North Carolina. We'd decided we had some old friends we'd not seen in a long time, and at our ages realize our clocks seem to be ticking at an accelerated rate, so we did it. It was a wonderful trip and now we were on the way back home.

While heading home and in lower Westchester County, New York, I needed to urinate. In recent years, my travel schedule is at least partially guided by planning a regular pit stop. Or, suffer the unpleasant repercussions. We were in Mount Vernon, one of the many suburban communities just north of New York City. As we drove around, we sought a restaurant, a gas station, or any reasonable place to park and use the facility there. It was becoming clear there did not seem to be any around, or at least we couldn't find them. At the same time, my sense of urgency was creating tension between Lois and me as we sought a location while driving aimlessly in Mount Vernon.

By sheer accident, she spotted a supermarket and after several turns we were there. Because Lois had been at Empire State College in Hartsdale for years, another Westchester community, she was aware of the surrounding communities and commented Mount Vernon, or at least where we were was a totally Black (African-American) community, and this was quite obvious as we drove around. As we pulled into the massive parking lot at the supermarket, this was further confirmed. Amidst the rest of the crowd I was the only white person. Outside the market was a large group of young African-American males, who didn't seem to be doing anything. They didn't look as if they were shopping, rather, hanging out, sitting and standing around, chatting with one another while many were smoking. It looked like a rough crowd. Having spent the bulk of my life in New York City, I definitely know a rough crowd when I see on.

I got out and quickly headed for the store. As I got to the store entrance, almost all of them stared at me. I was either walking quickly or perhaps jogging to be in the store, knowing from prior experiences supermarkets have toilets. Lois stayed in our car. Once inside, I sought a sign giving me information as to where to go, but there was none. As I looked around and moved about the store I accidentally met someone who seemed to be a manager and asked where the toilet was. He pointed to a distal location in the store, which led down a dark, long corridor and past some lockers where the employees kept their personal items. This was a remote, isolated place. I quickly went about my business, standing in this rather small, dark toilet facility. If anybody else were in this room or did come in, it would be tight and crowded.

My mind wandered to what would I do if any of those men outside the store came and bothered me for my money,

I had several hundred dollars in cash. My mind quickened in its anxiousness, I also had on the beautiful Omega watch on that Lois gave me three years ago. Would they be satisfied with my relinquishing everything in my possession, which I had decided I would do, or would they do something more serious to me? Would I bluff my way out or even put up a fight as I had done long ago when much younger? After all, having a USMC officer and trained how to combat others. I even created a mental/emotional scene that these men outside were skilled at robbing others and would be upon me shortly. I found myself overwhelmed with inordinate fear for my property, my money, but most of all, my well being and life itself. I was definitely going to be a victim of bad play. My psychologist buddies tell me "perception is reality."

Instead of finishing urinating and only because of my anxiety, I quickly wanted to get out of this toilet. I did, with my bladder probably still half full, but it didn't matter, I had to get outside and to a safer place. Then, I rushed out of the supermarket, and those same men were still standing where they had been when I rushed into the market. Again, they stared at me. I know this because I stared back at them. When I tried to get back into the car, the doors were locked. Lois had made a decision to lock herself in, which she told me once I was inside. She also told me she was prepared to ignore anybody who came up to the car and tried to talk to her. She would try to pass herself off as a non-English speaking person.

We drove off, found our way back to the safe Westchester parkway and headed north towards Rockport. In many ways I am ashamed of my bigotry, my almost innate prejudice to those who are Black. In retrospect, there was absolutely no reason for me to suspect anything of anybody. No one even gave a hint of doing anything. Perhaps I had created all of this unnecessary fear predicated on whatever racial demons exist in me. I've always thought of myself as an enlightened, sensitive, caring person. But, in this situation I clearly betrayed my strong, clear view of me, the egalitarian teachings of my parents and how I had behaved throughout my life. I had yielded to my bad thoughts. I didn't like who I was.

The last time I was comparably ashamed of my thoughts and reacting behavior occurred many years ago when several of us were visiting a dear friend in a New York hospital, he had AIDS. None of us ever spoke openly about this, but we all knew this was what he had. During our visit, I was totally surprised; shocked is a better term, at how little he resembled the healthy, handsome and attractive person I'd known for many years. We all chatted and joked around a little. At one point he asked me if I'd give him some water from a pitcher on the table, he was very thirsty. I did. He was terribly weak and while I held the glass he wrapped his shaking hands around mine while he drank. It took him time to swallow enough water. His hands and arms look thin as he gulped down the water.

We left shortly afterwards. As soon as I was in the hallway, I sought a public toilet but couldn't find one. My two other buddies and I went downstairs to a restaurant immediately across from the hospital. While they sat down, I quickly went into the Men's room and spent an inordinate amount of time methodically scrubbing my hands, even partially up my arms. I did this again and again, using copious amounts of soap and hot water. Here was the biologist, a college professor, an informed individual stupidly behaving as if I might somehow get AIDS from my dear dying friend touching my hands. This was the same unfounded emotional argument similar to the ignorant belief that someone can get a venereal disease from seating on a toilet seat, despite no evidence whatsoever to support such a view. Our friend died shortly afterwards.

Two totally disjointed experiences, remarkably different and many years apart, yet both predicated and governed by an ill-founded, emotional fear. I had created two scenarios that caused anxiety within me. I felt and behaved irrationally in both circumstances. How strange to be this way, how inexplicably sad to be so cruel to those unknowing and undeserving others. I wonder how many times each day in countless other situations millions of others behave this way. And we like to think of ourselves as so advanced, all so enlightened.

Our youngest son has a friend who is the editor of a magazine that recently celebrated its 15th anniversary of publication. It's <u>American Legacy, The Magazine of African-American History and Culture.</u> A while ago she sent me about a dozen earlier copies of this fine magazine, in which African-American accomplishments in a wide variety of areas are documented and described. The magazine also provides articles of how African-Americans have been exploited, abused and patently discriminated against by individuals and institutions, including our government. It is a paradoxical portrait. Despite all of the brutality, abuse and adversity, often beyond outright opposition, somehow African-Americans have historically made significant achievements in every area of our American society.

As for the HIV-AIDS epidemic, first noted in the early 1980s, people world-wide, especially in Africa continue to become infected and die from it. The original source of the virus is still part of a long controversy. In recent years there have been many educational programs about it, and a number of drugs used to treat it and sustain the lives of those with it. Ongoing research focuses on its prevention and perhaps its eradication, as has occurred in earlier infectious diseases. But, the battle continues, as do a variety of misconceptions, confusions and prejudices about it. Prejudice or "pre-judgment" is wasteful and consistently hurtful. It measures and influences individuals, groups and situations with a pre-conceived belief system clouding and marring experience. It's predicated on an inordinate fear or distrust, and the evasion of rational thought processes. Why do we do this? How did we become so distorted?

Addendum Reference:

Caste – The Origins of Our Discontents, Isabel Wilkerson, Random House, New York, 2020.

2011

A DEAR FRIEND

S EVERAL weeks ago, the wife of a dear friend called and told me her husband had committed suicide on December 4th, 2010. What does one say in response to such notice? "I'm so sorry." "I'm shocked". "Was something bothering him?" "Were there any warning signs?" "Was he depressed about his health?" Or "was it his finances?" Had he received some recent devastatingly bad or tragic news he couldn't handle? Did he have some terminal illness and wanted to spare himself and his family the deteriorating outcomes? Is there any question or bunch of questions that can be asked or answered resulting in some clarification, some rational explanation for choosing death over life? What was on his mind, if anything, as he turned the photograph of his wife downward and proceeded with such drastic action?

Here's a person I met almost 55 years ago. After being in the United States Marine Corps as fellow officers; we'd seen each other just about a dozen times afterwards. Still, we were close friends. So close I considered him a dear friend, and this is not a description I use lightly.

Yes, he was getting up there in years (he died a couple of months before his 77th birthday and was almost two years younger than I am). He had had a series of aging health problems, but none would of necessity be directly interconnected with his killing himself. Or at least that doesn't seem so. I'd spoken to him on the phone only a week earlier, and we'd been exchanging e-mails for a while. All seemed fine. We'd talked about reading a book, <u>Matterhorn</u>, written by a former Marine Corps Officer; and we discussed the upcoming holidays. He'd finished reading it, I'd just started. We even discussed an unfavorable review of the book written by a retired USMC colonel, my friend had sent it to me. And, months ago he'd read my book <u>Buddy Remembers – Then and Now</u> and had provided comments about it on the phone.

We first met in Quantico Virginia when we were in USMC Officer Basic Schools. That was in June 1956. We were part of the 3-56 Basic School Class; there were 557 of us. The class was further broken down into three companies, Echo, Foxtrot and Golf. We were in the Fourth Platoon, Foxtrot Company, 3-56 Basic Class, composed of 44 2nd Lieutenants, and would be living together in a Quonset hut for the next 8 months. We'd be kept incredibly busy all week long as USMC junior officers, classes, field trips, night maneuvers and other activities to simulate combat. Many of us were irritated by these activities. We were commissioned officers in the USMC and convinced we were ready to take on all sorts of FMF, Fleet Marine Force roles. Naturally, that wasn't so.

How or why we noticed one another is long gone, but somehow we did. It doesn't take long to get to know those you live within a Quonset hut for 8 months.

Perhaps it all started when each of us found out the other was from the New York City environs, he was from upper Manhattan near Baker Field, Columbia University's football stadium; and I was from Queens, but had played football at Baker Field while attending Columbia in the early 1950s. He used to sneak into Baker Field as a boy and watch the Columbia football games. He knew the names of many of the great Columbia players.

We began to bond from that point on. We had a lot of commonalities, we referred to similar childhood experiences, including religious backgrounds, schools, sporting events, and knowing a great deal about what goes on in the ever changing rhythms of the city. We became soul mates, bound up by those familiar life matters that made us comfortable with each other. There were no pretenses.

Over time, our frequency of communicating increased, especially when we'd drive to and from New York on liberty weekends. ("Liberty" is the term used in the military to denote time, space and freedom away from the military structure and its compliant routines.) This went on for the entire 8 months we were in Basic School, every weekend. He didn't have a car, but I had a trusty Volkswagen Beetle. Volkswagens were relatively new to the United States, and they were considered a novelty, and certainly no threat to the massive, gas-guzzling tank-like cars most Americans were used to driving. They were somewhat of a novelty in our country, built in Germany, and a continuance of the earlier and unfulfilled German Third Reich promises for a relatively simple "people's car" for the German population. Eventually, after the war, there'd be millions of Volkswagen Beetles all across America.

One of my (our) regular difficulties before our rushing off the base on those liberty weekends was to first locate my Volkswagen Beetle. Why would this even be necessary? Somehow, well before we were going on liberty, a group of my Marine buddies, maybe 6 or so, would arrange to pick it up and carry it to a place where it couldn't easily be found. They thought this was amusing, so much so they did it week after week. They were extremely effective in keeping me and a couple of friends looking for it. It isn't easy to hide a car, a non-military vehicle, even a Volkswagen Beetle on a military base.

My dear friend had as strong a desire to get to New York City as I did; so he was always helpful in hunting for my hidden vehicle. We'd look all over the base proximal to where we lived in those Quonset huts, after all there's only so far these buddies could carry my Volkswagen Beetle. He seemed as annoyed as I was, and it wasn't even his car. Sometimes we found it quickly, other times we lost several hours in our quest.

Gas was one dollar for 5 gallons (that's right) and my two passengers each paid seven dollars for the round trip. My buddy sat next to me in the tight front seat and we were joined by another friend who was also from New York, in the backseat, where he had more space than either of us. I did all the driving; my dear friend offered to drive, but I didn't take him up on his offer. They either talked or occasionally slept. We were rushing to the New York area for dating and a quick visit home. Both up and back, we'd make one stop for some food and a "head" (toilet) stop.

There's nothing quite like being encapsulated in a Volkswagen Beetle for hours with a couple of buddies. This is the equivalent of being confined in a tent in terrible weather with two or three persons, and with minimal space to move around. It was during these extended trips we became close friends. We'd talk about all sorts of activities, the week's military events, some of the personalities of our senior officer instructors, our college experiences, our families, where we'd eventually be assigned after this school program, and our longer range future goals. We were fluent in each other's lives during these cramped, hurried regular journeys to and from the "Big Apple."

On weekends, the entire basic school class would stampede out, all of us going somewhere else well beyond Quantico Virginia. There was almost a herd mentality to exit from there to freer, unstructured realms. Then, on Sunday nights, there'd be this frantic reversal rush back from all over the map for these same officers to promptly return on schedule to the base to begin another week of rigorous training and study. Some had driven so many hours they'd return exhausted, but still had to be ready.

Finally, after 8 months of Basic School, the 557 fresh, young, trained and eager USMC 2nd Lieutenants were spread all over the place. It's too long a story as to how this distribution of junior officers is done by the Corps, but it's far from just a random distribution; my friend was assigned to artillery at Camp Lejeune, North Carolina; and I was shipped to Camp Pendleton California to become an infantry platoon commander. Without request, my dear friend suddenly provided a set of complete maps for me to use driving my Volkswagen to California.

Except for when my friend visited Lois and me right after we'd gotten married and were living in Washington, D.C., we did not see one another. Later on in more recent years, we only had intermittent contact via mail and holiday cards. But, we did reconnect at various USMC reunions starting in 1996 when our Basic School platoon met in Washington, and later on with the entire Basic School class, at least those attending of those still alive. (As of this writing, 169 buddies, including my dear friend, have died).

At these reunions, it was as if there'd never been in any separation between us. The fluency was there. We'd both been away from the USMC for years. We wrote to one another, called, and later on exchanged regular e-mails. In late October 2009 we and our wives met at Gargulio's, a fine Italian restaurant on West 15th Street in Coney Island, Brooklyn. It was a glorious day. He'd been a career FBI Special Agent for many years and I had been a college professor. The third person on those trips to and from New York, the one who always sat in the back seat of the Volkswagen Beetle, he became a lawyer. All three of us had gotten married and had families.

About a couple of months ago, we'd chatted on the phone. My buddy told me he was having a lot of trouble sleeping and was using prescribed medication. He didn't like how he felt using this drug. I reminded him that many years ago I'd been deeply involved in sleep research at Columbia, and knew something about sleep medications. I urged him to talk with his physician, consider not using them; and even sent him some current articles about the disadvantages of pharmaceutical agents related to sleep. These articles were from Harvard Medical School's Health Watch for Men. The television commercials advertising and encouraging the use of sleep medications offers considerable information about the possibility of becoming depressed and how they can promote sadness; and urge that if in any way you have suicidal thoughts or considerations, you should stop taking the medication immediately and contact your physician right away. It is unclear whether he stopped taking the drug he'd been using. It is also unclear if the drug influenced him in any of these ways.

What was it about this person who decided to abruptly and inexplicably end his life, what kind of person was he, at least through my eyes? My dear friend was a person of integrity, someone with definite perspectives on all sorts of topics we'd discussed. For those who did not know him, he might have been considered a somewhat rigid thinker, but I didn't believe this. His early Roman Catholic school training, upbringing and education could easily give this impression. This is something I am quite fluent about because of our similar backgrounds.

His definite viewpoints were blended with his ability to listen to others' positions; he was tolerant and respectful of varying opinions and belief, yet steady and strong in holding on to his. He liked orderliness, preferred to be in situations where the rules and regulations were clearly stated; then he was comfortable in living within them. His morality was predicated on basic principles of trustworthiness, fairness, and justice.

He liked to excel at different things, and this led him to eventually learn to fly, to be a flight instructor with the FBI, and become an expert sharpshooter with different weapons. He was extremely well-informed and read a great deal, as he sought clarity in many issues. He was a no-nonsense, clear thinking person. When he didn't know something or didn't understand what I was talking about, he'd ask me to clarify, to be more thorough. Although I do not recall ever seeing it, I suspect he had a temper and could get quite angry; and as someone who has one, perhaps I'm projecting to him what I know about myself. He had strong religious perspectives, and he was terribly disappointed about the behavior and recent uncovering of Catholic priests who'd violated boys, or violated their priestly other vows and commitments. And, beyond everything else, he loved and deeply cared about his wife and family with a quiet, steady approach, just as he cared about our country and the Marine Corps. He worried about America's future, and we'd talked about this.

So, where are we regarding my dear friend's suicide? He made a choice, but this choice has left a lot of us deeply saddened. Could he have offered some reasonable explanation for depriving himself the rest of his life, and all of us deprived of continuing to know and love him while living?

The answers to such questions remain forever lost in his now-gone neuronal firings just before he took his life. The mystery of his decision continues for those us left without him. There is no need for guilt or shame by anybody, and that includes my dear friend. We are all lonely and unfulfilled in different ways at different times in our lives. He became desperate. He did not want to go on any further. I want to believe as the bullet entered his body, in that millisecond, my dear friend was terribly sorry he pulled the trigger, and wished he could somehow magically reverse what he'd done. By then, it was too late. No matter, now, he was and is a dear friend.

2011

DUAL JOURNEYS

WE just returned from a glorious holiday trip to Santa Monica, California. California is a beautiful place, despite floods, earthquakes, forest fires, mudslides, soaring state population (35 million), ever packed 12 and 14 lane highways, and massive state-debt. The weather was superb, every day sunny, warm and idyllic vacation days throughout Southern California. Beyond everything, it sure beat the harsh East Coast winter weather so dominant these past few months.

We were traveling with our dear friend Rosemary Mahoney. Lois and I first met Rosemary and Michael Mahoney on a peace march in the early 1970s; we were protesting the raging Viet Nam War. Since then, we've known each other in Leonia, New Jersey. Over the years the four of us traveled together to Charleston, San Francisco, Italy, France, and Martha's Vineyard. Michael died in the late fall, 2008. This trip was the first long-distance the three of us together had taken since. Without him, It was a departure from our past travel events and known situations; and a new experience for each of us.

We took hikes in parks, visited museums, walked along the public beaches, and had splendid meals in various restaurants, some with beautiful views of the Pacific coastline or mountains. The many state parks are easily available; they also enhance the public's awareness of the fragility and beauty of the land. We saw nature at its best. While there, I continually noticed how open and free life is in that area. The weather innately promotes outdoor activities by the visitors and permanent residents as they pursue good health and proper exercise for sound minds and bodies.

Yet amidst the beauty and benefits of Santa Monica, there are also large numbers of homeless men and women, wandering about, lugging their possessions, seeking basic comforts during the day, and then disappearing at night to unknown places until the next day when they too can share in the common outdoor comforts. Santa Monica's conditions are conducive to those homeless and alone. But, this is another paradox, along with such wealth and luxury, there are those who are lost and with so little.

The spectacularly designed Getty Museum and its gardens high above Los Angeles with unobstructed views, and the famous, still bubbling oil/tar pits smack in the middle of Los Angeles that have yielded thousands of fossils were two other highlights. While in the Payne Museum at the tar pits, Lois and Rosemary went off to view a film about these pits; I sat on a bench, forward of a massive wall photograph of this same geographic area. The picture might have been from the early 1900s; and I went about methodically counting almost 65 wooden oil-rigs constructed and neatly lined up like huge wooden soldiers, operating smack at this same location that now is a small park/museum amidst skyscrapers and other surrounding buildings and streets. Children enthusiastically run about, looked after by their parents as they view the bubbling tar and stare at the hundreds of fossil specimens harvested from the tar pits over many years of collecting. Most of these are long gone, some minute, others six feet in height and weighing 1500 pounds, ancestors to organisms still alive today. They were all here roaming about so long ago, hundreds of thousands of years ago, maybe longer.

There is much going on in California regarding the total environment. Many innovative projects are operating to conserve water, to reduce pollution and to recycle wastes. There's a sensitivity and intense commitment to the ocean. Communities, marinas, and businesses bordering it have strict rules and systems in place to prevent waste products contaminating it. Solar energy (Santa Monica is striving to become a total solar community), hybrid and electric vehicles are frequently observed throughout Southern California.

We visited a beautiful Japanese garden ("Garden of Water and Fragrance") in Van Nuys, which is contiguous with a massive water treatment/recycling center handling and purifying the waste water of about 800,000 homes, and the businesses and industries in that area. The beauty of the garden, the textures, the water design, stone and rock arrangements in carefully planned patterns, and of course the many plantings and the serenity coupled with the functional operating technology of the treatment plant was an enlightening experience. Humans can do such creative and purposeful projects enhancing our lives. The statement "life is good" covers all of this.

We did a great deal of driving on the Pacific Coast Highway, journeying south to San Clemente, Laguna Beach and Oceanside and the beach communities beyond Los Angeles, Redondo, Manhattan and Newport Beaches. And we visited the mission at San Juan Capistrano where the swallows used to return each year on St. Joseph's Day (March 19th), and observed young school children getting California history lessons. The swallows are no longer returning; they've gone elsewhere.

While driving, we passed the massive USMC Camp Pendleton base. Seeing it again reminded me of my time there so long ago. In the mid-1950s, I served in the 5th Marines, First Marine Division as a platoon infantry commander, a young Second Lieutenant. That was during peacetime. Our daily military training activities involved climbing the hills of Camp Pendleton; going to the barren desert well beyond Los Angeles before it became fields of energy generating windmills and walled luxury communities and posh golf courses; intense cold mountain training at Pickle Meadows in Northern California;, and repeated simulated beach invasions along the Pendleton coastline. We were practicing for whatever might happen and where the Marines must go in warfare, that's what Marines do. We didn't go but all were ready. Some of my buddies talked about anxiously wanting to go.

Then, but a few days home in Rockport after our glorious trip and the privileges, serenity and beauty in Southern California, another dear friend sent me an e-mail concerning the United States Marine Corps. It was about this same Third Battalion, 5th Marines, First Marine Division, the one I'd originally served in 1957, except these days it's doing battle in Afghanistan. This unit is fully engaged in the ongoing, relentless war efforts. In the past four days, 12 Marines from this group died in combat. That's so far, more will follow as our troops battle supposedly in our behalf.

Here are their names and ages:

Justin Allen, 23,
Brett Linley, 29,
Matthew Weikert, 29,
Justus Bartett, 27,
Dave Santos, 21,
Chase Stanley, 21,
Jesse Reed, 26,
Matthew Johnson, 21,
Zachary Fisher, 24,
Brandon King, 23,
Christopher Goeke, 23,
Sheldon Tate, 27

What do you notice from the list? Besides being all male, (females are in Afghanistan too and some have died), all are in their twenties, with their ages ranging from 21 years to 29. The young serving in our behalf have given up their lives before they even got started; they were not yet out of their twenties and their enthusiastic youth. If we had more information about each of them, we'd find they undoubtedly come from all over the United States. It's likely they're all enlisted, lower ranking personnel. And if we knew their military ranks, we could probably estimate how long they've been in the Marine Corps, with several of the older ones in for longer periods, possibly career Marines. The younger ones have to recently completed boot camp in either Parris Island South Carolina or Marine Corps Recruit Depot in San Diego California. No information is provided about their families, or whether they are married or parents, or anything about their past or future intentions.

In 2010, I posted <u>War is Hell</u> on my website, <u>www. joemuzio.com</u>. At that time, 1002 military personnel from all the U.S. branches had died in Afghanistan. Those figures did not address the number of wounded in the Army, Navy, Marine Corps, and Air Force, only those killed. The wounded figures are considerably higher. Now, the grand total killed through early 2011 is 1476, not including these most recent 12 Marines. The total for the US military branches of service and other nations involved in this 10 year long war so far is 2332. These figures do not include Afghanistan's casualties, or those of the few other countries supporting our efforts.

For more than 10 years the United States has been at war in Afghanistan.

Hundreds of millions of dollars have been spent; thousands of military personnel and their families have been significantly changed; those returning will have personality disruptions along with other scars from being there; and there has been no clear, rational, logical explanation for why the United States is engaged in this extended battle. Why?

In Viet Nam, more than 57,000 Americans died. Those of us who opposed the Viet Nam War as it dragged on, when the dead and wounded figures continued to soar and more body bags were sent home, might believe that comparatively, the death/wounded figures from Afghanistan seem a meager drop in the bucket. Even so, death is death.

There were many more protestors and rallies in opposition to the Viet Nam War. The possibility of being drafted into the military and dying certainly stimulated a number of potential candidates objecting to the war for strictly selfish, survival reasons. Some didn't wait too long and fled to Canada and other locations accepting them to avoid being drafted. They were "draft-dodgers." They violated the laws, and were able to live and flourish while others randomly went in their places to serve, to die or to be injured.

Maybe at this point, some might be thinking since there no longer is a nationwide military draft and the military services rely exclusively on volunteers signing up, then there has to be an expectation something like Afghanistan or Iraq or some other place will require their going there and fighting a war for the rest of us. Such a perception is fallacious; it suggests justification for the irrational or senseless expenditure of these persons' lives simply because they joined of their own free will.

Right now you might be wondering what possible connection is there between my description of a fine vacation in California and the deaths of 12 Marines in combat far away from California? Is there any conceivable relationship, even a remote connection between the luxury and advantages of our beautiful trip and the deaths of these Marines whose desires and talents they will never know? Perhaps there is.

This war is a remarkably unique one. While our young are sent off in repeated meaningless battles and die or become casualties, the rest of us take vacations, carry out our daily rituals, make no sacrifices, and pursue our lives unhindered. Few talk about it. The media provide minimal coverage to the continual combat going on for so long, and whatever we know is probably only partially so. This war does not touch all the rest, it's under the table and given little thought and scant protest. It only affects those engaged in it and their families and friends. Their misery, their losses are hardly shared with us. No matter how we try to ignore it, or analyze it, no matter the cause, it is terribly undemocratic. It is also immoral.

None of these young men (or any others who've died in war) will ever experience the beauty of a vacation, or develop from their youth into adulthood, to use their lives for any effort to better themselves and this world. They are devoid of opportunity and laughter. For them, there are no trips with their loving friends and family, no journeys to museums, no walking in serene Japanese gardens, and no views of the Pacific coast. While the rest of us get the benefits of their efforts, at early ages they only got silence forever.

Politicians, military leaders, others monetarily benefitting from the war and those writing history books for elementary school children tell us this is the price that must be paid to live in our democracy and to be free. How did any of us come to believe such blatant propaganda? What has happened to us?

In 1929, a book titled <u>All Quiet on the Western Front</u> by Erich Maria Remarque was published, translated from German to English. It's about World War I, the war that supposedly would end all wars. The front piece statement reads:

> "This book is to be neither an accusation nor a confession, and least of all an adventure, for death is not an adventure to those who stand face to face with it. It will try simply to tell of a generation of men who, even though they may have escaped its shells, were destroyed by the war."

We need to read this book for the first time or again, as well as others deploring the horror and sheer waste of war.

2011

REVOLUTIONARY ADVANCES: COMMUNICATIONS DEVICES, SMARTPHONES, TABLETS, CELL PHONES, COMPUTERS

E ACH new invention and technological development stimulates changes in our thinking and behavior. In recent years, a uniquely human revolution has been taking place with the exploding, almost incessant development of communication and technological devices. Computers, cell phones, smart phones and tablets are everywhere. The range and scope of them seems limitless.

We change because of them and with them. Our minds integrate these communication devices into our daily lives; our interactions with one another are modified; and how we spend time alone and within a group. More and more we are substituting digital communication for personal communication. In the past people used to look at each other, talk, listen and react. Beyond any fluid vis-à-vis chatting, our devices promote remarkably varied personal and business relationships. They involve more focus on solitary activities, the manipulating of these ever-present technical devices with swift, agile digits, especially thumbs. It's possible to see couples or groups of people sitting together, each engaging their devices as they communicate within the boundaries of their screens to near and far away contacts. While physically being with others, we are technologically capable of being with others simultaneously in another environment.

Bllions of these communications devices are already out there and billions more are on the way. This does not include the estimated hundreds of thousands lost, damaged or stolen each day, and requiring replacements and expenses. They are slick looking, light, ultra compact, and designed to operate in milliseconds. Some of the unique brand names and captions are: BlackBerry, iPad1, and then iPad2 ("Faster, lighter, smart covers, 10 hour battery"), Droid, Nexus, Android, iPhone 4, then 5, Appstore, iTunes, Webcam, Wii (now its successor Wii U), Galaxy, Knack, and endless play stations are examples of what's available. The Apple Company just announced a new encompassing mechanism, "iCloud." It provides concomitant storing and access for all of an individual's personal devices.

Ongoing conversations about our newer technological goods take place; as if they're alive, dear reliable friends we can't do without. There are discussions about Facebook, Twitter, Google, LinkIn, Skype and chat rooms, along with excitement about the benefits of Kindle and Nook. We visit crowded Apple stores and other computer stores like places of historical interest and significance. Our lives are encompassed with all of this.

Terms related to our gear are throughout our daily chatter: "dead zone,""Can you hear me now?", "Blog," "Web site," "operating systems," "mega bites," links, "platforms," "routers," "booting up," "being brought up to speed," phishing sites, surfing, apps, and "delete" are mere examples. As people "text," AKA "texting" or even "sexing," their language is quite different than common English vocabulary. Letter-symbols such as "R U," "IMO," "BFF," "BTW," "LOL," "OMG, and "WTF" are commonplace and expected substitutions for coherent language. Similar abbreviations have been in our language long before this revolution, i.e., SOS and TNT, yet hardly with such expansive substituting usage.

The Internet is the encompassing component within this technology revolution. We have instantaneous access to everything, everybody, everywhere, and all ways. Wikipedia offers quick information, albeit written by anybody and everybody, and therefore on occasion being inaccurate, possibly superficial and slanted, although it is subject to additional editing. A result of such communication is anybody's opinion can be promulgated and treated as valid, conclusive facts. All statements and beliefs can take on lives of they own; they are the new reality, yet subject to change by others, and then changed again, perhaps again. Accuracy becomes a forgotten or transitory term.

Along with these communication technologies we're experiencing newer invasive and potentially dangerous risks. We have become far more vulnerable to exploitation and abuse. There are expanding incidents of identity thefts; financial and personal scams; and questionable overseas appeals for money; and the creation of fake profiles predicated on stolen information. Pornography, posting of intimate photographs, either authorized or surreptitiously, virtual sex, human and drug trafficking, facilitation of prostitution networks, and unknowing children lured into inviting chat rooms are harmful/hurtful activities via these technologies. In addition, gambling sites entice individuals into these addictive, money consuming activities in their quests for emotional highs and sudden winnings. Also, we do not have data regarding the effects of the created violent video games consuming inordinate time from our youth and adults.

Plagiarizing, a form of stealing becomes remarkably easy and tempting. As sources of information are sought, other's writings can be appropriated with attribution disregarded. Since it's already on the Internet, others can erroneously and conveniently think it's public domain, therefore belonging to all of us. Anybody can transmit lies, rumors and misinformation, along with countless personal hoaxes.

Some faculty in high schools and universities are requesting students to "turn off" their devices, including computers typically used in classrooms. How come? Some students are more engaged in their pre-occupying communication worlds, playing games, doing puzzles or texting amidst classroom activities. Whatever happened to dialogue between students and students, and students and faculty as they exchange their thoughts and ideas? Paying attention to others' comments and preparing sound questioning and refutations promotes responsible thinking and intellectual development. Have we totally abandoned those remnants of the revered Socratic approach?

We are subjected to barrages of political and social manipulations. Our screens and minds are inundated with flashing advertisements visually moving about and bombarding us as they are constantly superimposed on our lives. Some are devised to be just shy of subliminal, catching your eyes in milliseconds while unknowingly transmitting neuronal messages into the brain for possible processing and persuasion. Electrical engineers, neuroscientists and behavioral scientists are seeking research data to determine any potential harm from continual radiation altering our brains' metabolism and pathways. Can holding some devices close to the skull and brain or near other body parts cause damage and possible cancer? At least the World Health Organization experts think so in its latest report; and this institution urges more rigorous study.

Will millions of university, community and home libraries throughout the world be disassembled as millions of books are digitized and then readily available for our readable slates. Books and document collections are an integral part of our humanity and cultures; libraries serve a community as more than simply repositories of organized information, history and writings; and many citizens prefer those bound, unique versions of poetry, short stories, novels and other historical writings along with the other multi-media materials publicly and freely available in libraries.

There is no going back to those "good old days," if they ever were. It is far too early to assess the impact these devices have in this ongoing technological communications revolution. In the July/August 2008 issue of The Atlantic, a major article appeared: "Is Google Making Us Stoopid? – What the Internet is Doing to Our Brains," written by Nicholas Carr. Coupled with this issue, Scientific American, September 2008 published a full special issue on "Will Technology Kill Privacy?" The focus is on "The future of privacy and can we safeguard our information in a high-tech, insecure world?" Now almost three years later, these dual critical issues about the mind and privacy require our concern, sound research, and more thorough public discussion and analysis. It remains highly questionable and unresolved who and what organizations have access to our individual and collective data and for what purposes. What is private and what is public? Who speaks for individuals?

While this revolution leaps along and engages us, is there ever time for quiet, untimed contemplation and spontaneous creativity? When are we able to have unencumbered thought processes permitting our reflection and insights? A formidable issue requiring attention is how such extensive technical usage ultimately influences our traditionally evolved writing and speaking skills, our thinking and understanding, even the ways our brains/minds neuronally operate in conceptualizing, forming new ideas, and solving problems.

Beyond everything else, we just might have unknowingly lost reasonable control of our individual inherent privacy and freedoms, having already surrendered them to a magnified, amorphous and encompassing global community forever capable of delving into our lives and minds.

Addendum Reference:

After Babel – How social media dissolved the mortar of society and made America Stupid, Jonathan Haidt, <u>The Atlantic,</u> May, 2022.

2011

SUGGESTIONS TO ENHANCE CHILDREN'S LEARNING

W HAT I am going to write about is complex, controversial and not easily clarified. In several weeks, millions of students will be attending schools across this country for the start of a new academic year. It's a fine time to initiate sound practices to help students do well and enhance their educational adventures. It is advantageous to develop positive, constructive habits early rather than expending time and energy to replace poor patterns later on. Recent research in the neurosciences indicates positiveness promotes optimism and hope as well as success, while negativism can result in pessimism accompanied by failure and even serial degrees of depression.

Since just about everybody in our country has undergone some formal education, they believe they are experts in it. After all, they went through it and therefore possess first-hand knowledge about it. But, their perceptions could be outdated or bias. Most parents accept our public school system as the primary place where much formal and informal education occurs. In addition, parents can and do play a critical role in making sure this educational commitment takes place in an effective, positive manner. Of course, if parents are dissatisfied with what they believe is occurring, then many options can be brought into action.

In many ways, I never left schools. After being placed in a pre-kindergarten nursery program at 4 years of age, the bulk of my life has revolved around all sorts of formal and informal educational institutions. Now being 79 years of age, the rough figure for all of these years in educational arenas is 75 years. This includes being a substitute teacher at the elementary and high school levels; and then many years as a full time college professor. (I served almost 4 years in the United States Marine Corps with responsibility for the education and training of military units.) I pursued advanced degrees, have a doctorate in education and carried out major roles in education: formal studies, curricula development, research, wrote, and consulted on many educational topics while on college and university-wide committees. Also, I helped raise three sons; and when they were younger had major concerns about their educations, all in public schools. These biographical details are cited because I consider myself highly qualified to discuss various aspects of education, and to have the ability to offer serious suggestions about ongoing educational processes.

Indeed, education is a difficult process. Why do I say this? Because we all have different viewpoints as to what constitutes an "education." The ingredients for an "educated person" or a "good education" have widespread descriptions. Much depends on who's doing the defining. Some people think having an education means a person can earn a great deal of money or have a prestigious career. Others think it's especially important to go to the "right" schools. This will inherently promote an education accompanied by success, whatever that is. Of course, exactly what a "right" school is can also be subject to all sorts of interpretations, many of these being erroneous illusions, even based on just hearsay information or vague impressions. The overall purposes of an education in a democracy can bring forth additional topics and opinions for further discussion. These will not be considered at this time.

Then there are others who aren't quite sure about any of this. They believe this educational responsibility belongs solely to the school system where tax dollars and trained experts function. It's left for those in charge to decide what is best for the child, including compliance with various layers of legislated agencies and related community bodies. Whatever the situation, the child is subjected to a wide variety of measurable and anecdotal variables: administrators; teachers' competencies; curriculum being used; other students in the classes; home life of the child; child's growth rate; motivation of the child; and the mental and physical abilities of the child. (There is considerable controversy accompanying the variations in all of these realms.) If it isn't already clear to you, I'm suggesting whether a child learns, even enjoys learning, and then progresses at rates usually pre-determined by others, and possibly becomes an outstanding student eventually leading to being a fine citizen, it is extremely difficult to identify all of the contributory factors, including these.

With this introduction, let me offer specific suggestions as to ways a child's learning can be influenced. Some of these have been known; others might be considered basic or simplistic and already underway; and others you might disagree with and evaluate as unnecessary. You probably have ideas and attitudes of your own, too. But, it's my suggestion list and is presented in no particular priority order.

1. <u>PARENTAL DISSATISFACTIONS</u>: Schools are uneven, and do some things well and other things poorly. Whatever your perceptions of the school system, especially if they are negative ones, it is advisable to avoid communicating them to your children. Children exposed to such negativity might be worried what their parents will or can do about this. If you have dissatisfactions, make an appointment with those running the schools, and openly and calmly present these specific concerns with the appropriate professionals. Whether or not there are changes will depend on a number of things. You might want to follow-up to determine if there have been any modifications influencing your child. Parents have to appreciate teachers and school administrators are hardly miracle workers.

2. <u>INVOLVEMENT</u>: Be directly involved and supportive to your children's education, at school, after school, even during holidays and vacations. Education comes in many different structures and opportunities. Make sure the children meet deadline dates for assignments, do their homework thoroughly, and you verify its quality. These assignments belong to your child. There is a wide girth between being helpful and doing it for them while they watch or are pre-occupied with other interests. Recreation activities, computer games, television, sports can take place after school assignments are properly completed. No sooner.

3. <u>READING</u>: Encourage your children to read a great deal. Reading improves comprehension, focus, imagination, and language usage, and opens up the rest of the written world to a child. The child becomes engaged in the material, even transformed. It also promotes neuronal firing at the various higher centers in the brain. If a child says "Reading is boring," or anything else "is boring," that's silly. If a child is bored, it's because he/she is boring, nothing else. Do not accept cheap excuses to avoid reading, or even doing writing projects. Show me a clear writer and I'll show you a clear thinker.

4. <u>BECOMING A CLEAR THINKER</u>: When children make foolish, inaccurate or illogical remarks, it is important they be informed of this. Often children pass on hearsay information, make unsound or unkind remarks about teachers, classmates or friends, and this cannot be tolerated. Statements of innuendo or gossip are negative and unproductive. What evidence do they have to support their comments? Are they accurate? If they've made a mistake in something they've said or done, they must correct it and/or apologize for it. And they have to make an effort to avoid doing it again.

5. <u>TECHNOLOGY</u>: The television programs your children watch, the computer games they play, and their communications on a computer or cell phone must be regularly monitored by parents. There is so much going on in our society potentially dangerous or non-productive for children. They can easily become victims by mentally reacting to certain programs or responding to those communicating via these mechanisms. Also,

some research data support continual, excessive usage promotes addictive traits. It also takes time away from other possibly beneficial activities.

6. <u>OPPORTUNITIES</u>: If your children have an interest in building something, playing a musical instrument, learning to swim (a must) or excelling in some other activity, encourage this. Make it happen. You will be opening their minds and bodies to other experiences, and with hard work and commitment, they might even find out they have talent in the area they've expressed interest. They learn the importance of perseverance and structure to excel.

7. <u>THE BRAIN AND MIND</u>: Children's brains and minds grow at varying rates, as do their bodies. Each child is unique. Brains and their neuronal connections are not fully developed until sometime around 30 years of age (recently confirmed by research). Accept the variability and avoid making comparisons between one of your children and another, or with other people's children. Such created competition is fallacious because it disregards inherent differences. Much remains unknown about the plasticity and operations of the brain and mind, with continued research there will be clarifications.

8. <u>LEARNING</u>: Sometimes we learn by trial and error, sometimes sheer discovery, other times we become educated in a more orderly and logical way. A fine professor from Purdue University once told me: "Learning isn't something done to the learner, learning is something done by the learner." We gain skills and

knowledge by doing things, and hopefully doing them well after we understand and practice. If they're done poorly, patiently correct the child so they better understand and will gain self-confidence in their achievements. Nagging seldom is an effective learning device; besides it's upsetting and time consuming to the nagger as well. Besides, children adapt to nagging by ignoring it.

9. LIFETIME LEARNING: Education is a lifetime process. This process is typically varied, personal and done independently. This translates into encouraging independent thoughts and behavior. Sometimes seemingly doing nothing, or day-dreaming can be highly productive for one's mind to imagine, create, problem solve while not being cluttered or overloaded with other time consuming activities. What might seem like idleness or being unproductive could be that moment a child is seriously engaged in figuring something out that was puzzling her/him. It could be a moment of discovery.

10. LEARNING BEYOND SCHOOL: Learning takes place in all sorts of settings beyond the school environment and schedules. Other settings where learning can occur are in neighborhoods, while on vacations, and while playing. There are all sorts of wonderful summer programs, musical and drama camps, sporting activities, adventure experiences, etc. Family travel to new locations where there will be points of interest, historical sites, etc. are other examples of the variety out there. These cost some money and time, but they can remarkably influence children in determining in

their areas of interest, possible areas of study, even future careers. Carefully selected ones specifically of interest to your children exposes them to new opportunities not typically offered in regular formal school.

11. <u>PUBLIC AND PRIVATE EDUCATION</u>: You don't have to spend all of your money on a private school, where in many cases the programs aren't remarkably different than what your child experiences in public school. Avoid believing a private school is the ultimate solution for whatever you think you want for your children. You might think such a private school commitment will guarantee your child's acceptance to a better college, but that isn't necessarily so. Besides, certain attitudes and belief systems can be promulgated in private schools and by the students attending them. Sometimes snobbery, pretentiousness and superiority attitudes can become more prevalent there. Do you want to prepare your child for the world they will inevitably exist in, or the world you think you want them to exist, or to possibly mimic your world?

12. <u>POSITIVE TRAITS AND LIFESTYLE</u>: Train your children to be forthright, to have integrity, and to stand up for their rights and the rights of others, but not by screaming or whining. Such training will help to prepare them for an increasingly complex, more populated and sometimes chaotic world. It is highly questionable whether our standards of living here in America can forever be sustained when 70 percent of world's population survives on so much less and under far worse conditions. Children should know this, along

with knowing how much we are destroying the beauty and privileges of this planet, nature, and its nonhuman inhabitants. Help them to become environmentally sensitive, and to prepare for possibly living with less materialism, too. Promote the concepts of reduce, recycle, re-use in their lives.

13. A LANGUAGE BEYOND ENGLISH: In recent years, there are frequent references to the "global" aspects of our lives along with expanding multi-cultural dimensions. From early on, encourage your child to become proficient in another language beyond English. The earlier this takes place, the easier it will be. One needs to appreciate another language, to understand and communicate in that language, along with cultures beyond ours. There are various ways this can be achieved. Certainly being bi-lingual or even multi-lingual will have lifetime benefits and promote improved relationships with others.

14. CHILDREN'S CHORES: Amidst all of this, children need other responsibilities. This translates into carrying out chores on a regular basis. They might not like this, but family members carry out all sorts of work that must be done for all involved; and children should not be exempt. If the chore isn't properly done, have them do it until it meets your satisfaction. This requires some monitoring and supervision. There is dignity in labor.

15. FAMILY MEALS: Whatever your definition of a family, strive to have your family take its meals together as a family unit (without phones and computers). Conversing with one another, sharing the day's activities,

developing listening skills, and while learning proper table manners on a daily basis can be quite enlightening and instructive. And during these meals, no technical communications devices are to be used or on, including phone interruptions. These detract and isolate the users rather than having them engage in the family's interactions. They are an interference to sound dialogue.

16. <u>NUTRITION AND SLEEP PATTERNS</u>: Finally, beyond all of these suggestions and considerations, it is vital for children to have proper, balanced nutrition (less sugar, fewer snacks, more vegetables and fruit) and appropriate amounts of regular, uninterrupted sleep patterns. There are data indicating children can be experiencing malnutrition and/or sleep deprivation; and these conditions directly influence learning, behavior and attitudes. Both of these areas are sorely neglected in our society. Considerable information is available about nutrition and sleep from a variety of reputable sources.

Addendum Reference:

After Babel – How Social Media Dissolved The Mortar of Society and Make America Stupid, Jonathan Haidt, <u>The Atlantic</u>, May, 2022.

2011

RECOLLECTIONS

I T was once said, "Your memories are your life." I do not know the source of these words. The fine American author William Faulkner once said: "The past is never dead. It's not even the past." Both of these statements can promote much discussion. Can we accurately define the term "memories?" Is there such a thing as just "a" memory? What did Faulkner mean? How could "past" still be with us?

There are some individuals who claim they remember events from the first few years of their life, although it's extremely difficult to know whether such memories are based on original, consistently authentic traces. Recollections can change over time; and many factors influence their storage and retrieval. They change as they're retrieved and then told again, and even take on newer dimensions with each new telling. The recalling of earlier events can have embellishments, possibly totally different versions of what took place so long ago. And, there are situations where the same experience is remembered quite differently by different people who were present. The prime sources to resolve these variables are located within the intricacies and still mysterious aspects of the human mind and brain.

Then, there are certain events in our lives accurately imprinted in our minds forever. They are vividly recalled both shortly after they occurred, and then way down the road. We have photographic recollection, as if we're reliving it in its entirety: a marriage ceremony, giving birth, graduation and similar joyous events stay with us and can be fully recaptured. When we recall a tragic, unexpected and especially shocking event, at that instant we know exactly where we were, who we were with, and what we were doing.

It was early Sunday evening, December 7th, 1941. My mother, father, my sister Maria and I were driving home to Sunnyside Queens from Aunt Elizabeth's house in Bay Ridge, Brooklyn. My parents were in the front seat of our 1941 black Pontiac, Maria and I were sitting in the back. As we were driving along the Belt Parkway, we were listening to the radio. Suddenly there was a somber, monotone announcement Japanese planes had attacked the United States and its naval fleet at Pearl Harbor. I asked my parents "Where's Pearl Harbor?" They weren't sure, no, they didn't know. Shortly afterwards the announcer went on to mention something about the territory of Hawaii and an island of Oahu. I didn't know where that was, nor how this place had any connection to the 48 United States of America. Nor did I comprehend the reason for this bombing. The next day at school, our 4th grade teacher spent a lot of time pointing to a world map and explaining its location and what this attack meant to us and our country as Americans. The United States was going to war. There would be years of sadness to follow. Early in 1942, my father had to register for the military draft, even though he'd served in World War I and was 51 years old; and my mother volunteered to train and become a neighborhood block air raid warden.

Soon after this, small flags appeared in windows throughout our neighborhood, and in the rear windows of cars. They were rectangular, the border was red, the broad background inside this border was pure white, and in the middle of the white field was a blue 5 point star. The same combined colors of the American flag. This was a visual public announcement that someone in that house or apartment or store (and cars, too) were serving in the military service. Months later, but not too long afterwards, added to these flags or replacing them were newer flags with a gold star in the middle instead of the blue one. This meant a person had died while serving in the military. More and more gold star flags began to appear. At school, we were issued plastic dog tags that had printed information about us. They had to be worn at all times.

It was the early fall, 1944. We had been in a war for almost two years. The war was not going well for the United States and our allies. President Franklin Delano Roosevelt was running for a fourth term as our president. Pictures of President Roosevelt in the newspapers and in the newsreels showed him to look old and tired, his face was drawn and he had dark, deep rings under his eyes. There was a lot of publicity in our school about President Roosevelt because he was going to be driving down Queens Boulevard towards New York City. After returning from a Sunnyside Robins football practice at Bryant High School, and still in our dirty football uniforms, a bunch of us stood on the corner of 43rd St. and Queens Boulevard. It was raining. We waited for him, standing partially underneath the concrete archways of where the now Number 7 train runs between Main Street Flushing

and Queens Plaza, and then into the city. We were trying
to avoid getting too wet. We waited a long time and we were
wet anyway. Finally, he swiftly drove by us in a black limo,
preceded and followed by other dark vehicles. There were no
other vehicles on Queens Boulevard. He could barely be seen,
but I wanted to believe he smiled and waved at us. I had never
seen a President of our country before.

About six months later, it was on April 12, 1945, a
couple of months before my 13th birthday. I heard on the
radio our President, Franklin Delano Roosevelt had died
in Georgia. He was dead and there was much sadness and
emptiness about his death. What would happen and who
would take place in his absence? We knew nothing about
the Vice President, Harry S. Truman, who abruptly became
the President. We spent time in our classes talking about
who Harry Truman was and whether he could lead us in this
ongoing war to save democracies against the enemies.

World War II had been going on between 1939 and 1945,
although some historians believe it started maybe shortly
after World War I ended long ago in 1918. After years of
reading about the war, talking about it in schools and seeing
motion picture newsreels about the killings, bombings and
maimed bodies, the European part of it finally ended when
Germany surrendered on V-E day in May 1945; then Japan
surrendered on V-J day, August 15, 1945. This was a week
or so after the atomic bombings and utter destruction of
Hiroshima and Nagasaki, and hundreds of thousands of
citizens dead. It was announced on the radio; people in the
neighborhood began to gather out on the streets in clusters.

On that hot August day, after gathering up newspapers
on every floor of the 6-floor apartment house we lived in,
they were stored in hallway closets next to the chute for the

incinerator, I went up on the roof and threw bunches of them down onto the street. Returning time and again, I made many trips to different floors to gather more papers and throw them off the roof. When I ran out of these papers, I went into the dark basement of the building where there were more piles of stored newspapers and magazines newspapers, and took the elevator back up to the roof for more random throwing. Some of the thrown papers got caught up on the fire escapes on the side of the building; most of them ended up joining the collective litter below in the streets. This went on for a long time. I never did figure out why I did this, at 13 years of age I didn't know what else to do. Eventually, we learned that 50 million people died in World War II. We were hopeful democracy had won over totalitarianism and everything would be better. And it was, for a while.

On November 22, 1963, Lois had a dental appointment with Dr. George Brazill Jr., who was located at Rockefeller Center, 620 Fifth Avenue on the 18th floor. I drove her there. Lois knew him from her nursing student days at Roosevelt Hospital in the mid 1950's. She'd observed him when he was a dental intern at Roosevelt and was convinced he was an exceptional dentist, and he was. I parked our 1963 red Volkswagen Beetle and waited outside of St. Patrick's Cathedral, directly across from the massive gold-painted Atlas/Globe outside the building. Suddenly, there were groups of people standing in clusters in the streets. Few others were walking, just gathered together. There seemed to be a quiet on Fifth Avenue, unlike the typical hurried movements of people, buses, taxis, and cars. Church bells were chiming. (Lois doesn't think this is so, but that's part of memories.) I didn't make a connection between these bells and the quiet all about me, but my feeling was the city had stopped moving. While I sat there and opened the car window, someone said "President Kennedy has been shot." Shortly afterwards, Lois came across the street, she announced the same thing as she got into the car. We sat there a few minutes, turned on the car radio, listened to further news about our President and said nothing. We both felt sick. Was he killed by a lone gunman, two or three partners, or because of a major still undetermined foreign conspiracy? We still do not know with certainty, despite studies, commissions, film clips, and endless theories and opinions.

On the morning of a sparkling, clear fall, September 11, 2001, I was driving on the West Side of New York, heading south towards the Brooklyn Battery Tunnel. I passed the massive Twin Towers on my left and just shortly later entered the New York side of the tunnel. The inside tunnel distance is about a mile or more, I'm not sure of its exact distance. It takes but a few minutes to pass through it to the toll booths on the Brooklyn side. Just as I came out of the tunnel, the radio announcer said there's been a plane crash into one of the Twin Towers, some sort of accident, and there would be more details as soon as they arrived, but right now it was unclear. The Belt Parkway winds through downtown Brooklyn and around the periphery of the Brooklyn along the harbor entranceway to New York City. By the time I got to the college in Manhattan Beach, just about everybody on the campus knew what had happened. Clusters of students and faculty stood around, but there was no clarity or understanding. Smoke could be seen all the way from the where the Twin Towers were located to our campus miles away. Somehow, everything about me seemed quiet, silent. Several thousand innocent people died, plus those sent to do battle against forces in other countries where our leaders believe the evil deeds emanated. Were those battles worth all the further deaths, the maimed and the personal and economic costs? This is terribly difficult to assess.

It is now past September 11, 2001 and we're at September 11, 2011. Ten years have passed. Memorials to those horrors ten years ago are almost completely prepared, lists of the victims are prominently positioned at these memorials, and the families of those dead along with many others will visit the sites where the Twin Towers once were in New York City, at the Pentagon in Arlington, Virginia, and a field in Shanksville, Pennsylvania. As just about everybody knows, these are the three locations of incredible human destruction, beyond all historical attacks on our nation's soil. The victims' names were read one-by-one, their families still sob even though a decade has gone by. Some carry placards with their names; many others with photographs from years before are held up, they are smiling, hugging others, bright and hopeful. Sadness permeates everything a decade later.

Some events described above occurred almost 70 years ago, with the most recent one just 10 years ago. Despite time gone, each is recalled with incredible accuracy. They are held within us. In each of these horrific and seemingly isolated events over many years there are still the untoward common repercussions of shock, death, separation, loss and loneliness. We are different. After each of them the world, families and relationships are changed forever, they will never return to what had been. They couldn't. As Faulkner reminded us, "The past is never dead, it's not even past."

Each day, individuals and families confront personal, sensitive tragedies. Beyond them, we hope, we care and we love; and we stay the course. We believe in possibilities, we dream, plan the future and pursue new projects. We strive to offset losses; we find ways to keep ourselves engaged throughout our individual and collective journeys; and take on countless missions. Until then, we continue to gather more memories, choose to recollect some, forget others and live out our lives. Amidst life's rhythms, we know full well what the ultimate outcome will be for all of us.

Addendum Reference:

The Anatomy of Memory – An Anthology Edited by John McConkey, Oxford University Press, 1996.

2011

UNWANTED JOURNEY

T HIS past Sunday we attended a chamber concert at the newer Rockport Music Hall. This facility seats about 300, it is intimate, with the interior building materials of warm wood and stone, done mostly by local crafts/technical persons; and there's a massive window behind the stage facing the periphery of the Rockport harbor outward to the ocean expanse, giving a totally unobstructed view of water and sky and distance to the audience. It was early evening and still light.

As I sat there listening to the music and trying to feel and understand it, I was looking at the slowly passing clouds, seagulls soaring, even a hawk or two, and an occasional boat moving through the glistening water, all of this directly behind the players' silhouettes vigorously playing their instruments, and my mind wandered to where I was just a week ago.

Last week, two days after consuming raw seafood at a local restaurant, I was taken to Addison Gilbert Hospital in Gloucester. I was there for three days. After several hours in the emergency room, I was admitted to the Intensive Care Unit (ICU). Due to arrogance and stupidity, perhaps even a dash of fear, I'd postponed, incoherently objected to going there in the first place and later on. I was adamant, even calling Lois a "traitor" for wanting to take me to a hospital. I knew I'd be fine, but such a belief was totally false. Lois tried very hard to convince me, but I wouldn't yield. Beyond being born in a Sanitarium in Brooklyn, being hospitalized in the United States Marine Corps with a concussion many years ago, and doing sleep research in various New York City hospitals and medical centers, I have not been a hospital patient; generally I'm ignorant of hospitals' daily operations and rhythms in behalf of their guests.

My initially meager (in denial) symptoms of inexplicably falling down several times, awkwardness, not being able to get up despite being athletic and still in good shape, and some internal abdominal discomforts, all of this delayed my journey to the hospital. How foolish on my part. Later I found out from the competent doctors and nurses if I'd stubbornly delayed getting there just one more day later, they couldn't have brought me around and I would have died. I do not say this lightly. After all, there are limits to internal resilience and adaptations along with medical/technological capabilities, especially in the aged.

Such sober and convincing statements by the professionals caught my attention, especially when repeated by those in charge. So too when I found out our youngest son Matthew was flying in from San Francisco, after a mutual friend, Rosemarie Reed told him about my situation. On this matter, Matthew was furious he'd not been contacted by one of us. But, I'm going ahead of myself.

Earlier in the day before the day I did go to the hospital, as I was going to move my car, I fell into the bushes next to the car, getting caught in the protruding thorns and brambles, and cutting my legs, arms, hands and face. The more I struggled to get up, I would fall back and the more cuts there were. After looking for me and seeing the car door open, and hearing me call out, Lois found me next to the car. She then struggled for more than 30 minutes to get me up, after using a garden shears to cut away the bushes restraining me; this matter was taking on proportions I did not realize or understand, and yet refused to accept whatever was taking place. No matter how she instructed me to "roll over," "get on my hands and knees," "cross one arm over the other," I couldn't do any of these, and kept falling back into the bushes. She put a yoga mat under me and urged me to get on it, but still I couldn't. The falling-down score card was 3 different falls for this day. She spoke of getting me to the hospital but I would have none of this. How foolish and stupid.

The next day I fell again in the house, next to our bed. Now, it's a total of 4 falling-downs. This time with Lois quickly calling first our son Frank, who was at work. He was in Salem, distal to us, and he called Edward, who was in the next town over in Gloucester. I was incontinent and yet unaware of this situation. Each time I struggled to get up on my own, I hit the back of my head repeatedly on a small chest next to the bed; it was a series of sharp blows, but without the protection of a football helmet. Together, and primarily because of Edward being quite strong, they were able to get me up. Then, they brought a metal chair into the bathtub, sat me on it, and Edward bathed me. He then helped me dry off and get dressed. Since his arrival, he was calm, cool, collected and highly supportive. Because of his strength, he was able to move me in ways Lois couldn't alone. His behavior helped to calm me down, although when either of them spoke about going to a hospital I continued to say "no." They didn't listen, thank goodness.

No more delay, no more cheap excuses, no more protesting on my part, at least not as vehemently. They put me in the car and rushed me to the hospital. Much of the rest of this tale is still vague or unknown to me, and I rely on Lois and Edward and the hospital staff for clarification. I've been told even at the hospital while being admitted I was putting on my clothes and planning to leave, despite being confused, incontinent and outright hostile. I kept saying I would not be staying there, busying myself with getting my sneakers and socks on, trying to get into my Bermuda shorts. Fortunately for all of us, the staff knew what to do with patients like me, they must have been highly experienced in similar circumstances. My babbling was disregarded.

Many urine and blood tests were done; cardiac rate, blood pressure, respiratory rate and body temperature were monitored continuously. Later on when I'd been stabilized with IV isotonic saline (to counter dehydration) and a combination of IV antibiotics, and oxygen supplied, I would then have x-rays, CAT scans and an MRI. The early data indicated trouble: 144 Heart rate highly elevated, but no adequate blood pressure (70/nil rather than typical 120/65 mmHg); shallow respiratory rate of 33/minute (normally 10-15/minute); body temperature of 104.7 F (normally 98.6 degrees F +/-one degree). Because of a lack of adequate blood pressure in the renal arteries, the glomerular filtration rate (gfr) typically taking place within the microscopic levels in my kidneys was not occurring; the net result is toxins are now accumulating in the body rather than being removed via the massive dual kidneys apparatus; White blood count 17,000 (normal range is 5-6 thousand). All of this indicated severe trouble. Major systems were not functioning or gradually shutting down completely. There reaches a point where things might not be reversed.

When a person is in a hospital, it's a totally alien world. Much technical equipment, unfamiliar surroundings, unusual noises, all sorts of people in unique attire coming and going, and language and abbreviations are used almost in some code chatter. Just as when a recruit joins the USMC, personal items are stripped away, inventoried and removed from sight. The rear-exposing hospital gown is placed on the person and depending on the situation, you have new, totally unknown roommates, or if you're lucky enough a private room with no companions. Anyway, who wants to talk or see other sick individuals and their families at that time? If the patient is conscious enough to be aware of surroundings, there's an inherent state of anxiety coupled with an unknowing sense as to what's going to happen.

To allay all of these unusual subjective conditions, there are kind, attentive, often humorous staff members moving about. You are theirs and they have full power, control, and influence on you. Fortunately, they carry out their serious, sometimes unpleasant chores with balance and civility. They know their missions and go about them. Your internal life activities are technologically monitored, you can see and hear them flashing across the nearby screen. Because of my science background, I knew the data were not especially comforting. It was much worse than that.

Every person I came in contact with at the hospital, from the smiling woman who spoke with me as she swabbed the floor of my room, those drawing blood and setting up IVs for fluids and antibiotics, especially the nurses, the doctor in charge of the ICU, they worked vigorously in restoring me to some normalcy. When I was more coherent, I spoke with many of them: one nurse in the ER who patted me and told me they would "fix" me; another nurse whose husband died 6 years ago; another nurse whose husband is dying from smoking and can't stop and will die soon but she's not told anybody at the hospital about herself; an aide who was hit by a car, has titanium rods in his leg, had to leave the U.S. Air Force because of his tumultuous divorce and the debts he and his then wife acquired; and another nurse who recently moved against her husband's wishes to a place she thinks she's finding out she's allergic to the materials in the new apartment, but she hasn't told him yet. They efficiently and sensitively moved along in their restorative chores each day, despite all sorts of personal adversities to make me better.

And, while we invest trillions on supposedly trying to make 13th century primitive countries receptive to democracy, bribing officials, wasting lives of our troops, many coming home maimed and disrupted, we don't provide the kinds of appropriate salaries for those holding us together in hospitals, clinics, and other public facilities. We waste so much while others silently work day and night for us, including those who will not survive their illnesses. How pathetic and unappreciative we are in all of this.

As I was improving, but not sure of this, surrounded by Lois, Frank, Edward, Jeanne, Mia, Joe Grant and knowing Matthew was flying in from California and would arrive soon, I looked at each of them so deeply concerned about me and my life. I glanced at each of them, while they talked amongst themselves and realized how close I'd come to death itself, according to the staff members and my precarious health repercussions. In a flash, an unspoken moment I thought of the beauty and benefits of my life, how incredibly fortunate I was to be loved and cared about, and the thought came to me if I did die, it was OK. It was not what I wanted, but the presence of those loving me so deeply and my loving all of them somehow released me to believe perhaps my time was up, and all the rest of them would be well, comfortable and moving on in the endless movement of life itself. In that instant, I felt ecstatic and strangely prepared.

Eventually, thanks to the full forces of knowledge, technology, the attentive efforts of the staff and my innate recuperative powers I was much better, not yet whole, but so much so it was time to leave the ICU of Addison-Gilbert Hospital. As I went around the ICU, I wanted to say "goodbye" to those wonderful staff members on duty. I asked the day staff to tell the other shift members of my appreciation to them. We hugged, held each other briefly and some of us cried as I said "thank you."

After being home two more days, I returned to the ICU; Lois and I had sent roses to the staff, they were on display on a table; those working moving amongst patients, charting, hooking up technical equipment, looked up and were pleased to see me walking and smiling; and there were more hugs and tears from them and me. I was one of their success cases and they knew what they'd accomplished. They knew and so did I how grateful I was to all of them. When I went outside the hospital, it was a crisp, clear-blue sky, fall day. I recall looking up and realizing how fortunate I was. My life had more time.

Afterthoughts: Have I learned anything from this experience? Certainly.

First of all, pay attention to the messages your body is sending. Machiavelli once said: "Illness and wrong turns at first are difficult to recognize and easy to fix. Later on, both of them are easy to recognize, but there's not too much you can do about them then." There is no such thing as an unimportant symptom, and there's no reason to be foolish or arrogant as I was. Being a biologist and married to a nurse, I should have been much more balanced in what was taking place in my body.

Secondly, be careful what you consume. Just last Sunday, October 23, 2011 and Monday, October 24, 2011 <u>The Boston Globe</u> ran two front-page articles, "On the Menu, But Not on Your plate," and "From Sea to Sushi Bar, A System Open to Abuse." Investigators gathered 183 samples, sent them to a laboratory in Canada where via DNA testing and other methods discovered 87 of them, 48 percent were sold under the wrong species name. Many were mislabeled, sold as one species but always a cheaper or less advantageous one had been substituted, and even included frozen products rather than being the stated locally caught fresh ones. A number of them were identified as causing significant gastrointestinal problems, as well as unlabeled farmed and overfished species. Some were totally mislabeled, either intentionally or otherwise. Examples of such practices are: Haddock was ordered and Pacific cod was given; cod was ordered, haddock was served; Red snapper was ordered but Tilapia was served; white tuna was ordered, and Escolar, a toxic substitution already banned in Japan was provided to unknowing consumers.

The seafood industry is wide open and not subject to the more rigorous controls on meat and poultry, but even these areas have major biological issues, too. You cannot automatically count on the quality, sanitary conditions, labels and integrity of those typically merchandising seafood, shellfish, or raw products. Of course our mothers knew best: Smell the product, check out its eyes for clarity, and they will give strong indications whether it's fresh, stale or even rotten.

If in doubt, don't eat it, or refuse it. One needs to be better educated, ask questions and always be careful. Remember the clothing chain Syms logo: "An educated consumer is your (our) best customer," or words to that effect.

A third lesson is the sheer fragility of one's life, especially as one is aging, or if it is a child or infant. In the aged, resilience and adaptations are probably not as keen as they used to be; in the very young, they are not fully formed yet. Once body systems start to shut down, it is extremely difficult to offset, sometimes impossible to restore them to their homeostatic responsive conditions. Without appropriate, rapid health care, and not just on matters such as potential "seafood toxic poisoning" (check out the Center for Disease Controls (CDC) web sites on this and related conditions regarding incidents of food poisoning), a person's life can slip away and by then there is little that can be done despite all of our medical/technological advances. The margin is a thin one and often unpredictable.

2011

STONINGTON AND FOXWOODS

Recently, Lois and I took a trip to Stonington, Connecticut, a beautiful coastal town. In many ways, it's similar to Rockport, MA, where we live, but we wanted to take a short trip elsewhere. Everything about it tells you you're in New England. There are white clapboard, old buildings with names and dates on them going back to 1775; narrow streets, some cobblestoned; and many shops and restaurants with attractively decorated windows and storefronts for the upcoming holidays. There's a village barbershop where mostly men and some children sit and visit, and there's plenty of gossip.

Wherever we walked residents said "hello" and smiled. Children's voices could be heard throughout the town. The wind lashes across the streets, and you can see harbors, inlets, piers, boats and ocean in every direction. We stayed at a lovely inn on the water, met some nice people, had wine and cheese in the evening, walked all over town, and ate in local, casual restaurants where people knew one another. We even met an older United States Marine who'd served in Vietnam, (a person can be a "former" Catholic, but not a "former" Marine), he's now an accomplished professional photographer, and he sat and chatted with us.

Stonington is not far from Foxwoods and to Mohegan Sun, the two prominent gambling locations in Connecticut. We decided to go to Foxwoods because it was the closer of the two, according to the receptionist at the Inn at Stonington. Lois loves to play roulette. She remains calm, analyzes the wheel, spreads her bets and sometimes wins a few dollars. If she loses she sees it as a form of entertainment for a small price and without major commitments. Then, by prearrangement we meet in a designated place, and we leave. We have no interests in free drinks, free food, shopping, or anything else offered at these gambling palaces. Normally we spend at best a couple of hours there, no more. Once we leave and are outside, I feel relieved to breathe untreated fresh air.

What do I do while Lois plays roulette? After wasting about $20 - $30 on slot machines which doesn't take too long, I grab a cup of coffee, buy a newspaper and find a place to sit and read. This isn't completely true, I also wander around the various casino areas, to observe, eavesdrop and watch the flow of the thousands of people there. I call it "people watching." Our son Matthew and I have studied people and their movements at several airports, their patterns, conversations, and related interactions as they await flight arrangements. We refer to this as "people watching" too.

As I go about my journey, my mind explores what is going on? How did this form of entertainment become so popular? Is this pre-occupation with gambling some substitute for other activities citizens are running away from? Are there ever any winners, I mean real winners who leave with more than they totally lose that day and over time?

At this point you might wonder why I go to the gambling casino in the first place. That's a fine question. I'm not a gambler. Primarily because my father over his adult life was at different times both a legal and illegal bookmaker, he instilled in his children the awareness of foolishness in gambling. His mantra was "only the bookmaker wins." He would tell us many tales of gamblers who lost everything, their lives, jobs, marriages, and never won; they'd borrow from loan sharks and then they'd be in serious trouble; sometimes they did dishonest things in their addiction and fury to win. But it never happened. Their ultimate win and salvation was always just around the corner, about to happen, but it didn't. They always lost, no matter what they claimed, because they selectively remembered winning and had amnesia about losing, or at least breaking even.

Another reason I go to the casinos every so often is to examine this portion of the American society and how it absorbs time, energy and money. Somehow, over the years I've considered myself a non-trained combination of being an anthropologist/ sociologist. And, now since I spend much more time writing, all of these things are brought together. Some people study the homeless; others observe corporate America; and then there are those more curious about health care or alternative life styles or professional sports. Others prefer politics.

I'm also curious to see how these operations function. What overall benefits, if any are there to the casinos and gambling? Are the complimentary meals and sometimes free accommodations offered to some of the gamblers in reality "free?" How is it so many people can believe in the gambling activity, thinking they will become winners and magically by chance make easy money?

Let me briefly describe the typical gambling casino structure at Foxwoods, the buildings and arrangements. I've also visited the casinos in Atlantic City, Mohegan Sun, Lake Tahoe, and upstate New York, and all of these have certain operational similarities. Never having been to Las Vegas, now the family recreation capital of America, I can only wonder about the concentration of such casinos. These American versions are popping up throughout our country on supposedly especially American Indian properties. As we drove through beautiful Connecticut countryside, a massive, shining glass structure suddenly appeared on the horizon soaring into the sky. It didn't fit the terrain, the geography. It was an anomaly to the otherwise natural surroundings. By following the signs to each attractively named casino area; you can make a choice of where you want to go, but all of the facilities are massive gambling halls. Cars and buses pull into layered garage facilities (valet parking is available); the license plates are from all over the East Coast. The people seem to hurriedly disembark almost as if they are on some type of mission as they rush into their chosen casino areas. There's a speeded up pace to the combined human movement, a rush to get on with the activities.

There's a great deal of noise, especially from the endless rows of diverse slot machines giving off bells, clangs, whistles and multi-colored lights. Occasionally, someone screams out at winning, or almost winning. Certain areas are specifically designated for the major gambling ventures of roulette, blackjack, craps, and even a massive hall for bingo players. Within the casino structure are literally thousands of slot machines lined up in carpeted, darkened areas.

For the unknowing, the slot machines are also referred to as "one-arm bandits." These machines have a large metal arm on the side, the gambler pulls it to get the gambling process underway; but, these days the machines also have a large "push" button on the keyboard, so less effort is expended having to pull the metal arm, and there can be much faster repetitive gambling, and losing. The "one-arms" are still there but seldom used.

It's significant in these casino areas there are no windows to look out or clocks to tell you the time, they tend to be dark, subtle areas. Whether the area is designated "non smoking" or for smokers, the air seems terribly stagnant, almost creating some sort of respiratory dead-zone, but the gamblers' preoccupations give no indications of unhealthy breathing, even those chain smoking.

Sometimes there's a public address announcement calling out a name to remind someone his/her bus is leaving shortly and the rest of the group is anxiously waiting in the designated departure area. Please hurry along, wherever you are. Amidst this chaos waitresses in abbreviated outfits and uplifting exposing bras are walking around hawking drinks for the gambling participants. Since the drinks are gratis, they rely on the good will and generosity of the gamblers for their tips. You'll excuse me, but many of the waitresses simply do not look attractive in these distorted and revealing outfits.

There are many security personnel walking about, along with other employees available to assist by answering questions, pointing out where to obtain cash, where the rest rooms are, etc.

Amidst this predominant atmosphere and in strategic locations there's a piece of sculpture depicting some element of Indian history, folklore or identity may be found. There is even a specific area designated "museum." Beyond the casino areas are attractive areas for shopping, eating, and for consuming all sorts of materialistic items too numerous to list here.

It is difficult to offer generalizations about the bulk and variety of the gamblers, although my observations give me the opportunity to offer some reasonable categories. As one might expect, there are the very old, the middle aged, and then the younger population, some seeming to be teenagers wearing athletic sweaters for their favorite college or professional team. Some families have young children with them, but they are not permitted in the gaming areas, so they wander in the food and shop areas.

Large numbers of the aged use walkers, or motorized vehicles provided by management, or canes, while others transport supportive oxygen breathing apparatus. Many of the guests appear to be shabbily dressed, some having hurriedly arrived from work or even in dirty clothes. There is no one overwhelming racial observation, but this particular day there appeared to be a large number of Asians at many of the table games. Some tables are designed specifically for their cultural game preferences and languages. I do not know the names of them. There are also gaming tables preferentially for Hispanic speaking populations.

Yes, I realize to examine and discuss gambling casinos is but a fragment of the American scene (gambling casinos in Europe are remarkably different in format, yet my focus is exclusively on our country's), but they are definitely a major component of harvesting money from the citizenry. Many states in concert with the remaining American Indian tribes on reservations have found a legal and favorable method to gather more money from the citizens, so they form more and more gambling casinos throughout the country. For example, Massachusetts recently approved three gambling casinos to be strategically distributed in the state and one slot machine operation probably at a racetrack, Suffolk Downs, or even Logan Airport to capture travelers' monies there.

If the issue of gaining public approval is put to the voters, they have to decide whether or not to endorse the casinos, they are subjected, perhaps brainwashed in respect to the supposed long-term benefits of them. There will be construction jobs; and the casinos will employ thousands in good paying jobs. Promises are made more money will be available for schools, senior citizens, and even possibly to reduce their ever-soaring taxes with this supposed newer influx of money. It all sounds so advantageous, except the additional money did not swell the coffers for education, senior citizens, or other programs. In addition, with attendance at racetracks diminishing, officials and politicians along with self-interest groups are placing slot machines at the tracks to gather more money from the citizens.

How or why did our government officials in the first place get involved in selling the gambling concept to the citizenry? What lies and deceit are underway? Perhaps the ultimate but unspoken goal is to have gambling machines and lotteries along with easily accessible ATM machines in every store and shopping center in America, or wherever there's human traffic. Then, it would be so terribly convenient for all adults and inadvertently children to literally piss away their meager or hard earned dollars on a chance of "hitting it big." It might even be perceived as a new form of slavery, that is, commitments to an addiction predicated on hope and pleasure, but the statistical odds are calculated and pre-determined to always favor the "house." These are major profit-making institutions.

To my knowledge, the ratios of the "house" split with those gambling, as well as the profits, casino executives' salaries, taxes, the American-Indian share, and proportions distributed for the stated purposes beyond the gaming enterprises are not easily available or regularly promulgated public information. Where are these vital figures and why are they so closely guarded? How does one obtain them? Who audits the reported figures?

While in my observations of the gambling casino and my musings, I came upon what I believe is a refreshing and critical concept, one that could easily be accomplished at the gambling casinos in our country. Because there appear to be so many individuals in generally poor health, the casinos could initiate a concomitant facility right at the casinos, a comprehensive variety of medical and dental health clinics. The clinics would serve the populations frequenting the casinos. Examples of services that could be offered are: "how to stop smoking;" "coping with gambling addiction;" and "a basic understanding of statistics and chance." Maybe it would be helpful to have a properly equipped gymnasium, including a walking track, so the gamblers would also have the opportunity to engage in physical exercises while frequenting the casinos.

Will this ever happen? Highly unlikely. It certainly isn't in keeping with the underlying purposes of the gambling casinos. Their goals are to separate us from our money under the guise of entertainment, enjoyment, the adrenaline rush, and possibly obtaining free money. And all of this was done to supposedly provide additional funding for the sound community purposes of education, senior citizens and other needed areas. What happened?

THE SHAPE-UP - 1951

W HEN I was 19, I had a summer job in Long Island City, Queens. The job was at the General Electric (GE) Appliance Warehouse on Northern Boulevard. I had just finished my freshman year at Columbia and after having played freshman football that past fall was in excellent physical shape and full of energy.

Early each weekday morning at the warehouse, there was what is called "a shape up." The "shape-up" hiring procedure has been part of the waterfront/longshoremen scene for a long time. It was accurately depicted in the great Elia Kazin film "On the Waterfront." In addition to the regular union workers and truck drivers, there was a varying need for additional workers who were considered daily extras or temporaries. About a half hour or so prior to the starting work time when workers punch in on the time-clock, all those interested in working stood on the dock outside the foreman's office. There was no guarantee you'd get work just by showing up; and if you did get work one day, that didn't mean you'd get work the next day.

The men who showed up for this hiring procedure were certainly a mixed bag in ages, physical conditions, and overall appearances. Besides the younger transient college age like myself, there were older men, some who seemed down on their luck, others who had a slight odor of stale alcohol, and still others who like the rest of us had heard about the possibility of work, but looked ragged and stood in small groups chatting and smoking with those they seemed to know from other shape ups in local factory/warehouse areas.

The GE foreman's name was Charlie. He had a slight limp and a shoe was built up to compensate for one leg being slightly shorter than the other. He would come out of his office after he and the others in the office had determined exactly how many added day workers were needed for that day's work. While he looked over who was available, everybody got quiet and hopeful; Charlie would point out different persons to work. The rest dispersed, went home or to a local diner for coffee (or a local bar) on Northern Boulevard. That summer, I worked every day. Charlie must have liked me and knew I worked hard wherever he assigned me.

The key to getting hired was to be at the "shape-up" every day. Typically, newcomers didn't get picked; you had to persist by showing up day after day, and on time. Those not hired could come back the next day. If you didn't get work one day, keep showing up, be patient. If Charlie saw you were consistently interested by your daily appearance, looking alert and able, maybe even vying for his attention with a look at him, this meant you were serious and definitely wanted to work. A couple of my friends from Sunnyside and Woodside would be there intermittingly, sometimes a few minutes late while we waited on the dock for Charlie to come out of his office. Charlie didn't like this; to him, it was a lack of commitment. When they weren't picked, this simply reinforced their future expected disappointment, and they stopped showing up. This was the end at the "shape-up" for them.

Once you were hired, there were just three places in the GE operation you could work; and like so much in life each had advantages as well as disadvantages. You could be selected and told specifically to work in the warehouse for the day. This involved unloading the freight trains that had almost mysteriously rolled into the warehouse during the night, and were jam-packed with stacked cartons of all sorts of heavy appliances from the General Electric factory in Paducah, Kentucky.

This work was continuous, labor intensive and hard throughout the day. It involved being lined up outside the freight train platforms, and then using a heavy steel hand-truck, (I call them stevedore's trucks). One-by-one you'd enter the freight train, and load and wheel each packaged appliance from the freight train to those designated warehouse areas where these appliances would be stacked by category into high columns by a more trained person driving a machine called a "High-Low." Several "High-Low" operators would be whizzing around throughout the warehouse carrying out this repetitive and dangerous responsibility. There was the possibility of a boxed appliance somehow slipping off the lift the higher they were meticulously stacked in the warehouse; or even a mistake in the freight trains as they were unloaded.

These industrial heavy steel hand-trucks used in the warehouse were unlike any you might find in a typical hardware store. There was nothing flimsy or unsteady about them, they lasted forever; they were quite large, made with thick, heavy wooden, slightly curved handles and had steel reinforcement throughout. The two wheels on the bottom were made of thick rubber, probably 8-10 inches or more in circumference to support the weighty, bulky appliances as they were moved about.

The steel blade on the bottom of the hand-truck had a wide edge which slid under the appliance carton. Since this blade was repeatedly rubbed against both the steel floor in the freight trains and on the concrete floors in the warehouse, it ultimately had a sharp, worn but firm edge, almost like a thick cutting blade. When you were using one of these hand-trucks, you were aware of this, and always extra careful not to have that sharp edge of your hand-truck near another worker lined up directly in front of you while waiting to get into the freight trains, or as you moved about the warehouse. The unwritten rule was to keep the blade down while you were waiting, never protruding upwards. You could do some serious damage to another person. If you're wondering about the details provided on these warehouse hand-trucks, I'll come back to this later on.

The second work assignment possibility was for Charlie the foreman to point you out to a specific driver and a particular truck loaded with appliances (done by the night crew), and you would be the third man on the truck. The driver and his helper were senior, older men who were long in the Teamsters' local; I think it was Local 807 or Local 847. Each truck's crew was involved in delivering appliances to homes and apartments throughout New York boroughs; each borough was broken up into delivery regions. There might be as many as 10-20 trucks going out per day, depending on the total number of deliveries. Once these regular union employees, many who'd been in World War II, knew you were there only for the summer, you were referred to as "college kids" or "Joe College." The kidding from them was relentless and often humorous. Many were friendly guys, hardened by life, yet quite inquisitive about college and you. Some had children of similar ages to the college students working there.

As the second helper, you did most of the less skilled labor involved in the deliveries, being sure to pay close attention to the driver's orders, such as guiding him when he was backing up the truck; or jumping up on the back of the truck and moving the appliance to be delivered to the edge of the truck's platform (there were no lifts on the back of the truck); breaking down the massive cardboard cartons the appliances came in; or even keeping your mouth shut unless you were specifically asked something by either the driver or his buddy.

After a full day of deliveries, the trucks returned to the warehouse, sometimes called "the barn," where there was a night crew that emptied the trucks of old and returned appliances, and then went about the activities to re-load them with the next day's appliances designated by the dispatcher's lists. There was logistical precision and rhythm to this ongoing process to complement the daytime missions of getting General Electric appliances efficiently delivered throughout New York City.

The third possibility was to spend the working hours breaking up the older and broken appliances returned to the warehouse from those places deliveries were made. Only a few at the "shape up" were assigned this daily work. This involved using a sledge hammer and other tools to disassemble these appliances for salvaging and recycling. It was done in an open area behind the warehouse and involved a lot of sweat and hard work, especially on those hot New York City summer days. But, at least you were outdoors and left alone to do this. It's noteworthy there were no safety goggles, no helmets, no metal-tipped shoes, no cover-alls, nothing to protect you as metal and plastic pieces were flying about from your vigorous sledge hammer swings. Sometimes you got hit directly in the face or arms, or reflexively closed your eyes as you hit the appliance with the sledge hammer. There didn't seem to be any safety regulations, instructions or inspections by any safety officials. At least I never saw any.

Of these three job possibilities, my definite preference was to be out on the delivery trucks, and for so many reasons. Traveling through a particular borough during the summer, and observing all of the street interactions, having quick breakfasts and long lunches in different places the driver knew were special, and spending time with the crew talking and kidding around, these were all advantages to being on the road in preference to being in the massive, hot warehouse or out in the yard breaking up appliances. And, the drivers always knew great places to have lunch or supper, depending how long you'd be out on deliveries each day.

There were other advantages to being on the trucks delivering appliances. You would work hard making the delivery, then drive to the next delivery point. This was time to relax. Some places you would get a tip, and the crew would split tips at the end of the work day. There was a lot of variability, with each delivery being different. Also, by manipulating the time needed for each delivery, (this was the chore of the driver), and exaggerating the delivery procedure, there were overtime hours that got built into the day's work sheet. On many of the deliveries we'd have to problem-solve: Removing the old appliance before putting in the new one; figuring out how to get the appliance up winding stairs;

making sure the appliance fit into the doorways, sometimes we'd have to take the door off the refrigerator to make it through the doorway; and even explaining the new appliance to the new owner who'd been waiting for it. These owners preferred this rather than reading the accompanying written instructions.

One day at the "shape up," I was told to remain and work in the warehouse, probably with 10 other workers. We would unload several freight trains that had arrived during the previous night. This warehouse work crew typically was a combination of seasoned, regular union workers who consistently worked in the warehouse along with perhaps 2 or 3 of the summer college students and a few other day workers. The work was continuous, boring, and so repetitive you could almost fall into a pattern of non-thinking labor. In and out of the freight train; load up with an appliance on your hand-truck; transport that appliance to the correct area; leave it there for the drivers of the motorized High-Low machines to lift and stack it to its proper place; and then return again and again with your empty hand-truck where you'd wait in line to get another appliance. By the end of the day you were tired, sweaty and glad the day was almost finished.

This day, I was standing in line leaning on my hand-truck, waiting for my turn to go into the freight train to pick up an appliance. In line several guys ahead of me was "Big Teddy," one of the union regulars who'd worked at the warehouse for years. One of the drivers I'd worked with had warned me awhile ago to stay away from him, but he didn't elaborate and I didn't ask why. A summer worker going back to college wouldn't ask why, at least not this one. He always worked in the warehouse, and his name told you part of the reasons why. He was about 6 feet 4 inches and probably weighed at least 275 – 285 pounds, maybe more. Even though I knew large football players at Columbia, this guy seemed especially huge. His thick belt holding up his baggy trousers hardly contained his massive overhanging gut. His work shoes were worn down on the outside soles. Usually, he had a cigarette fragment hanging from the corner of his mouth. Seldom did he speak, and if he did it was some rough, brief comment. As a senior union person, "Big Teddy" worked only in the warehouse. It would have been extremely difficult for him to go out on the delivery trucks, climbing up and down on the truck, or even fitting in the cab of the truck with the driver and the other helper.

Maybe there was another reason he didn't go out on the trucks. "Big Teddy" smelled. He had terrible body odor. It was not like any odor of sweat or dirty clothing I'd experienced in athletic locker rooms or gyms, but now knew what a pungent, rancid, offensive, body odor was. On those rare occasions I did work in the warehouse, he smelled so bad I made it my business to stand further back from him when lining up to go into the freight trains.

It was "Big Teddy's" turn to go into the freight train. Ahead of him already in the freight train was also another regular worker. He was well known to "Big Teddy." Then, before this other worker came out of the freight train with his appliance on his hand-truck, suddenly, inexplicably "Big Teddy" moved into the train before it was his turn to enter. You'd have to know the inside of the freight train and the operating procedure to get the appliances out of the train to understand this was terribly unusual and made conditions crowded because of the stacked appliances, the workers unloading them, and the worker with the hand-truck in there.

Suddenly there was a scream in the train; with the train partially unloaded the scream echoed off the train's metal and out onto the platform where the rest of us waited our turn. Those outside the train rushed to its wide-opening and saw the worker who'd gone in before "Big Teddy" lying on the ground, screaming and obviously in much pain, his hand-truck overturned and empty. There was some blood on the metal floor. Still standing was "Big Teddy" leaning on his hand-truck quietly looking at the situation. Those workers inside the train were leaning over the other worker, trying to help him get up, but he couldn't, so he was left there and tried to comfort him.

What happened was "Big Teddy" had rammed the sharp, well-honed metal blade of his hand-truck directly into the backs of this worker's legs just about at the level of his Achilles tendons, severing them. The worker collapsed on the train floor. These Achilles tendons extend from the lower end of the calf muscles or gastrocnemius muscles. Normally, when these muscles contract they lift a person's heels, and thereby allow walking or running smoothly, correctly and effectively. Some athletes, dancers, or industrial workers sometimes might strain their Achilles tendon as they try to do a slightly irregular movement; it would take months of healing and rehabilitation to offset the resulting damage. This happened to the great Joe DiMaggio and he was out for many months. But, intentionally severing them with the steel blade of a hand truck, this was an entirely different story. Recovery from this kind of injury takes a long time and sometimes has lifelong effects in a person's ability to walk correctly. Just try to walk or run without being able to lift your heel, it can't be done.

The screams resulted in other workers gathering at the train and an ambulance was called. Word quickly spread through the warehouse and work stopped as others came to gather outside the freight train. Soon, the worker's screams transformed into quieter moans, as he seemed to phase in and out of consciousness. Someone brought a towel or cloth and tried to contain the bleeding in his legs. After a while, an ambulance arrived and the worker was taken by stretcher outside the warehouse to a local hospital in Astoria, Queens. He was gone. Then the warehouse activities started up again and we all returned to our work functions.

Nobody, at least publicly ever said anything to "Big Teddy;" nor did he say anything, no explanation, nothing. All of us just let it go. Later on, the word in the warehouse was "Big Teddy" and this worker hadn't been getting along for some time; "Big Teddy" viciously decided to resolve the issue in his own brutal way. Why did he do this?

Eventually, there was some sort of abbreviated investigation by somebody in the warehouse. "Big Teddy" continued to work. We all stayed away from him, and if near him during warehouse work, kept a close eye on him. When I left there in late August to return to college, he was still working, still smelling and still staying mostly to himself. This was one bad mean dude.

After finishing my sophomore year at Columbia in 1952, I returned to work at the GE warehouse. "Big Teddy" was there; and so were the drivers and other workers I knew. The damaged worker whose Achilles tendons had been severed never came back.

Here it is almost 60 years later and they're still in my mind and thoughts.

EVERYBODY'S HERITAGE

E VERY so often we wonder from "whence we came." We want to trace our "roots," our "family history," or our "heritage." These are just some of the terms that describe our long ago genetic backgrounds. We want to satisfy our curiosity. We seek clarity via the examination of the past.

Most of us have some information about our grandparents; and even occasional photographs, stories or vague details regarding our great grandparents. Beyond these generations, it typically gets fuzzy. In some cases and for so many reasons, it borders on the impossible. Some of us give up in our efforts, we stop trying, and rationalizing it doesn't matter at this point.

With the more recent electronic developments facilitating our access to historical records, birth, wedding and death certificates, and municipal and church/synagogue documents, newer services have developed to help individuals collect fragments of their family relationships. And, if one Googles the term "genealogy," right now there are more than 500 million reference points! For example, Ancestry.com has provided services to many millions of people; there are many other sites including Family Tree Maker able to assist in tracing lineages; and there are individual experts offering guidance and services for fees. Someone once joked he paid $10,000 to comprehensively identify his "genealogy." But once he knew it, he then paid another $10,000 to bury it.

There are some families who have a lot of information about their past relatives going back several hundreds of years. But, this is comparatively rare. This includes written documents, old faded photographs and letters, and compiled genealogy lists. A clear example of one family's quest for gathering information about its history concerns Lois Grant Muzio and her first cousin Connie Grant Collin. Their great aunt Martha had some handwritten notes along with some documents related to earlier family members, some going back to the California gold rush, papers supporting candidacy to join the Daughters of the American Revolution (D.A.R.), and a genealogical charting of family members traced back into the 1700's.

Using the computer program of Family Tree Maker, Connie spent many months digitalizing and continuing to add data to this charting. These records indicate family members who came to the North American continent from England and Scotland. During Cromwell's time, they were given a rather questionable choice: Either go to jail, or instead leave the country and rapidly exit to the colonies. They made a wise choice. In 1652, Peter and Thomas Grant along with 10 other Grants came to the Boston area. Some of them settled in Woburn, Massachusetts, others in Berwick and Kennebunk Maine, and Stevens Point, Wisconsin. When Lois and Connie get together and review these genealogical charts, their spread out documents including dates and names take up considerable table space.

Regarding my Italian relatives and their roots, there are only scant data. So, instead I take the easy route and simply announce my family's genealogy begins rather abruptly at Ellis Island, in the New York City/New Jersey harbor. We start around the late 1880's. That's when my grandparents and some of their children arrived in America and took up tenement life in lower Manhattan. Once when I did ask my mother about our "roots" she simply commented: "You needn't bother, we all came from peasants in southern Italy." She went on to say: "And we're all short and built close to the ground so we can pick the crops." That's my mother's analysis of our genetic heritage. She left it at that.

In addition to these more personal interests, there are the difficult, complex, scholarly and scientific investigations seeking to better understand when primitive yet unique human traits began to appear in our evolutionary journey. Biologists; sociologists, anthropologists and other multidisciplinary researchers are engaged in the study of human evolution. Still, there remains both confusion and controversy in this realm. Today, much remains unknown, and the studies will continue to promote further clarification.

Of course the ultimate, most encompassing area to trace one's genetic background is still being explored. The elaborate worldwide Genome Project focuses on genetically tracing all of the more than 20,000 genes making up humans. Such investigations are underway in research centers, universities and public and private organizations. Relatively few complete human genome sequencings have been done. The costs to do them have dropped dramatically and more will be done soon. Eventually this area will yield much more accurate data of biologically who we are, both in normalcy and in the many diseased conditions afflicting humans. There's already a newer television program, "Finding your roots," hosted by a Harvard faculty member. The focus is on DNA and tracing family linkages, and some have been quite surprising to the participants.

As we move on, one wonders why such newer, intense formal interest in our heritage. Do we expect to unlock significant secrets about our long ago past? Will whatever we discover give us a richer understanding of ourselves? Equally vital is whether or not what we gather up is accurate and reliable. After all, wouldn't it be some sort of cruel joke if we predicate ourselves on fictitious data?

In any final analysis, will it matter now and in our future?

Addendum References:

The Code Breaker – Jennifer Doubna, Gene Editing, and The Future of the Human Race, Walter Isaacson, New York, Simon and Schuster, 2021.

The Gene – An Intimate History, Siddhartha Mukherjee, New York, Scribner, 2016.

2012

JACKIE ROBINSON - PROGRESS=CHANGE

I T was the spring of 1946. My childhood buddy Larry Sulllivan and I went on a long journey. We were 13 years of age (I would be 14 in a few months, Larry was 13 until the following February). While sitting in the schoolyard in Sunnyside, Queens during our Easter school vacation, we spontaneously decided to hitchhike to Washington. D.C. In pure impulsive excitement coupled with foolishness, and the reasoning of children with immature brains, we were going off on an adventure the next day.

Without parental notification or authorization, (we did leave our parents a note), little money, and a poor understanding of highway travel, we found our way to New Jersey and Route #1, the north/south corridor road from Maine to Florida. After many hours, occasional directional errors, pouring rain throughout our voyage, lots of kind drivers, and enough money for two bowls of hot soup in a Baltimore diner, we did get to Washington. The Traveler's Aid staff at the major train station, Union Station, somehow found us a room to stay in, and gave us some funds to carry us through our visit. We were most cautious with their generous gift to us. We visited many national monuments including the House of Representatives, the Lincoln and Jefferson monuments and other historical sites we'd never seen before and had only read about in our schoolbooks.

It was here in our nation's capital we saw for the first time segregated, "Black," "Colored," "non-White" and "White Only" signs at the train station and elsewhere. These signs marked the public toilets, drinking fountains, and restaurants. Outside the station, we noticed only black passengers seating in the back of the public trolleys and buses. When they got on, they casually would move to the back. This system existed, thrived, was silently and obediently complied with. That was life in our capital. It seemed to extend to areas outside of the D.C. area, too. We found this out because we erroneously got on trolleys and buses going to the suburbs, and saw continued segregation away from the capital.

Having lived our formative years in the New York City area, this was indeed, a strange, peculiarly structured world. We knew nothing like this. We couldn't understand this arrangement. How could it exist in our country's capital? It was inconsistent with all we learned in school: our civics classes never discussed this; nor did our Declaration of Independence and our Constitution. There were "inalienable rights of life, liberty and the pursuit of happiness"for all. Weren't we all free?

We attended school and played with black children, and they were our friends, and we knew black families. We were so beyond the deadly Civil War and its repercussions; our country had already been in two World Wars supposedly to sustain democracies throughout the world. Yet we were witnessing outright, endorsed, practiced segregation and the accompanying denial of other basic rights. I won't even attempt to get into what this must have been doing to the minds and spirits of those subjected to such practices. We talked about this after making our observations, for a long time and after we got home. We didn't live it or face it on a daily basis, and it faded into our mental backgrounds and regular activities. But it was still there.

All of this was occurring in America right on through post World War II, and years before the Brown v. Board of Education case, and the progressive and long-sought after Civil Rights Acts of the 1960's. Until these legislative acts and various court decisions, as well as national leadership, America was a distinctly segregated nation in virtually every human endeavor.

It was still years before a black woman, Rosa Parks or any other courageous person refused to give up her/his seat on the bus; or when others sat at a Woolworth's 5 and 10 cent store counter and wanted to be served food and beverage like white customers; or sit-ins; or the Freedom Riders; or the civil rights marches. We need to remind ourselves despite court decisions and legislative actions, many powerful groups across this country refused to comply with the conditions set forth and continued to endorse created segregated practices.

A year after our hitchhiking journey to Washington, on April 15th, 1947, Jackie Roosevelt Robinson, the first black baseball player broke the long standing color barrier in Major League baseball. Robinson came up from the Brooklyn Dodgers' farm team, the Montreal Royals of the International League. Branch Rickey, the president of the Brooklyn Dodgers made this happen. He had the courage and perseverance to break this barrier, but with much resistance from a variety of influential sources. He also was a keen assessor of baseball talent and his thorough understanding of outstanding baseball talent played a critical part in his inevitable decision. And he was a businessman and realized the potential monetary benefits to finally include talented black players.

Mr. Rickey held a number of lengthy preparatory meetings with Robinson in order to determine his suitability for this unique challenge, and to help prepare him for impending racial difficulties he would encounter. Robinson would have to sharply inhibit his personal anger and possible reactions to all that would spew out, the racially predictable reactions from baseball club owners, fans, and other players. Both Rickey and Robinson were special human beings, they were heroic, and changed baseball, society and American history forever.

Despite all sorts of individual and collective opposition from fans and ballplayers and others, including the baseball club owners who voted 15 - 1 against this integration move, still it was going to happen. Jackie Robinson's athletic talents could not be denied. His abilities certainly were well beyond what some white players in baseball had. Somehow, just try to imagine being a black person and how you might feel about this significant racial breakthrough: a black ballplayer finally getting into the major leagues.

Throughout Jackie Robinson's life, from early childhood right on through college at UCLA where he was a gifted athlete, he repeatedly met racial humiliations. So too did his older brother Matthew, who in the 1936 Olympics ran second to the great Jesse Owens, yet was completely snubbed in Pasadena, California when he returned from them. This offended Robinson a great deal. Robinson served as a United States Army officer during World War II (no combat). In 1944, as a 2nd Lieutenant in the U.S. Army at Fort Hood, Texas, Robinson was given a general court martial for his refusal to move to the back of a bus on the military base when ordered to do so by the civilian bus driver. (According to the Uniform Code of Military Justice, there are three levels of court martial: summary, special and the most serious, general, which also results in the most severe penalties.) This incident, in which Robinson was eventually acquitted was demonstrative of his character and determination, and in some respects good fortune to have important political and legal forces come together in his support. In Jimmy Breslin's book, <u>Branch Rickey</u>, there are about 10 pages focusing on documented statements from this military court case involving Robinson.

Until this exact instant on April 15th, 1947 when Robinson ran out on Ebbets Field in Brooklyn to play first base, black baseball players did not play in the majors. There didn't seem to be any written code, regulation or document stating this, it just was the accepted long-standing situation. Blacks did play in separate, totally segregated Negro Leagues. Typically before the start of the regular Major League season there were those rare "barnstorming" occasions when a collection of all-white major league players would play exhibition games against all-black teams. These games were played in segregated-sitting ballparks and were well attended by blacks. Many blacks were curious to see how their players would do against the white ones. Sometimes the games were won by the major league teams, other times by the Negro League players. If a black pitcher struck out several known white players in a row, or another hit well against a white pitcher, it got publicity in the local newspapers.

The history of the Negro Leagues is a fascinating journey of athleticism, discrimination, and patience by hundreds of outstanding Black athletes and thousands more of the segregated Black fans. It manifests American racism at its worst levels. There were players in the Negro Leagues certainly equal or better than some Whites already playing in the major leagues. Yet they were barred from playing, just as they had been banned from schools, jobs, military services, drinking fountains and transportation, hotels, neighborhoods, and just about every other conceivable realm enforced by bigoted forces, rules and traditions. The most powerful democracy in the history of civilization discriminated against those of color. How could this be?

No matter their talents, skills and outstanding athletic abilities, they were excluded from full baseball opportunity because of skin color, their race. These ballplayers were underpaid, had poor equipment and uniforms, and played in inferior ballparks. They stayed in segregated cheap hotels and private homes whenever they traveled; ate in segregated restaurants; and their trips between cities on their schedules were on unsafe, decrepit buses. Often the players drove these buses. But play baseball they did, and they met the needs of their black fans and their own desires or need to play ball. There was constant adversity to overcome.

Robinson was treated viciously and with disdain from the first day he played for the Brooklyn Dodgers. There were all sorts of insults, taunts and death threats, both on the baseball field and when off of it. This was so for his family, his wife Rachel and their children. Such gross and nasty racial activities were carried out by fans and the players on other teams in all of the cities where the Dodgers traveled, and even by some of his teammates. Some opposing players attempted to "spike" him, others threw at him when he was batting, and a few would try to spit on his baseball shoes, sometimes succeeding. There were all sorts of verbal abuses, especially involving the "N" word. Because Robinson had made a deep promise to Rickey, he would not react or retaliate to these horrible examples of racism. He was a silent hero. This caused only confusion for his tormenters. It was the classic Biblical "turn the other cheek."

Earlier efforts by some of Robinson's white teammates to petition the Brooklyn Dodgers' ownership to prevent him from playing did not prevail. One person crucial for Robinson's acceptance on the Dodgers was Pee Wee Reese, the renowned shortstop and team captain. Eventually, those more reluctant teammates recognized his extraordinary athletic abilities; a few became friends with him. Shortly after Robinson's successful rookie year and his overcoming many adversities, other black players joined him in the Major Leagues: Roy Campanella, Don Newcombe, Larry Doby,

Satchel Paige and many others came along successfully. Some Major League teams were noticeably slow in having black players for a while. Were they resistant to change?

I saw Robinson play at Ebbets Field in Brooklyn. He was a most gifted athlete, exceptional beyond so many others. He could play a number of positions, infield and outfield, but not catcher or pitcher; he could hit or homers and to all fields; and could he run, sometimes stealing home from third base, a highly unusual ability. Earlier Major League players, including Ty Cobb and Lou Gehrig did steal home. In the old days, they did it frequently. Robinson did it a total of 19 times in his career, plus once in the 1955 World Series against the Yankees. How often do you see anyone steal home in the Major Leagues today?

In the early 1950's while a young student at Columbia, one of my professors presented a question to the students: "What factors most contributed to influence blacks in our country and to encourage them to seek better lives, better careers and better living conditions?" The question stirred various responses; all sorts of reasons were offered and discussed. Then, the professor offered his views. He said there were two primary factors. This caught our attention because it seemed too simple, too direct.

He went on to name these two factors. One was many blacks had gone off to war between 1941-1945, some 800,000. They served in segregated military units, typically led by white officers in charge of them. Sometimes they were given most difficult assignments. Some upper echelon military leaders hoped they'd fail, and such failure would then be attributable to their inferiority, lack of commitment, and other racially-biased reasons. But, this did not happen. Historical wartime records, along with individual recollections indicate they performed well and with honor in combat. Despite their having lived in a racially segregated America, they fought for it. Sometimes they interacted with white military units.

When they traveled to distant military places and foreign countries, they were treated far better than they were in their own country. Citizens in other countries did not treat them with the discrimination they were so accustomed to at home. They mingled, socialized, dated, had sex with the women there, and in many cases married women who loved them. This was an eye-opener, to be appreciated and loved by those outside their own country in so many positive ways they'd not ever experienced. They became enlightened by this humiliating and horrible paradox: they could serve, die or be maimed for their country in wartime battle, but did not have full citizen rights and privileges in that same country. Also, upon returning they were given the educational benefits of those who served honorably, the highly effective G.I. Bill of World War II. This too changed their lives.

Then, one of the students asked the professor "What might the second reason be?" He smiled and simply said the word "Television." He went on to describe how this medium opened many Black American citizens' minds to the possibilities and benefits shared by so many in our country, yet most of it never reached Black communities and individuals across our country. They could watch programs clearly demonstrating how white families were living; and there were the accompanying powerful visual advertisements emphasizing the glaring discrepancies between what was going on for the rest of America, but still excluding blacks. Blacks were becoming emotionally sensitized to an entirely new world. They saw what they did not have and compared it to what they did have. They wanted to share in it. Why not? If others had such goodness, comforts, seeming wealth and other materialistic benefits, why couldn't they? No doubt there were other contributory factors. These two cited factors of so many years ago are still with me.

On April 16, 2012, 65 years after Robinson broke the baseball color barrier, all Major League teams honored this uniquely gifted and first black player - every player on every team was wearing Jackie Robinson's number "42" instead of their own regularly assigned baseball numbers. And, all of the teams recently retired this number "42" forever. In all of the Major League ballparks, number "42" is posted along with the other retired numbers for those individual teams. It will never again be available for any future player. (Mariano Rivera of the New York Yankees is permitted to wear number "42" until he retires, he was exempted or grandfathered.)

Robinson's Major League records are readily available; for the nine years in the majors, they are extraordinary; his lifetime batting average was .311; he was Rookie of the Year in 1947; later on the Most Valuable Player; selected many times for the All-Star games; and he is in Baseball's Hall of Fame in Cooperstown, New York, the first black player so honored.

Moving ahead to 2008, Barack Obama runs for President. He is the first Black Presidential candidate to do so. He wins the election by a significant margin and in January 2009 becomes our 44th President. This election transcended pre-conceived notions about ever electing a Black president. We already had overcome comparable thoughts about a Catholic by having John F. Kennedy as our president, but until then it was not yet clear whether the voters could support a Black person. Millions of white citizens long beyond those earlier brutal days of segregation and bigotry did enthusiastically support a black man to be our national leader in a global environment.

The night of the election results in 2008, Jimmy Breslin the noted New York writer was at a public school in Brooklyn named after Jackie Robinson. He commented it was because of Robinson, Barack Obama was able to become America's first Black president. Naturally, there were many other factors contributing to this outcome. This election confirmed what a great democratic nation the United States of America can be, offsetting the racial bias that had been a part of our history for so long.

However, in these ensuing presidential years, 2009 to present, President Obama has been subjected to subtle and not-so-subtle discriminatory statements, comments, jokes and abuses. For example, even after intensive investigatory procedures and the presentation of authentic documents, still there are rumors promulgated about his birth, his education, his religion, and other detracting concerns having virtually nothing to do with his qualifications or Presidency. Some of these efforts are clearly racial.

As with previous presidents, there have been many validated threats on his life. The estimates are about 12,000 per year, far more than any of his predecessors. There are those in e-mail and public communications stating specific ways to kill the president; and incidents of citizens who publicly state they will not, cannot vote for a ... and they use that "N" word again to express their disdain and hatred. The Secret Service and other law enforcement agencies investigate these threats and pursue identified individuals with such bizarre thoughts. Fortunately for all of us, so far they have been most effective and successful. We've already lost too many national leaders to assassinations.

The aspects of racism are complex, historically deep-seated, and often beyond a clear understanding or explanation, at least so far. Racism elicits some of the worst possible thoughts and behaviors, including beatings, hangings and other bizarre, primitive, and illegal actions. People's minds and behavior aberrantly take over their rationality and good senses, and bring them closer to those more mysterious animal roots within us. Why would the mere "darkness" of a person's skin evoke so much hatred along with other peculiar and compelling distortions?

Throughout society and our individual lives, there are always turning points, tipping points, processes superimposing or at least encouraging a new direction or change upon us. Bob Kennedy once said "Everybody wants progress, but progress requires change, and most don't want change." As creatures of habit, we are all resistant to change at one level or another. There are also factors and forces attempting to inhibit such change, efforts to block or impede any disruptions in the way things are, or the habits some try so desperately to hold on to. But change does and will take place, although slower and more unevenly than some would prefer. Inevitably, the change occurs and is operational; later on reflections cause us to wonder why it took so long, or why was there resistance to it in the first place. This is the way new patterns and new thought processes and behaviors result, this is progress. Today, it is extremely difficult to understand exactly what were the cumulative forces and reasons for the pervasive exclusion of Black athletes in the major leagues for so long, or other organized sporting activities, or anywhere else. That's so true for all the other realms of racial discrimination.

We are a remarkably different American society since those days so long ago when two 13 year old boys hitchhiked to Washington, D.C., and shortly after when Jackie Robinson first stepped on Ebbet's Field. Yet every so often, the ugly head of bigotry continues to raise its head intermittingly yet pervasively. Change and progress have been occurring and will continue, that is the nature of being alive. Our ability to democratically elect a black President is the clearest example of both.

Footnotes:

The September, 2012 <u>The Atlantic</u> magazine contains an analytic piece, "Fear of a Black President," by Ta-Nehisi Coates, pages 76-90. It is informative, thoughtful, enlightening and balanced.

For those interested in documented acts of violence and hate, you can delve into the publications of <u>The Southern Poverty Law Center</u>.

2012

PERVASIVE MISREPRESENTATION
OF ITALIAN-AMERICANS

A MERICANS are inexplicably fascinated with incessant tales, movies, news articles, gossip, or anything else about the Mafia. This historically infamous group in Italy and later on in America has long been involved in so many illegal activities. The Italian Mafia's origins are predominantly in Sicily; and it still functions there despite efforts to eliminate it or marginalize it. Its roots are long entwined with poverty, limited educational and employment opportunities, and in some situations oppressive and corrupt governments and officials. Some of the Mafia's organizational components bear a striking resemblance to well-run corporate tables of organization and procedures.

Without question, there has been a Mafia here in the United States. It has been involved in criminal behavior, with intimate ties to politics, businesses, and legitimate services and enterprises. In recent years, thanks to continual federal, state and local law enforcement efforts, the Mafia is a remarkably weakened and less influential force in our society.

Many of the earlier major Mafia leaders have either died by syndicate assassinations; or become so old they've retired; or have been confined in federal prisons for long periods of time. Some turned on their brother members and have gotten into the witness protection programs as they seek remaining new lives in anonymity.

The overbearing result of all of this habitual preoccupation is Italian-Americans are stereotypically seen as criminals in our society. We're presented almost as genetic gangsters; even as dangerous buffoons; there are jokes that degrade us; and sometimes we're portrayed as being of lower intelligence. We are viewed as exploiting others and carrying out illegal activities. Sometimes we supposedly hurt and/or kill other citizens. The composite creation of these negative portraits is a chronic reinforcement of terribly distorted thinking, attitudes and perspectives regarding Italians and Italian-Americans.

Initially, I was terribly reluctant to start this writing with such a vivid and harsh presentation. It would only call attention the most erroneous considerations of us. These repetitive, illogical and harmful approaches we've been subjected are all untrue. Most of us are law abiding, productive, competent and positive individuals. We have achieved a great deal in many areas, including music, the arts, the academic world, in the sciences, business and politics, and we consistently exhibit admirable qualities.

As an Italian-American and the child of an Italian immigrant, I know something about being discriminated against. I've experienced crude jokes and degrading comments when I was a child, a young adult, a United States Marine Corps officer, and later on even as a college professor, sometimes by supposedly learned others. Throughout their lives, so too did my parents and my sister Maria along with other family members and friends. To us, it was commonplace, sometimes expected.

Are Italian-Americans the sole ethnic group supposedly involved in such aberrant behavior? (Please note the term "Mafia" is used generically, thereby disengaging it from its Italians/Italian-Americans exclusivity.) No other ethnic or racial group is exposed to such consistently destructive and inaccurate presentations. Beyond everything, why is there little publicity about a Russian mob in our country as it deals in loan sharking, gambling, prostitution and killings? Criminal mobs in Mexico have killed thousands related to drugs and illegal immigration, sometimes in our country's border states. Is there an Asian Mafia? What about a Jewish or Irish Mafia? How about a Cuban Mafia, or a Hispanic Mafia or an African-American Mafia? Even recently another unusual and totally unexpected group has been identified as the Amish Mafia. Peace-loving, passive Amish are relying on their own protective enforcers to handle unpleasant matters amongst them.

Over the years, there have been numerous weekly television programs making Italian-Americans appear to be especially dangerous, even sometimes outright silly. The long-running and syndicated television shows "The Sopranos" and "Jersey Shore" repeatedly portray Italians/Italian-Americans as manipulative, empty, explosive, inane, vulgar, and chaotic. A while ago, there was another supposed "reality" television program about mobster John Gotti's widow, Victoria, and her rude, out-of-control spoiled children living in their Long Island mansion. Their disrespectful behaviors were noteworthy.

Another example of misrepresentation is a recent television "reality" show, "Mob Wives." Overly made-up but rough, uncivil Italian-American wives in Staten Island,

New York meet, go to the gym, have harsh confrontations and talk about when their husbands might be released from federal prisons. Often their children don't know their fathers are in prison. In one show, a devoted wife is on the phone, writing down her imprisoned husband's food preferences. She is arranging for his favorite food items not available in prison to be brought there. Does anyone want to know what a convicted felon's culinary preferences are while he's incarcerated?

In addition, there are innumerable films emanating from Hollywood that repeatedly show characters as violent Mafia members. More recent re-runs on television of "The Godfather," parts I, II and III, and "Goodfellas," along with another film, "Casino" these clearly demonstrate Italian-Americans as distorted personalities with a variety of negative traits. While these films are powerful art and visual forms, portions are outright nasty and vicious, and quite insulting to Italian-Americans. Not surprisingly, such films did extremely well at the theater box offices and in rentals for home viewing, along with their repeated showings on television. Audiences inexplicably love them, sometimes quoting lines from them or imitating characters in supposed humor.

Upon further analysis and reflection, I ask these questions: Are the traits presented in these media demonstrative of who we are as Italian-Americans? What purposes are served by such bombardment of publicity? An equally vital question is why do decent, productive, law-abiding Italians/Italian-Americans accept such presentations without even a whimper of protest? Is there something now in our collective psyches to inhibit reasonable reactions to all of this?

Since I have never been comfortable with these humiliating and insulting portrayals of the miniscule minority of such Italian-Americans, there must be a more rational explanation. Italian-Americans are an easy target. We get battered, yet say little. Our silence allows all this negative publicity to flourish as we tolerate it. I wonder what all of this garbage does to the self-images and development of young Italian-American females and males. Does it promote certain terribly damaging and unsavory feelings, attitudes and beliefs about themselves? Are we all less because of this? Have we lost our courage to react and to set the record straight?

Paradoxically, while Italian-Americans continue to be debased, there is comparatively minimal treatment on recent White-collar criminals exploiting this nation. The financial debacle in 2008 is second only in its untoward repercussions to the Great Depression of 1929. Recent prosecution and conviction of some insider traders, Peter Madoff, Bernard Madoff's brother, and UBS bank officials are most welcome. Some of the Wall Street crowd, the bankers, the mortgage loan executives, the corporation CEOs, and the hedge-fund operators, some conducting Ponzi schemes, continue to operate just as they had. Illegal insider traders keep right on working. Inadequate and irregularly enforced Federal regulations have not dealt effectively with the stealing and cheating of billions of dollars, perhaps more.

I want to go and open a window and shout out "We're not going to take this anymore." (This was in a film, "Network" years ago. Sound familiar?)

Besides such an ineffective but symbolic action, there are far more positive actions Italian-Americans and others could take to offset the damages. What follows are just suggestions.

Consider taking a trip to visit Italy. We are frequently ignorant about our heritage or deep cultural roots and achievements. Such a voyage will promote greater understanding and appreciation for Italian culture and the beauty of the country and people. Visit museums and take children with you to confirm the significant historical contributions of Italians. Make an effort to identify the scientific, musical, architectural and art activities of Italians and Italian-American authors. Perhaps it would be beneficial to learn to speak one of the Italian language dialects.

Read <u>Sprezzatura, 50 Ways Italian Genius Shaped the World</u> by Peter D'Epiro and Mary Desmond Pinkowish. Read Alfred Lobrano's <u>Limbo: Blue-Collar Roots, White-Collar Dreams</u> to better understand Italian Americans and our personal uneasiness despite our accomplishments. Another important historical enlightenment is <u>La Storia – Five Centuries of the Italian American Experience</u> by Jerry Mangione and Ben Morreale.

Give thought to become active in Italian-American political and educational organizations throughout our society. The Calandra ItalianAmerican Institute of Queens College/The City University of New York offers social, cultural and historical programs focusing on positive and unique Italian-American experiences. A fine place to learn more about Italy and Italian-Americans will be found at the website: hhtp:www/i-italy.org/. Consider joining UNICO National, the largest Italian-American service organization in the United States. The Craco Society provides excellent data and heritage assistance to those especially from southern Italy: <u>www.thecracosociety.com</u>. This group now has almost 500 members interested in their roots in southern Italy.

As I approach the conclusion of this writing, I also recognize we're at the tail-end of 2012, soon beginning 2013. When the calendar and the clock announce it's a New Year, it's a wonderful time to reflect, to make resolutions, and start anew right from the beginning of a brand New Year. We need to appreciate the Reverend William Sloane Coffin's statement: "If you don't stand for something, you're apt to fall for anything."

Whether you're an Italian-American or of another background, you need to be offended by any racial/ethnic misrepresentations, even degrading jokes. Jews throughout the world are painfully aware of how the holocaust during World War II devastated their people and culture, and they have pledged "never again." Other specific groups who suffered the same outcomes in that war, for example, millions of Russians, and thousands of gypsies, gays, Catholic priests and nuns have to be equally vigilant. Blacks or African-Americans are frequently the recipients of prejudice and distortion, along with other ethnic and religious groups, and they require the same intense focus.

We can continue to strive for a zero tolerance of any form of bigotry, distortions, or crude and cruel jokes. Goodness can become a habit. Speak, write and directly confront inequities and falsehoods presented about Italian-Americans, or any racial or ethnic group or individual. We can modify our thoughts about prejudices, bias, inaccurate statements, and become better communicators. There is no need to belittle one another. And, you can communicate your displeasure about negative portraits of us and others to the various media corporate offices if you believe this is so.

2013

RECENT SUPREME COURT DECISION

W HEN my sister and I were growing up and being tutored by our father, who never went behind the 6th grade in the New York City school system, but was an extraordinarily wise and experienced person, he taught us everybody has a price or wants something. It might even be money, but the secret is to find out what it is they want. He was partially wrong, at least by today's standards.

A couple of days ago the Supreme Court in a typically tight 5-4 ruling, determine there cannot be any ban on corporations spending in political campaigns or elections. This decision overturned two earlier precedents and significantly raises all sorts of concerns for the American public about the financing of elections and investing in politicians. Prior decisions already had given First Amendment rights to corporations and the remaining trade unions.

The Court's decision results in money becoming the sole powerful influence and control in our political system. It's quite straightforward: large organizations, corporation boards and executives, individuals with deep pocket (often the same) can spend whatever they want to make sure their spheres of interest are given full intentions by their paid-off candidates. Such an arrangement insures elected officials are now working for them and their well-trained lobbyists at the expense of the broader American public and any general good. It might even be considered bribery. Essentially, it's an updated manifestation of what a former General Motors executive (Charles Wilson) once said years ago while holding a cabinet appointment: he proudly informed us "What's good for General Motors is good for the America." We can never forget that the corporations and their executives created our problems.

From now on, when candidates or elected officials, Republicans or Democrats say or do anything the voters and the citizens will have to figure out which organizations and wealthy individuals paid them for their words, thought processes and decisions. Money can be flying all over the place without any clear understanding or awareness of its effects. Advertising and persuasion in all forms will intensely shape and dictate thinking and behavior. How voters go about analyzing such situations becomes overwhelming and an incredibly difficult matter to decipher. Will voters believe their votes do count?

For a long time we've been talking about campaign finance reform in our country, ways of positively and effectively preventing large organizations and powerful individuals controlling election outcomes and those in office. With this decision, it seems they now own the First Amendment. What's next?

December 1, 2012 - To the Reader – an update

We have just gone through the most expensive presidential election in our history. It was the first since this highly controversial court decision. Huge amounts of individual and corporate money was expended, especially by the Romney supporters in order to influence this election's outcome. Fortunately for America, these efforts did not work. But, this doesn't mean they couldn't succeed in future elections.

2013

THE 85ᵀᴴ ACADEMY AWARDS CEREMONY

W HILE on vacation in Santa Monica, Lois, our dear friend Rose, and I watched the entire Academy Awards festival. This was from the early beginnings of the "Red Carpet Show" in the afternoon right on through the Best Picture Award given by Jack Nicholson and Michelle Obama (that's right) at about 9 PM. You might be wondering why we would spend so much of our valuable time locked in to such trivia. Typically, I don't watch such events. But, it was because my deceased sister Maria's talented filmmaker son David Owen Russell had written and directed "Silver Linings Playbook," and it had been nominated for 8 Academy Awards. We were rooting for him, and were looking forward to his acceptance speech if he won. I was most curious whether he might mention my sister and her role in his life. Via deep-seated familial connections defying explanation, we were supportive.

We watched almost 6 hours of slender, made-up women in striking gowns, and men in formal attire, with silly commercials dispersed throughout. Of course, while watching we made our own comments and jokes in response to theirs and the entire presentation. Preceding the Awards, the Red Carpet event was pure gibberish taking place between noted celebrities and those interviewing them. The prime focus of these interviews was how women look; the designer names of their gowns; and of course, mention of their borrowed, high-end jewelry. Their empty chatter and inane remarks was somewhat overwhelming. As these self-indulgent celebrities spoke of their "craft," terms such as "amazing" "talented," "unique," "awesome" and even "surreal" were thrown about.

The film industry is a massive multi-billion dollar operation employing thousands of behind-the-scenes individuals who are paid far less than the "stars," the directors, the corporate studios and the producers. While there's a great deal of ongoing dialogue about "artistry" and significance to the broader society, let's not kid ourselves, this is all about making money. 6 of the 9 films nominated for Best Picture ("Silver Linings Playbook" is one of them) have each already grossed more than 100 million dollars! Over time, DVD and overseas sales will surely increase these figures. The film industry is a unique American success story.

Of these 9 nominated films, so far I've only seen two of them: "Silver Linings Playbook" and "Lincoln." This makes me most reluctant to offer any comments about the qualities of all of them. My mind does wander to films from long ago and I do wonder now that I'm older what is going on in the current film industry. Whatever happened to developing films of the caliber such as: "On the Waterfront," "To Kill a Mockingbird," "Streetcar Named Desire," "Raging Bull," "Platoon," "Deer Hunter," "Apocalypse Now," "Julius Caesar," and even the epic "Gone With the Wind"? Are any of these nominated ones of such artistic dimensions?

Approximately 1 billion people out of the 7.6 billion in the world supposedly were watching this all-day event. It represents at least some of America's values being projected throughout a complex, often hurting world of diverse societies. And what are these values presented? They are: money, glitz, power, self-love, sex, drugs, empty comments never to be remembered, polite digs, dance and song, and a neurotic focus on amusement and entertainment. We are exposed to this; we talk about it, and have our children share in it, and I guess we want to believe the rest of the world wants and seeks just what we have. America is a nation transmitting entertainment and created joy.

The MC Seth MacFarlane was in my opinion atrocious. His opening adventure was a musical dance and song number titled "We Saw Your Boobs." He was joined by a noted gay chorus surprisingly degrading and insensitively mocking women's bodies. Why? He read his prepared script perfectly; it was done by an immature adult who thought he was being funny. During his monologues, I counted at least 10 inappropriate, racist, sexist, disgusting, and poor-taste remarks. He slurred Jews, blacks, conservative rights, gays, and especially women. He even had a crude remark about the assassination of President Abraham Lincoln. Offensive digs at violence that occurred between a show-business couple, and George Clooney's predisposition for younger women while enthusiastically laughed at, were further evidence of his poor behavior. His jokes were similar to those that so dominated television, low-level comedy clubs, and resort hotels upstate New York and Las Vegas in the 1950s and 1960s.

Early in the show we witnessed an awkward interaction between the MC and a large screen presentation of William Shatner in his Captain Kirk uniform from Star Trek. We also viewed a rambling, almost incoherent dedication to 50 year history of the 007 James Bond series, with the focus on their musical scores. There were other comments about cocaine growing on trees in Hollywood, and other drugs readily available and used by some of these celebrities. Why the talented Mark Wahlberg allowed himself to be up there with an animation talking bear "Ted" was a puzzle to me. He deserves much better.

The Award recipient entertainers smile, emote, and even humbly commend their losing competitors, their mates, children, and parents, sometimes their God for their good fortune. How the President's wife got involved in this show-business fiasco with Jack Nicholson can be interpreted as some form of "payback" for all of the Hollywood support to President Obama's recent presidential campaign. Now we have the ultimate blending of our political system with show business. (An earlier first-lady, Laura Bush participated in a portion of the Awards ceremonies; and President Franklin D. Roosevelt also did many years ago. The motives in this situation remain questionable.) Jennifer Lawrence ("Silver Linings Playbook," David's film), tripped and went down on the stairs she climbed receive her Award. This was one of a rare reality, non-staged events.

There were a few exceptions: Awards for the various documentaries gave some credence to our being more advanced. These films made us think and wonder. And a couple of individuals spoke about the disarray in the world, but they were rare, brief, and hardly audible amidst the clutter.

If all of this seems harsh, you're right; it is and has to be in any analytical, sensitive response to what occurred last night. I wasted almost a third of a day of the remaining limited days of my life.

Today, February 25th, the day after the speeches and Oscars, I am getting <u>The Los Angeles Times</u> and <u>The New York Times</u> and see how the critics reacted to this pretentious, empty, uneventful, and poorly created debacle.

My pledge is never again to watch these self-absorbing Academy Awards. I will continue to embrace people, books, and documents who give me further thought; to strive to keep my mind and spirit open, even at this advanced age to the goodness in others, clear ideas, the beauty in nature; to love those I can; to avoid hurtful behavior to others; and finally, to speak out and write on matters I have strong feelings and beliefs. If anybody missed this Academy show, you didn't miss a thing.

2013

AMERICA'S FOOTBALL HEROS

COLLEGIATE and professional football players are integral components of our nation's entertainment and amusement worlds, similar to film and rock stars. These football players are cheered on by adoring fans; they are America's modern-day equivalent of ancient Roman gladiators, except without fighting or having vicious animals eat them, or those watching them in the arena signaling "thumbs up" or "thumbs down." Today there is much greater notoriety, publicity, adoration and potential monetary compensation.

Why do so many adults and children adore college and professional football players? These athletes are known on a first name basis, as if they're family members; people want to touch them or get their autographs; and devoted fans cheer them on while wearing their favorite player's team shirt with that player's name and number on it. Athletes use their Twitter accounts to communicate with their fans, and likewise fans have ongoing dialogues with players. Fans seek a closer identity, a more intimate relationship with their heroes. Somehow, they want to be in the athletes' world and entourage. Athletes' lives transcend the fans' lives and fantasies. Even so, as these athletes pursue their dreams, they are being exploited. One wonders if fans give thought to such a concept.

Colleges evolved into the farm system and training centers for football athletes. Some powerhouse colleges are known as "football factories" rather than as just institutions of higher learning. The more competitive collegiate football divisions prepare talented players to possibly enter the professional ranks via a yearly, highly publicized draft system. While on this athletic journey, some are permanently injured and paralyzed, but there are no consistent authorized insurance policies or catastrophic coverage for damaged high school or college players to offset their lifetime woe.

College recruitment is a major aspect of all of this. The majority of the college athletes are black; sometimes since early childhood, they have been groomed and prepared. They are superior athletes. Their prime focus is on making it, it's the route for fame and fortune. They are wooed by intense college coaches who are paid millions of dollars. These highly compensated coaches are expected to have highly successful football programs for the "good" of the college or university. (This interconnectedness is never quite clear.) Families of the athletes are exploited, too, with false promises and sometimes monetary rewards including bribes if their offspring can be lured to attend a particular college. Once at college, their time and energy are devoted almost exclusively to football: year-round conditioning, training, studying plays, attending football camps, and practicing, all leading up to those glorious fall Saturday games.

This exclusive focus offers minimal involvement in the ongoing collegiate educational activities. The athletes more intellectual developments are typically restricted. There are reported incidents of easy academic programs arranged for them; tutors help write their papers; others take examinations for them; and intimidated professors tacitly grant them favored academic leeway. Players' grades are manipulated to higher levels to maintain eligibility. Athletes receive money from influential alumni "under the table," and for "no show" campus jobs. Criminal behavior by some players has been ignored and minimized. After all, how could they play on the team if convicted of theft, rape, etc.? The topic of drug usage and performance enhancement agents is seldom discussed.

Such factors might encourage these athletes to see themselves as privileged recipients of celebrity entitlements.

Academic leaders including college presidents, faculty, athletic directors and coaches "wink" at what is taking place. So do the players and fans. The combination of such clandestine supposedly helpful activities coupled with the love given by frenetic adoring fans and others eventually disadvantage the athletes now and later on. The bulk of the nationally successful college football programs have consistently low player graduation rates.

Meanwhile, the relatively few collegians who enter the pro ranks are temporary highly rewarded millionaire employees. Temporary because their careers last but a few years, provided they are not seriously injured before then. Partially because of their ill-preparedness, self-importance and limited education, they are hardly sound managers of their lucrative finances. These athletes waste their earnings, live lavish life-styles, make poor investments, become financially broke, and often file for bankruptcy, or criminal behavior.

After years of playing football, athletes' brains/skulls have been repeatedly forcefully hit, and injured with perceived and/or unknown concussions, along with limited recuperative periods. Some of these damaged warriors are combative off the football fields, get into disputes with wives and friends, confrontations in local bars, and have difficulties with law enforcement officials. The intensity and fierce competitive levels of being professional football players only magnifies these long-term damages. Increased incidents of suicide amongst current and retired football players have been cited, as for those in the military services who return from combat situations. Perhaps combat and violence on the football field and in military combat operations promote similar overlapping long-term deleterious outcomes.

More dementia and early Alzheimer's disease issues have been documented amongst retired professional football players. (There are no cumulative data regarding college football players who did not enter the pro ranks.) Recent increased opportunities for autopsies of former NFL players have confirmed incidents of extensive brain damage. Without accepting responsibility, the NFL and owners have set aside monetary amounts to compensate and care for such identified retired players who manifest the signs and symptoms of early dementia and Alzheimer's. Another perplexing question and perhaps related to football violence is why professional players have life spans considerably less than the average comparable population (approximately 20 years less)?

Recently, NFL officials, team owners and the players' union have sanctioned more intense analytical studies and scientific research. Improved equipment, rule changes, and more rigorous penalties for blatant violence are being explored. Such responses to documented chronic injuries came about primarily because of the noticed growing number of damaged and retired football players. Also, immediate families are making this a public issue; they witness and live with these victims while exhibiting aberrant behavior patterns, so they too are victims. Can the violence of football be sharply inhibited, and less conducive to concussions and other severe injuries?

Studies at the University of North Carolina and at Boston University's Center for the Study of Traumatic Encephalopathy have correlated head trauma and degenerative brain disease, known as chronic traumatic encephalopathy (C.T.E.). NFL officials vigorously dispute such a finding, with the assistance of some NFL-hired physicians. The Institute of Medicine (part of the National Academies of Science) announced the investigation of young athletes and military personnel concussions. In late January 2013 the NFL players union funded a $100 million interdisciplinary project at Harvard to explore all injuries.

These newer research commitments will never restore those already damaged. Once these highly conditioned athletes do retire either because of earlier devastating injuries, loss of their speed, timing and athletic abilities, or simply aging, their long-range health prognosis continues to be in jeopardy. It is hardly a graceful retirement period for them, or their families and friends.

Player performances are finished; their modern gladiator days are over; the adoration is waning; and the players' football jerseys with their names and numbers are now worn by fewer adoring fans, and then none. Soon they are forgotten as American heroes. The writer A.E. Housman reminds us in the poem "To an Athlete Dying Young," how the athlete's "name dies before the man."

If as individuals and a society we tolerate damaged brains, minds and bodies, and shortened lives as the price to play football, then this is the ultimate manifestation of exploitation of athletes. Will those who control local community, high school, college and professional football leagues focus on physical and ethical responsibilities to acknowledge and prevent damages? Parents, coaches, physicians, and the football players themselves need to make critical and informed decisions. Or will money/income, massive business interests (pro football is currently a 9 billion dollar industry, along with innumerable related industries that provide services and products), publicity, fan adoration, and insensitivity win out? Thousands of former pro football players and the families of deceased ones have filed a number of suits in federal courts.

ATTENTION MUST BE PAID

Arthur Miller was a gifted, sensitive playwright; he captured much about the American scene and its diverse personalities in encompassing situations. Miller would grab hold of historical and upsetting human conditions and then meticulously created characters that interact in flawed and heroic ways so we might better understand life, human frailty, and possibly even ourselves.

His outstanding plays are; <u>The Crucible</u>, <u>A View from the Bridge</u>, <u>All My Sons</u>, and <u>Death of a Salesman</u>. These plays continue to speak to us in personal ways and emotionally touch us. The focus of this essay is <u>Death of a Salesman</u>, it first appeared in 1949.

In May, 2012, Lois and I saw <u>Death of a Salesman</u> for the 4th or 5th time. This recent revival was directed by the skilled Mike Nichols, and starred Philip Seymour Hoffman (Willy Loman); Linda Emond (Linda Loman); Andrew Garfield (Biff Loman); and Finn Wittrock (Happy Loman), along with other exceptional cast members. The stage setting throughout is bare and haunting, with spaced, subtle music originally written for the play by Alex North. You can be simultaneously drained and enlightened by this play. It's raw drama about fallibility, mistakes and falsehoods. Once you leave the theatre, it can remain with you. Here it is more than a year after we saw this play and it's still in my mind.

Miller provides us with various interconnected themes: a family in serious interpersonal trouble; decisions made to avoid or deny truth; self-deceptions and inadvertent interpretations as the characters pursue dreams and unrealized goals; the consequences of an individual's actions; and ultimately the underlying human issue: "who are these people, and can we and do we identify with them?" We are viewing those human flaws of pretenses, denials, and avoidance of responsibility throughout the Loman family.

Is there anyone not familiar with the underlying themes of it? Sometimes even those who've not seen the play know about this man being a salesman and his flaws make remarks about Willy Loman. Willy is a long-time salesman on the road a lot; he continues to puff himself up and delude himself about his supposed success and "making it." But, over time, he is essentially failing at what he does, selling. He doesn't see this, as matters are spinning out of control. Linda shores him up with false praise and continuing hope, and wants to believe things will get better. They don't, they only get worse. Their sons also move along in their distortions as their lives have developed.

"Death of a Salesman" transcends the Lomans' singularity. Those operational behaviors portrayed on stage are hardly exclusive to the characters. It is a powerful metaphor for all of us. In a taut scene near the end, Willy, his wife and their sons interact. Everything has come apart, with much revealed, most of it is heart-wrenching. Willy is especially fractured, but there's plenty of damage to go around. He's piecing together his life as a failure; despite Linda's love and support she seeks to magically hold this family together. His sons construct what has happened to their father as well as themselves. Any repairs seem most unlikely, there's no going back, and the future is at best dismal.

We approach the play's ending. The packed theater audience is collectively holding its breath. No one coughs, no one moves about, some lean forward in their seats to capture the somewhat muted words on stage. There is absolute silence, only full focus on the players.

Then, at that instant, Linda partially turns towards the audience, stares outward, speaking almost in a whisper, enunciating slowly: "attention must be paid."

Linda's words are a crying out, a desperate warning. Is she talking just to her family or more inclusively to those in the audience, and perhaps beyond the theater itself? After a pause and no sounds whatsoever from the audience, the play moves to its final scene, Linda's plea is far too late. The Loman family is destroyed. Willy is dead, Linda is still confused yet seemingly calm, and their sons are still groping to understand what occurred. Tragically, everybody loses. Slowly, the curtain comes down.

The word "attention" has many meanings. It comes from the French "attendre," to "look after or to perform a service," and implies "increased alertness." "Attention" grabs us as an immediate warning to evade being distracted, and to give up whatever we are doing so we can pour our energy and reacting senses in a new and fully concentrated level.

"Attention must be paid" is a compelling mantra, in everything, individually, collectively and globally. Everywhere we're experiencing chaotic matters: countless destructive issues throughout the world; a human population exploding; wars and expanding terrorist violence; and repeated environmental disruptions with ongoing pollution of oceans and the atmosphere. This is a planet heating up with excessive carbon dioxide; nuclear/industrial accidents; major droughts; poor crop productions; deforestations; losses of biological species; trash/garbage accumulation; and newer mysterious bacterial and viral entities, with other bacteria now resistant to antibiotics. There is the continual exploitation of non-renewable natural resources. Added to these chaotic matters are endless social, political, and economic problems remaining unresolved well beyond national or geographic margins.

Cumulative data from highly reputable worldwide scientific researchers and institutions repeatedly confirm humans doing irreparable damage to this planet. With the human population exponentially increasing, and billions seeking more materialistic existences, accelerated destruction has become more prevalent and severe. The scholarly predicted human carrying capacity of this planet is about 10 billion, (some think less) and we're already approaching 7.5 billion.

In addition to these quantifiable issues, we are amidst massive public electronic communications transformations. (There are more cell phones in India than toilets.) Far away events become proximally known, are discussed and possibly impinge on us instantaneously. We share in daily world events and tragedies as if they're occurring right next door to us or in our living rooms. The bulk of them, at best are disconcerting, and at worst tragically sad. Each next day they are replaced by newer ones equally heavy. Events of the day before are pushed aside and barely have time to hold any focus. Everyday there's a new happening out there; we now are able to participate in global gossip.

The result of such massive intrusive "24-7" and "tech savvy" obsessions is fewer opportunities for unencumbered thinking, for quiet, uninterrupted contemplation, and spontaneous creative thought processes. When can there be sensory sensitivity and attention to the diminishing beauties of nature itself? Or time to even glance at the stars? Where will our empathy come from?

Can anyone specifically clarify the positive benefits of all these electronic communications that include the Internet, Facebook, Twitter, games, chatter, etc. and pervasive electronic "fingering" and texting to improve our problem solving abilities and capacities to think more analytically and effectively?

The world's most competent and thoughtful scholars and researchers are informing us that not enough "attention has been paid." They might not use exactly these words, but the alarms have been sounding for a long time. We need to rationally consider the disturbing concept that humans are not as evolutionarily advanced nor as intelligent as we've been led to believe, or we want to believe, or might hope. What else can explain the ever-expanding and intensifying global chaos?

The history of the human journey indicates significant scientific and technological advances that have remarkably changed and improved existences, especially throughout the Industrial Revolution to more modern times. In certain parts of the globe, various diseases have been controlled and conquered; vast modifications in living conditions and life opportunities have taken place; and in so many ways a portion of the world's population has heretofore unknown benefits, conveniences, and privileges. The criteria to measure standards of living confirm the extraordinary lives many of us have as billions more seek comparability. Still, the bulk those billions linger and die in poverty and disease.

No organisms have ever confronted so much simultaneously. The grim pronouncements predicated on cumulative data cited above simultaneously are terribly overwhelming and unpopular. Those uncomfortable with these data or not believing them promote efforts to neutralize them; some continue to have faith and are unwilling to grab a hold of them. There are still others who believe ultimately we will have resolving, almost miraculous solutions down the road, and so we needn't worry or panic, or concern ourselves. We might as well just "mosey along." Such illogical thinking and behavior will only accelerate further downward outcomes.

Our lives develop as we follow patterns, get involved in many interactions and become committed to outcomes that don't always happen. Expectations can supersede reality. Then, disappointment and confusion set in. We look to comprehend something, and whatever we do understand contains knowable and unknowable errors, including self-created ones. As we seek answers, we give significance to many matters, sometimes yielding excuses.

The Loman family members were self-deceiving in their hope and persistent optimism. Despite their beliefs and efforts, the outcome could not be what they wanted. As they come apart, it is their tragedy. What happens when the deceptions are so much greater, when billions of humans are involved, and there are no adequate sustainable resolutions to offset the tragic conditions global chaos has superimposed upon the planet and us? A major unknown is how all of this documented aggregate global disruption and knowledge about nature influence how we think, feel, create and interact on a daily basis and on long-term levels called the "future."

References:

"The Future of Science in 50, 100, 150 Years." <u>The Atlantic</u>, January 2013.

"America the Clueless" Frank Bruni, <u>New York Times Sunday Review</u>, May 12, 2013.

"The Art of Paying Attention," <u>The Atlantic,</u> June 2013.

2013

RETIREMENT

" **H**E is free to explore whatever he wishes to bind thoughts and feelings of a lifetime together." Statement from an article about Oliver W. Sacks, who turned 80 years old on July 9, 2013.

A friend who'd retired a short time ago was visiting us. After we'd chatted awhile, she hesitantly asked me "what do you do with all of the spare time you have, now that you've been retired a while?" I've been retired since 2002. So this "a while" is quite a while. This question caught me by surprise; nobody's ever asked me this. My immediate answer was "I've become more introspective, reflective, and freer." This brief response contains serious and attractive words. Yet without any specifics they're ambiguous and meaningless. It calls for an in-depth review of almost 11 years into retirement, and a more thorough response.

Throughout your life, you pursue a career, or more than one. Your days and years are dominated with daily job responsibilities that absorb most of your time. There's comparatively little time to carry out those things you dream about or might prefer to do; or to be free to even occasionally think more abstractly. Consumed with routines, days slide by you; patterns tamper with freedom. You even think about putting off those more preferable activities until later on after you're retired.

After almost 50 years of being in the education/research world, and having been deeply involved as a professor and then as a department chairman for 15 years, the rest of my life changed the day I made the decision to retire. I was drained and depressed; it was time to get out, to leave what I had habitually been doing for too long. In retirement, it would be a new, unknown and different world, moving from fully planned days to completely unplanned ones. Being unencumbered by a job or profession, it would have to be a freer world. When I first retired, I didn't know what to do or how to spend my time with this new freedom.

We've been in Rockport for the past 5 plus years. It was after 46 years in familiar and comfortable Leonia, New Jersey. These recent years have flown by, or seem to have. It's calmer and quieter up here, more beautiful in this countrified, less populated community on the ocean, reached across a bridge so it's part of an island. It's far less cluttered with the intense, hurried-up existence, pace and noise of the New York/New Jersey locations. The beginnings and endings of the seasons seem to be more clearly recognizable. Whatever the season, the air is clean and crisp and smells good. There's a daily closeness with nature all about us. The newer living environment has a wonderful influence on me.

Seldom am I in a rush to do anything anymore. The movement is slower. I think more about my life and those about me, and consider "dark, delicate, precious time," a somewhat foreboding statement made by my favorite

American author, Thomas Wolfe. Along with these thoughts, I take walks on quiet roads from which I observe nature. Every so often I walk along one of the most beautiful beaches I've ever seen. This includes beautiful beaches we'd been to in the Hawaiian Islands. I carry a garbage bag and pick up flotsam pushed up on the tidal shoreline. If the weather's good, I sit outside on our beautiful property and watch birds and other animals moving about, or just sit there listening to wind or the quiet itself. It's during these private activities when my mind wanders to all sorts of random topics.

I love spending time writing and reading, and listening to music. Each day I'm up quite early, when it's barely light, and carry out a cluster of exercises to sustain muscle mass, energy and endurance. Then, I do writing, even on days I don't think I might not have anything to say. With no need to focus on a regulating ticking clock and superimposed routine behavior, I'm more engaged in putting my thoughts down on paper or computer. This focus led me to write a lengthy memoir about my parents, <u>Buddy Remembers – Then and Now</u>. Writing this book has led to book signings, speaking engagements, and meeting other people. After all, now, I'm a memoirist! I've also started another book. (An article recently appeared urging you should never ask a writer what he/she is writing about.)

The music I listen to changes every couple of weeks. Lately, Gershwin, Neil Young, Mozart and Bach have been the main composers. Next week Brahms, Chopin, and Copeland. There are so many brilliant composers; just as there are outstanding book authors. There are far too many to ever hear them all.

Since being in Rockport, I've also taken to writing personal essays. This is a fine introspective and absorbing experience. There's great freedom in this realm to explore. It activates my mind. About 27 or so personal essays are posted on my web site www.joemuzio.com. Thanks to our dear friends Diane and Tom Ford, who gave these to me, I've become more familiar with Phillip Lopate (The Art of the Personal Essay, Portrait Inside My Head, and To Show and To Tell) and Edward Hoagland (Sex and the River Styx). Then, there's Bernard DeVoto's The Easy Chair written in 1955. These readings and others have made me more fluent, sensitive and comfortable about essay writing. The writing you're reading right now is but an example of the personal essay.

Writing "Letters to the Editor" in the local newspaper became another sound outlet to publicly share my thoughts on controversial community topics in Rockport and Gloucester. What I write is bothersome to a few individuals. But that's OK, they weren't written to please others or to gain favor with anybody. They're offered as possible alternative ways of thinking and expressing one's self.

In the silence of early mornings, isolated from virtually all other matters and with clear mind I do more reading at that time, too. Since being a young man, I've continue to reread Thomas Wolfe's massive writings; recently the autobiography of Neal Young; the biography of Rachel Carson; one on Whitey Bulger; and A History of the World in 100 Objects kept me absorbed. A short while ago I came upon a book given to me by a dear friend, George Rooney, now deceased 5 years, for my 60th birthday in 1992. It's The Fragile Species, essays by Lewis Thomas; it's a beautiful read. Lewis Thomas is one of those writers with great skill and clarity, and a pure dose of humanity,

I've read and reviewed about 60 plus biological sciences scholarly books for an educational/library service. These reviews are sent to thousands of colleges and universities.

My interpretations and criticisms, along with their accuracy and clarity count. It's a way of telling others my analytical thoughts matter; that I still have value to myself and those beyond. This helps me to learn about current research and the theoretical developments in the biological sciences and related disciplines.

Lois and I have many bookcases and shelves loaded with our books in our house. These books are the accumulations of our professional careers, visiting old bookstores, and newer acquisitions from local bookstores. Others are gifted to us over the years by family members and dear friends. These are special; it means those that gave them know and care about who we are and what we read.

Maybe a quarter of the thousand books still have not yet been read or only portions of them. This bothers me, but I keep on buying and getting new and old books. I've come to recognize there will never be enough time left for me to read all of them. I wander to the bookcases throughout the house, and examine some of them more carefully. If it touches me in certain ways, even its attractive bookbinding or the title can hold me, I go ahead and read it. It's somewhat of a losing race against time, but a process that challenges me.

These past few years I've been writing letters to dear friends and those few remaining relatives to tell them how important they have been in my life. This process promotes reflective thinking, pulling out memories from long ago often forgotten by those who receive the letters. I've written to Lois and each of our sons and grandchildren. I want them to know how vital they've been to me all these years. They have shaped and loved me in so many ways.

It takes time to put one's thoughts and feelings into clear written language. Such carefully composed letters transcend hurried e-mails, sudden phone calls, poorly structured "text" instant messaging. It's a permanent trail of what you wanted to say to someone else, long after a "delete" or "send" button is touched, or hanging up the phone. It's further evidence you're less in a hurry.

As we age, there have been more deaths of dear friends and some relatives. With each one, I have the combined experience of loss and joy. Some I've been asked to eulogize. This takes time and effort to write a eulogy, sometimes a few weeks; I want so much for it to be special, totally individualized, truthful and vital to the survivors, including me. The loss of close friends, and eulogizing them gives me a newer awareness about the innate coupling of life and death. Being a biologist, I know full well this duality.

I've met lots of people in Rockport and Gloucester willing to linger and chat with me. Most are friendly, curious, and willing to share their thoughts and feelings in an open manner. They are unpretentious, and willing to be helpful to others without seeking some personal benefit. When they drive by, they wave or honk. These easier characteristics can't help but rub off on newcomers.

We talk and share ideas. Those who've done improvements in our house are highly competent, work hard, charge fair prices, and always finish the jobs they undertake. One is a fine house painter; another a competent, friendly plumber; an outstanding contractor; a neighbor who used to repair foreign cars in Cleveland and knows so much about technical matters; a stone mason and his assistant who've done work for us and who still joke with me; a couple who own a lovely B & B in town; the person in charge of the town's recycling/separation transfer station; the women who work as tellers at the local bank; the postman or postwoman and those working in the local post office; a caring dentist; and a concerned, attentive primary care physician who sits and chats regardless of his schedule.

There's a three-generation extended family from Sicily via Toronto, Canada that own a Trattoria in Gloucester where Lois and I regularly dine. They remind me so much of my original Italian American family, giving, friendly, gracious and open. Sometimes one or two of them will sit down with us while we eat. Where I go every morning and have coffee and get <u>The New York Times</u>, a group of local older men sit and talk; they've known one another for many years, some their entire lives, and they chew on all sorts of topics. Occasionally, I'm invited to join them, but am reluctant to disrupt their well-established habits, and often just read my paper and observe and listen.

These people have varying levels of education, knowledge and opinions about America, this community, world situations, poverty, the environment, and politics. In each situation, they present their thoughts clearly and without rancor; are curious about my thoughts; and wonder about their future and their families. Dialogues go on in a civil manner and with respect for conflicting positions.

The general consensus is long-standing wrongs are not being corrected in our country; with too much inequality, corruption and dominating special interests lobbying for their monetary causes. Some express distrust for our political institutions and large business and banking organizations. Much seems to be puzzling and chaotic.

I also recognize many of these issues have a long history and over time have not been resolved. This is the disturbing reality. It's true throughout generations.

What happened to "selflessness," "common good," and "concern for others" in our society? I think about the importance of kindness and civility to others; to offer assistance to those more in need; and recognize the importance of forgiveness. Whatever we do accomplish is often due to the help and guidance of those about us. Sometimes the poorest, the lonelier and the more down-trodden are where they are because of factors well beyond themselves. There are people who have a great deal of "bad luck" coupled with poor decision-making; others do not know how to effectively problem-solve; or to think more clearly. We must do what we can to counter these situations with goodness and integrity, and certainly avoid stereotypic conclusions and hurting anybody. These are hardly new concepts; since early childhood I heard about them and learned them from my parents.

Only a year older than Oliver Sacks, here I am healthy and just as free to "bind my thoughts and feelings together" into some reasonable longtime perspectives. In retirement, my life is clearer and freer. I am determined, perhaps driven to be thoughtful and involved.

Readings related to societal forces and issues:

Collapse, How Societies Choose to Fail or Succeed, Jared Diamond

The Cheating Culture – Why More Americans Are Doing Wrong To Get Ahead, David Callahan

The Great Unraveling – Losing Our Way in the New Century, Paul Krugman

The Greatest Story Ever Sold – The Decline and Fall of Truth, Frank Rich

"The Stench of The Potomac," Frank Rich; New York Magazine August 12, 2013, pages 16-21

A Special Issue of The Nation, October 8, 2012: Focusing on the Supreme Court; Corporations; and Isolating America's Workers.

2013

VIOLENCE

D URING late August 2013 there was a shocking but perhaps hardly noticed brief news report about a 23-year-old senior college student from Australia was attending school in Oklahoma, he was out jogging in a public park during the day. Three teenagers who later on claimed they were "bored" and "didn't know what to do" decided to follow this jogger in their car. They didn't know him. Then, with a 22- caliber pistol shot him several times in the back. He was dead. The teenagers were apprehended and have been be arraigned. They are being held without bail until a trial date is established.

Several days after this brutal incident, in Spokane Washington there was another equally obscure news report. An 88-year-old man who had served in World War II in Okinawa (he probably was a Marine), was waiting for a friend outside a pool hall. Details are unclear as to what promoted this incident. At least two, possibly three teenagers confronted him and went on to beat him so severely he died.

One teenager had been captured and later on two others were identified. These teenagers are being held without bail.

You might be wondering why these two incidents a short time ago are of interest to me a couple of months after they happened. They reminded me of a similar incident that happened when I was a youth. Three older teenagers, I knew but did not hang out with them from our Queens neighborhood decided to steal a man's car as he got out of his car to mail his income tax return. When he protested and offered resistance, one of them had a gun and shot him dead. Eventually, two of them were convicted and electrocuted at the Sing Sing Prison, New York; and the other did a long prison sentence. This was a tragic, senseless, stupid killing that to this day defies explanation and understanding.

Beyond the transitory news reports about these two violent events in Oklahoma and Washington, isolated and apart in a nation of about 307 million people might almost go unnoticed. But, they're not. Similar incidents are reported throughout the country every day. One can only wonder how many incidents do take place across America.

So too are the families of the accused murderers in Oklahoma and Washington forever disrupted and suffering. Eventually, following trials and probably convictions, the teenagers will receive prison sentences and will remain in confinement for extended periods of time. Perhaps the verdicts will result in death penalties for them. These long periods of incarceration will require taxpayers' dollars. If the teenagers eventually do get out of prison, they will be old, battered, hardened adults; their life journey carried out primarily in confinement. All of this is just waste, lost lives, lost time and lost energy. How pathetic.

I've fantasized about journeying to Oklahoma and Washington, and being able to meet and talk to these teenagers. I want to have the chance to chat with them. This is highly unlikely, probably impossible, but I still would like to do it.

After introducing myself and reassuring them I mean no harm, I would ask them these questions: In Oklahoma, "What was on your mind when you shot this jogging individual?" How did this act alleviate your "boredom?" "Did you give any thought to what the outcome was going to be?" The others in Spokane would be asked: "What were you thinking about as you beat this 88-year-old man to death?" What could he have possibly done to warrant your unchecked lethal violence towards him? "Now that you're in jail, what will happen to you?"

And, if somehow I had been able to visit those violent persons in Oklahoma and Washington, their responses to my questions about their insensitive and destructive behavior would likely be they do not know why they did what they did. Down deep, they are clueless. Their predictably feeble responses have no conceivable way to offset what they've done. Capriciously, they killed and now, they too are destroyed. They too are dead.

Since I'm not a psychiatrist, a criminologist, a law enforcement officer, or a sociologist, whatever the answers to these questions would probably give little clarity about their mindless actions. Right now, the combined 5-6 individuals are in confinement, being guarded, fed and housed while they await legal disposition. The legal system is underway, involving lawyers, judges, further investigations by authorities, and setting up court appearance dates. Two families and the friends of those two killed have suffered and will not be as they were before these killings.

Between 2000 and 2010, there were 165,068 reported murders in America. This does not include figures from Florida; this state does not report its figures, why not is inexplicable, but I'm sure they are available somewhere. That's about 14,500 murders annually. What happened in Oklahoma and Washington is occurring in every city and town, more recently in schools, movie theaters or malls. This averages out to about 400 times every single day nationwide. It is noteworthy that many murders remain unsolved, with others taking decades to bring to justice. This translates into the stark reality that each year we can conjecture that thousands of murderers continue to walk and live amongst us, perhaps even committing further murders.

Rapes (CDC, 2010, 1 in 5 women, 60% unreported) and other violent abuses to women, sexual assaults, physical altercations at sporting events and bars, road rage confrontations, bullying, child abuses resulting in murder, gang murders, and murders related to drugs and other random acts of violence are cumulatively dominating our society. Incarcerations related to these and other violations result in more than approximately 4 million persons in prison.

Is violence unique to the American psyche? Throughout America's history there are innumerable examples of violence. Our origins were predicated on violent upheaval against oppressive England. Do our beliefs in access to guns have anything to do with this? (Russia has much stricter gun laws yet has an even higher murder rate.) Does violence in the entertainment industry, in computer games and certain sports (cage fighting, football, etc.) contribute to violence by the citizens? We don't know any of this to be true. They could be conveying a great deal about our society. Perhaps they are even manifestations of the growing random violence throughout our nation. Rather, it's part an epidemic of brutality and insensitivity.

What can be said about all of this violence? There is no one explanation as to its manifestations, no single causative agent. As a biologist, I do have certain perceptions regarding violence. These perceptions are predicated on readings, especially those related to clarify human evolution. In the past few years, I have read and reviewed about 10 books on the human brain, recent advances in the neurosciences and the historical human journey. We are simply not as "modern" or "advanced" or sophisticated as human beings as we would like to believe.

Much about human behavior remains unknown, or at least unclearly or only partially explained. Our evolution certainly is not complete; according to those studying the topic, we are still in major forms of evolutionary development. Another way of saying this is despite our discoveries, technological advances, our capacities to problem solve and to exhibit seemingly humanistic traits, there are still within us primitive tendencies, animalistic remnants that inexplicably present themselves at violent levels beyond rationale controls. This is hardly a wordy excuse for the continuing human slaughter, or leniency to those giving us violence and disruption.

Since there is such a large population committing acts of violence over time, maybe it would be helpful if in addition to just incarcerating those captured and convicted, if there were carefully designed research projects carried out on them while in confinement. Based on interdisciplinary data, the causative and contributory factors promoting violent acts might be identified. Such long-range studies could yield invaluable data for analysis to give us clearer insights into the "models" or templates of violent behavior.

This disorder of violence could be thoroughly dissected: genetically, neurologically, psychologically, environmentally, sociologically, historically, economically and politically. Then perhaps we would better understand its multiple interrelated components. We would be moving well beyond isolated and erroneous opinions and bias that do little to enhance our comprehension. Our next interest is how to prevent this chronic human disorder, if we can prevent it or bring it to minimal levels.

These violent incidents that occurred in Oklahoma and Washington two months or so ago have already been publically forgotten, and replaced by many more recent ones. They have quickly been absorbed into the complex ongoing activities and rhythms of America.*

*This essay was completed on October 24th, 2013. This is the second incident this week when a juvenile in our country is involved in the death of a teacher: 1) In Nevada, on October 21st a 12 year-old student killed himself after killing a math teacher and wounding two other students. 2) In Danvers, MA. on October 23rd, a 14 year-old student is held for killing a high school math teacher.

2013

MAMA MUZIO'S COOKING

Somehow, during this time of year near the upcoming Christmas/New Year holidays, I have clearer remembrances about her special cooking competencies and skills.

My mother, Philomena Brancata Muzio, eventually known just as "Billie" was an extraordinary cook. This laudatory statement is not made simply because she was my mother. It's based on many years of witnessing her detailed preparations for our Sundays and holiday's massive menus to accommodate relatives and friends, eating her meals on a daily basis, and observing the ways she cooked. She had a lifetime commitment to her Italian cooking heritage. Based on all of this, she deserved major awards from European and American culinary organizations and cooking institutions. But she never got any. Beyond our relatives and friends her cooking talents were never acknowledged. Maybe it's because of the singularity of her cooking abilities.

Her culinary talents were exclusively for just one realm: basic nutritional Italian-style meals strictly from southern Italy, where she was born. Food preparations and cooking were done in one habitual way. While she was a naturalized citizen, and a totally Americanized woman in other ways, including speaking and writing perfect English, paradoxically she only knew and cooked Italian meals. Her cultural experiences, perhaps coupled with some innate but still unknown genetic programming made it impossible for any deviation.

When it came to any other cooking, my mother was totally ignorant. Nor was she ever interested in cooking non-Italian foods, although her sole exception was to roast a turkey and roast beef every Thanksgiving and Christmas. No French, no Chinese, no Indian, no Thai, no Irish (she believed the Irish diet was limited and probably promoted malnutrition), no Japanese, no Russian, no German, no Jewish, and certainly no awareness of what ultimately became known as fusion cooking.

For those more accustomed or interested in eating diverse ethnic foods, and willing to explore all kinds of food on a more international and enlightened level, this singularity must seem mighty peculiar. It wasn't a total rejection of non-Italian food, just never cooking any of it. There were occasions when as a family we did go out to eat; and then we would go to a local Chinese restaurant or rarely to an American style restaurant for a special, totally different meal. Also, we did go to Katz's delicatessen in lower Manhattan for massive pastrami or cornbeef sandwiches, loaded with spicy mustard and large pickles on the side. Once in awhile as a family we went to a Swedish restaurant in New York City; the only other restaurants we consistently went to were known Italian ones in Brooklyn, Queens and New York City.

Once when I asked her "Mom, where did you learn to cook?" her response was vague. She spoke about watching her mother and following her mother's orders as a child; then shopping and cooking with her older sister Elizabetha when they were both rather young; and eventually being given more and more cooking assignments as she grew up on Baxter Street in lower Manhattan. It's clear her lessons were considered "on job training." Without knowing it or labeling it, she was an "experiential learner." Billie was practicing a sound educational tenet that "learning isn't something done to the learner, learning is something done by the learner."

In all my years living with my parents and then afterwards as a grown up while visiting them, I never saw a single cookbook on any sort of food in their (my) home, not even Italian foods. There were no written recipes kept in a kitchen drawer, or on a bookshelf, or in a wooden box on a kitchen table readily available for consultation. Nothing was put down on paper or available in a cookbook. Everything was kept in her stored-up mental encyclopedia, the ingredients, the ratios of them, the step-by-step cooking procedures, the cooking times and temperatures were exclusively available to her. If my mother and her three sisters or friends did share a recipe, it was done openly and verbally, but not written down. Upon reflection, there did not seem to be any cookbooks or written down recipes in my mother's three sisters' kitchens, either. Yet, they too were excellent cooks who'd been prepared in early childhood.

Billie's ability to remember played a critical role in the recipe's ingredients and final outcome. It's as if my mother was some sort of secret foreign agent who early on learned never to write down anything for fear those messages would be read or stolen by the enemy or an unknown cooking rival. Maybe she'd been influenced by one of her careers. During World War II, when she worked for the Federal

Government's War Manpower Commission, she learned then to avoid writing down vital information that might be stolen or read by others.

Significantly, as I analyze my mother's approach to cooking, it is noteworthy she never used nor owned a Kitchen Aid mixer, a Cuisinart stirrer, an electric can opener, or any other automatic GE kitchen appliance so frequently seen in more modern kitchens. No food blenders or processors were in her kitchen. She used traditional manual equipment only, lots of pots and pans, kitchen utensils and a large wooden cutting board from one of my father's restaurants. Her sole purpose and focus was to keep things simple, unencumbered with gadgets and gear. Besides, she never was comfortable with automation. Newer, advertised gear made her flustered, and so, she evaded all of it. All of it.

Also, she only used the same heavy metal pots and pans that had been with her since she was first married in 1928. When she died in 1985, those very same pots were in her kitchen cabinets and still regularly used. I'm sorry to say the present location of these pots is unknown. There's a possibility my sister Maria incorporated them into her major cooking equipment after our mother died, but I just don't know. Maria's motives would have been to ultimately determine if by using our mother's cooking pots, she finally had the ability to prepare certain Italian dishes, especially my mother's pasta sauce, as well as my mother did. Maria repeatedly tried to mimic my mother's recipes and mixing procedures, but never was the outcome the same. There were other occasions when inquiring guests and family members asked Billie about a particular recipe for a meal they'd enjoyed. She would tell them in detail, but they somehow never could duplicate the flavors. Why was there this culinary mystery?

Oh, there was one concession, one long time commitment to American food my mother made: it had to do with the supposed dietary benefits of the gelatinous dessert product Jell-O. Somewhere she'd read this was vital for children. She insisted my sister and I eat it regularly, even thought the advantage my mother preached has never been confirmed by any reputable dietitian or nutritionist. This ongoing childhood ritual for me was quite traumatic and warrants a totally separate tale by itself. These unpleasant Jello-O childhood memories have inhibited me from eating Jello-O or just looking at it ever again. To this day, I cannot eat Jell-O or even see it without reflexively gagging and recalling her insistence.

When my mother was a child, her mother gave her and her sisters various chores to be done on a daily basis. One of hers was to knead dough for making bread. Sometimes she was sent to the local stores with a list given to her by her mother. A long time ago my mother told me how tiring it was to knead the dough but she had to keep on doing it. There were no complaints to be made.

After she married, she continued her earlier childhood habits and did her shopping exclusively at local neighborhood markets, a separate one for meat (including a poultry shop where she's pick out the live chicken to be slaughtered, plucked and prepared while she waited for it); another for vegetables and fruits; a different one for fish and seafood; and a fourth store for cheeses, breads and other items.

Shopping at a supermarket? What was that? Even after this kind of massive one-stop store became more popular after World War II, I do not recall her ever shopping at one, at least in the years we were together as a family. She needed to touch, smell, fully examine whatever she was buying, almost diagnostically, and then certainly to talk with the individual store owners to make sure she was getting only fresh products, and to find out about their lives at the same time. When we lived in Brooklyn, trucks carrying vegetables or seafood would come through the neighborhood, and families would buy directly from these merchants. "Fresh" was the key stimulus word. For example, if she was buying fish in the fish store or the merchant selling from a truck, she had to smell it, look into the eyes of the whole fish, and perhaps gently poke at it. She might even have asked the fish store owner when he'd been to the wholesale Fulton Street market last. This logistical combination would give her more complete information on which to base her final selection decision. This was a major process, the way some military leader was preparing for combat and needed all sorts of plans that had to be carried out.

In those days our refrigerators were small, especially in the apartments where we lived. There was little space for freezing items. Her purchases revolved around making sure there was no waste. Whatever she did buy was going to be eaten shortly or within a few days. When she asked either my sister or me to do the shopping, it was with a specific list of items along with repetitive verbal instructions where to get them, and what to look for in the products. It was awkward for us to smell the fish to determine its freshness, but my recollection is we did as instructed. She was far more lenient with my father, who'd been in the restaurant business for years; and she trusted his food judgments much more than her children. After all, he was constantly buying or going to the wholesale markets for his restaurants or diners.

My mother was a strong advocate of child labor. Her spirited involvement in using her two children to actively work in support of her intense culinary efforts probably stemmed from her childhood experiences, already cited above. Besides household cleaning chores and cleaning up after supper meals on an alternating nightly basis, my sister Maria and I had regular chores directly related to food shopping and food preparations. This child labor involvement was within the context of our mother holding down a full time, 40 hours-a-week position throughout our growing up years. Detailed shopping lists prepared by her were carried out by Maria and me; grating large sections of hard Romano cheese or the stale Italian bread (to make breadcrumbs); mixing the multiple ingredients she selected for meatballs; and washing the cooking pots for repeated use are those that flash back in my memory. The way the ingredients were brought together, even what they were in totality, remained locked solely in my mother's mind. It was her secret.

Of course there was always a potential reward regarding the meatball preparations: whenever my mother wasn't paying attention while she was partially cooking the meatballs in the olive oil, one or two of them could be "stolen" by Maria or me. One or two removed from the dozens being prepared went unnoticed. Or if she did notice this loss from her massive frying pan, my mother never said anything. Another benefit for grating the Parmesan (or Romano) cheese was to have small portions of it while grating. Sometimes I ate so much cheese I had a couple of sores in my mouth; other times if I wasn't careful while grating, I'd have a slight scrap on one of my knuckles. That's when my mother would comment about paying attention. Those flavor and odor remembrances are still with me! The aromas from Billie's cooking spread throughout the apartment or house we were living in, and you just knew she was actively engaged in her cooking missions.

When Billie was cooking, she was completely focused. She was like an accomplished surgeon carrying out a brain operation, or a skilled mechanic intensely working on a high-end foreign car. She made sure she was working without interruption, measuring, adding ingredients, tasting, and evaluating what she was doing. No interruptions were tolerated; and if she was interrupted, she would be upset, and ordered the interrupter out of her special, solo territory, her operating room, the kitchen. All that was missing from the entrance to her kitchen was a posted sign "Do not enter, outsiders not welcome."

Now that you have this background, let's get to the actual meals. Some of these meals were governed by the Roman Catholic holidays and family patterns. Another paradox: Even though my parents were not a devout religious couple, we still abided by the traditional governance rules and regulations of the Catholic Church when it came to respecting the various holidays and fasting practices. There was a religious calendar on the kitchen wall also providing culinary guidance. On Friday nights, pasta fagiole or lentil soup, followed by some type of fresh fish was served with a variety of cooked vegetables; meat was not to be eaten on Fridays. During Lent nothing was served that had been given up as a personal sacrifice in preparation for Easter; and no meat was served on Wednesdays or Fridays.

For Christmas Eve, there was a variety of seafood dishes, and absolutely no meat products. Traditionally, at least 7 seafood dishes were served. This particular meal is known as "Italian Feast of Seven Fishes." I can't accurately recall if we had this many seafood dishes, and they were all freshly prepared. (Some Italian-Americans serve fewer than this number, others more.) No one ever clarified this "Italian Feast of Seven Fishes." I recently spoke with an Italian from Canada, the owner of a Trattoria in Gloucester, MA. He claims there is no such "feast," it's just some habit that developed because in Italy seafood on the coastlines was so plentiful and meat less available. Some of the fishes and seafood I recall being served were soft shell crabs, cuddle fish, scungilli, baccala, anchovies, and lobster in marina sauce. As a child, perhaps even later than that, several of these were unknown to me; and no one bothered to explain what they were, but as prepared by my mother, they all tasted wonderful, along with their aromas and textures. Invited family members and friends would be there for the entire evening, or just drop in for a few portions of my mother's special Christmas Eve servings on their ways elsewhere. There were different vegetable dishes too, mostly with tomato sauce and garlic. Red wine from gallon bottles kept on the floor near the dining room table was had by all, including small sips by the children. Sometimes for the young ones, wine was mixed with cream soda in a tall glass with ice.

Any holiday meal except Christmas Eve would start with a massive antipasto made up of different meats including thinly sliced Genoa salami, suprasetta, and peppers, anchovies, several types of olives and cheeses, and basic lettuce greens. Sometimes fennel or celery with provolone cheese accompanied the other ingredients. The antipasto was essentially a complete meal in itself, eaten with fresh thick slices of Italian bread, to be followed by a series of courses. After the bulk of the meal was over, you could barely stand up and manage to get to an unoccupied couch or chair for a much needed nap. Following respite, espresso, desserts along with mixed nuts, fresh fruits and various cordials were served, which had been brewed by Billie's younger sister Lucille. This pattern was followed again and again, with no variation.

During the week, our family always ate different pasta dishes on Thursday evenings and again on Sundays. I can't recall when there was any variation in this. The fresh vegetables served were usually one or two of the following: escarole, broccoli rabe, spinach, eggplant parmigan (eggplant in many other ways, too), asparagus, artichokes stuffed with Italian style breadcrumbs and lots of garlic, and carrots, again with garlic and olive oil mixed in. Sometimes sweet potatoes were served, although not when pasta was served that evening. The meats were simply prepared, moist meatballs with the pasta; and flattened veal slices, or fried pork chops, again having been cooked in olive oil, and of course chicken in many varieties, especially chicken cacciatore. There was always an accompanying bowl of salad greens, arugula, and Romaine lettuce, mixed with tomato slices, mixed olives, garlic, vinegar and olive oil. Desserts consisted of bowls of fresh fruit, some thick chunks of different cheeses, and cakes and pastries. The pastries were from a local Italian pastry shop.

If either my sister or I did not eat our complete dinner, then there could be no desserts. My mother believed it was a serious sin to ever waste food. Any food left over was to be eaten the next day for lunch or incorporated into the next night's dinner. Sometimes as a treat, my mother made pizzas. She'd use ingredients from scratch, again following some recipe kept within her memory, probably from childhood. The pizzas could be eaten cold or hot, just as the leftover spaghetti dishes could. These seemed to have enhanced flavors the next day.

There must be hundreds, maybe more outstanding Italian cookbooks. My advice is quite simple for anyone who wants to become a skilled cook of Italian meals: Spend years in the kitchen of an Italian-American or Italian woman/man and simply observe everything she/he does. Then, memorize it all, or take careful notes and return to your own kitchen and assiduously practice what you've learned.

If you need further culinary help, get a copy of <u>Shut up and Eat!</u> (Tony Lip and Steven Prigge, editors; New York, Berkley Books, 2005, hardcover, 2006, softcover.) This is a fine array of classic, easy to make recipes provided by well-known Italian-American celebrities. The accompanying stories are wonderful, too.

When my mother died in the spring of 1985 so did her culinary skills and secrets. They're gone. To this day, I still do not know the whereabouts of Billie's heavy kitchen pots and frying pans with the thick wooden handles. They were integral to her culinary magic.

2014

BLACK MALE JAZZ PIANO PLAYERS

SOMETIMES when you're sitting around your mind wanders to seemingly insignificant matters. It's open to all sorts of random thoughts; some are coherent ones, others less so. Inexplicably, they rush in, moving about as you hold on to some of them for more dissection. Typically, we're purposeful in our thoughts and actions. You might even wonder, why this is happening?

Each day while I drive around, I've been serially playing CDs of different jazz piano players I've received as gifts or bought over the years. Each piano artist has a distinct style, unique in what is emphasized and improvised. There's no confusion in discriminating one from another. Even when the same piece of music is played by different pianists, it's possible to determine whose performing.

Listening to the music, these thoughts came to me: How come so many of the jazz piano players I'm hearing are black male pianists? Are they just more gifted in both jazz and the piano, just as they are in certain professional sports, excluding golf, tennis and ice hockey (at least so far)? Is there any valid explanation for their piano talents and artistry? Or, am I making all of this up to support some created, pre-conceived notion?

A while ago, I heard a silly joke: "What is a black piano player?" After some thought, the best possible answer given is: "It's a piano player playing on a black piano."

In recent times I'm uncertain whether it's appropriate to refer to a person of color as "black" or Negro, or preferably "African American." The answer from a person who is one, and not some person being politically correct, is from my dear friend Bill Rivers. His advice is "Joe, it all depends on the situation." So, I'll use the term "black" throughout this writing.

Besides black American jazz piano players, my mind wandered to black women who are well-known jazz singers or jazz pianists. Am I imagining this black jazz piano predominance? Well, I called my dear friend Tom Ford, who's a jazz expert and asked him about this matter. While Tom is hardly a biologist, he quickly responded "it's clearly in the genes, in the gene templates." Tom has made this same statement on a variety of topics in our many discussions over the years. Then, I corresponded with another friend, Don Mazzoni, who's also a jazz expert.

Thanks to Tom and Don, along with my contributions, here's our combined compiled list of black male jazz piano players. Undoubtedly, some have been inadvertently left out. In no order, these are the names that came up: Art Tatum, Errol Garner, Junior Mance, Willie the Lion Smith, Ray Charles, Jelly Roll Morton, Thelonius Monk, Duke Ellington, Count Basie. Fats Waller, Fats Domino, Scott Joplin, Bud Powell, Eubie Blake, Stevie Wonder, Herbie Hancock, Chick Corea, Ahmad Jamal (recently appeared in

Rockport, MA.), Oscar Peterson, Billy Taylor, Cecil Taylor, Teddy Wilson, Jacki A. Byard, Ronnie Matthews, McCoy Tyner, Barry Harris, Hank Jones, Earl Hines, Gene Russell, and Tommy Lee Flanagan.

One more added to this list.......Marcus Roberts; he has the talent to play the piano in styles accurately interpreting many of the pianists cited above. He's black too, and in addition, blind, yet a brilliant pianist. He happens to believe Art Tatum is the greatest jazz pianist. I haven't heard all of the above pianists, but my favorites are Junior Mance and Errol Garner.

(This list contains none of the thousands of jazz pianists who've played in small clubs, bars, and resorts over the years across the expanse of America yet remained essentially unknown.)

Roberts, like some others on the list was trained first as a classical pianist; there's at least one who can't even read music; and those who had little formal piano training. Others attended noted music schools while some barely attended any schools; some became pianists by sheer accident and curiosity, and there's a few that are blind. All are part of this diverse group ultimately reaching professional success and notoriety, and involving endless hours of practice playing.

A further electronic search and reading reveal hundreds of male, female black and white pianists, including a selected list of the 100 most outstanding. Examples of brilliant white male jazz pianists are George Gershwin, George Shearing, Dave Brubeck, and of course, the wonderful "piano man" Billy Joel.

So, where does all of this piano giftedness come from and why so many black jazz pianists? As in many things in life, it is difficult to identify all of the causative factors. It's tempting to single out one reason or force, but this excludes or ignores other potential contributory causes and motivations. In earlier writings, I've speculated about complex, multi-causational contributions to success in learning, in relationships, athletic achievements and politics.

When an individual achieves in any area, there can be common ingredients: parental support; teachers who saw something in that individual; inexplicable motivations within the individual; a capacity to work or strive with intensity and energy, the popular term these days to describe such a state is "a passion;" and positive encouragement and interest by those about the person. Added to these are undoubtedly innate abilities to possibly excel by playing a musical instrument. Certain individuals simply are more attracted to such activity; they seek out the experience with fluidity, and persist despite barriers, setbacks, even discouragements. I prefer terms like "mission" or "purpose" that drives an individual. Whatever inspired these jazz artists, money was hardly a factor.

Black musicians got to be dominant with difficulty. Blacks have been forced to find their ways by so many routes, including serving as entertainers for portions of the population. Some were from families active in church groups where spirituals and hymns were memorized and sung. There are others who brought forth rhythms and songs from Africa, the Caribbean, and the American South. Such background factors made others recognize and appreciate their sheer talents.

Are their special talents realms predicated upon some unknown or unspecified ethnic/racial backgrounds? Is it possibly within the inherent genetic/cultural talents? Is it because of some serendipitous or creative instant? If it's true that genetic pre-dispositions or more complex genetic factors do exist, we will have to wait for reputable research studies to confirm this concept.

Perhaps you're wondering why a particular racial or ethnic group collectively becomes involved in some identifiable role in our society. This too is a complicated issue. Humans find a place to fit in and belong. Once there, they persist, some flourish and excel. As each group seeks identity as well as benefits, it carves out a niche and can remain dominant there. Lois Grant Muzio offers a belief in the "principle or path of least resistance," to fulfill some need or purpose in the community or social structure, and where others do not object or are less threatened by such presence.

If you think you know reasons that might account for black male jazz pianists' prominence and their abilities, please let me know.

2014

WHY ARE THERE "MULE LADIES"?

O N March 31ˢᵗ, 2014 when I picked up my <u>New York Times</u> I was stunned by a large photo on the front page of a bent over older woman leaning on a cane while she carries a massive package on her back. The accompanying caption of the photograph reads:

> "At the border between Morocco and Spain's enclaves in North Africa, Moroccan women carry goods over the line for meager pay."

On that same front page is the first column of a lengthy article titled "A Borderline Where Women Bear the Weight" by Suzanne Daley. Wanting to know more about this brutal oddity, I continued to read the rest of the article on page A8, which includes additional photographs of the women and the bundles they carry, and a map of the area considered in the article.

Why am I providing such background details? Because after you've read my writing you too might want to read the entire article and verify the information reported in the New

York Times for yourself. The contents of the article are so overwhelming they require our attention, along with any resulting despair readers might have.**

If not, I offer here a summary:

At the Moroccan-Spanish border, hundreds of women, some in their 60's referred to as "mule ladies" carry on their backs and/or roll huge bundles of goods that weigh between 150–175 pounds (some up to 220 pounds) about a quarter of a mile up a hill. These women earn 3 Euros per trip, between 15-20 Euros per week ($20-$27), although they do not always get a package to carry.

The border is only open certain days and certain hours. The women in this region do not need a visa to cross the border. There are dangers at the border; including possible stampedes moving through the border turnstiles. Some women are whipped by men with belts; are injured in this work by getting broken legs and arms, and others serious health problems from their experiences.

These impoverished "mule ladies" do this work so the goods being brought in evade duty charges when they come into the country. Because the massive packages of goods carried into Morocco are considered "hand luggage," they are therefore not subject to any duty charges. Thus, the import taxes are considerably reduced for the Moroccan traders. About 412 million dollars worth of goods arrive in the Morocco port per year.

When I first read the weight these women carry, my reaction was it was just not likely. How could frail women carry almost a couple of hundred pounds? Throughout my lifetime, including as a teenager, I carried certain loads. When I was about 14, I worked for a grocery store on Queens Boulevard in Sunnyside. One of my jobs once a week was to carry a couple of sacks of potatoes on my shoulder a block away to the barbeque Broiler Restaurant. Each potato sack weighed 50 pounds and I would make two trips. As a young college student, I worked at a GE warehouse in Queens and handled large appliances, but was able to move them about on a stevedore's hand truck. Later on, when I was in the United States Marine Corps and 23 years of age, in tip-top physical condition, I carried a 50—60 pound pack on my back on long marches. In the past few years of living in Rockport, MA. I've been carrying 40 pound sacs of pellets from our garage up to the pellet stove in the living room, a distance of about 40 feet or so. But never did I have to carry 175 pounds or more of goods on my back as these older women do daily.

Why do they do this? Without asking each of the hundreds of women who do this painful and arduous hauling, it would be unlikely we could ever identify all of the reasons. A few reasons must be the more obvious ones: Poverty drives them to do this; poor education and inadequate other employment opportunities are other reasons; living in a culture that does little to prevent or offset such hard labor are also involved; and no doubt the subjugation of women to accept such work is an additional factor. It is noteworthy the cited article does mention these women are either widowed or with infirmed husbands unable to do work, so they must support entire families on their own to stay alive.

Some officials in Spain and Morocco have commented this is a matter between the two countries, yet no correctable solutions have been offered. The women doing this work have proposed there are needs for more orderly procedures at the border, and their desire for the merchants to make the huge bundles they carry smaller. No changes have been taken. The underlying force to leave matters without change is directly related to the existing monetary benefits for those controlling the bundles moving across the border, the profiting merchants. Any improvements in conditions would cost them money. They do not want to do this, despite the observed slave-like atmosphere.

Those remote from situations or ignorant about such matters can easily brush them off as isolated incidents. There can be all sorts of comments and questions about these women: Why do these women do this work and maybe if they refuse to do it, this would improve matters? Why don't these women move away? Why don't they just improve themselves and get better jobs, or get better educations? Why should I worry or even be concerned about these things, aren't there more important matters? Why bother about these women, they choose to live these lives and isn't this their problem? Why are they forced to do it? Recently men who are unemployed have been trying to carry the bundles. If they succeed, will the work conditions improve because they are men? Why are women subjugated to slavery like this? Why don't those who control this matter have the workers use wheels underneath the packages? Why can't the leaders in Spain and Morocco resolve such brutality, it's their problem? None of these questions corrects this matter.

One needs to be reminded how in a world population of about 7.4 billion humans, given the expanding ranges of poverty, abuse and deprivation throughout, comparable examples of harsh labor are occurring daily all over the globe. Many forms of slavery persist. Why in supposedly modern times do we silently allow such dehumanizing activities to continue to exist throughout the world? International, regional and philanthropic organizations supposedly address these types of issues, but inexplicably many remain unresolved or unknown to others. Perhaps they continue to exist simply because large amounts of money can be made insensitively via the exploitation of others. Some ethicists and economists refer to this as "unfettered capitalism."

** If you are interested in viewing a 5 minute video of this matter, then go on your computer to <u>New York Times – Archives,</u> and place the term "mule ladies" in the search box to watch this deplorable circumstance.

2014

PHILOSOPHY

LATELY I've been asking people I know and even those I don't know well: "What is your 'philosophy of life'?" Some people find this offsetting and wonder why I'm asking. After a pause, some even ask me what is "your philosophy oflife?" By asking this question, perhaps I've created some confusion. I wasn't referring to the classical concepts and scholarly definitions of the term "philosophy." Nor was I ever expecting they had knowledge or understanding about those classified and studied as the great philosophers at colleges and universities. I wanted to know what drives them, what shapes their attitudes, beliefs and character to be who they are in their lifetime journey. What do they stand for? Since I've been asking so many people, I also decided in fairness to present in writing my "philosophy of life," or at least to make a serious effort to do this.

My "philosophy of life" is predicated on many forces and factors. By citing some of them, the reader will have a deeper understanding of what contributed to it. There are many individuals who have contributed to how my "philosophy of life" has been shaped, modified, and developed. Certainly Lois and the many years of knowing her and benefitting from her mind and her counter points to mine have been critical. Having children and being involved in their lives as they have grown and developed gave me certain perspectives about family and how each child is unique individual

I was brought up in a close-knit Italian-American family, with all of my relatives being uneducated and for the most part low-level employees or entrepreneurs most of their lives. I lucked in by having the parents I did. Both were loving, attentive and supportive. Both parents emphasized and demonstrated goodness to others, being helpful to those about them, and striving to improve themselves. My father was an aggressive no-nonsense businessman, and in addition a bookmaker at the racetracks and then off the tracks. He had definite codes of conduct instilled in me from early on.

My family members were Roman Catholics, but not devout ones; I attended Catholic schools for the first few years, and afterwards was a devout, intensely practicing Catholic, paying close attention to the church's teachings and procedures. It was only after attending college, reading a great deal and somewhere while I became a USMC officer that I came to realize I did not believe in God or the Catholic Church. Since then, I put little value in attending any religious institution or its teachings, yet know some individuals rely on church/synagogue/masque attendance for their own benefits.

Paradoxically, in some areas my underlying behavior and thoughts are still dominated by certain Catholic perspectives inculcated in me since being a child. Most are sound ones because they focus on being a "good" person, not hurting others, being generous and caring, and recognizing the flaws in the human condition.

A vital component of my philosophy is to strive to excel. From when I was a little boy, I have tried to do well at whatever was being undertaken. This has been so in my learning activities, schoolwork, sports, games in the schoolyard and even chores I was assigned by either of my parents or others. Throughout my education I worked to achieve high grades, studying regularly and intensely. My friends used to kid me about such a commitment, but I did it anyway. I wanted to be recognized as a person who cared about what I was doing. When I work, it has been my consistent lifetime practice to work hard, to do the job thoroughly and without excuses. Regarding sports, even though I was not especially tall or large in size or talented, my goal was to be at a level of excellence for myself and those about me. Such a pattern often resulted in my being selected, chosen or elected as the leader, the captain of the team. This was also so in the USMC and at the college where I spent the bulk of my professional years.

My philosophy is to treat others with kindness, direction and openness. I like to meet people at all levels, giving the same attention to those lowest on the totem pole as those at the top of it. I identify with those who are down-trodden, believe they need extra attention and support; offer suggestions for their improvement; and appreciate their unpretentiousness and the levels of work they do to make the entire operation succeed. When I was a substitute teacher in high school and later on as a professor, I operated with the belief that every student with encouragement and assistance, coupled with their efforts could become a more complete student and person.

Learning to give to others and enjoying doing so is a significant part of my philosophy. Recognizing how vital it is to love those about me in my family and in friendships gives me a greater sense of interconnectedness and reliance as well as appreciation of others. Without loving others I do not believe there can be any meaning to life itself.

There is something about some of those who are well-off or anyone who is pretentious that I find myself deeply upset. It puzzles me why they are this way. Such individuals in my mind believe they are genetically advantaged over the rest of the population. Many have inherited their wealth and position; others were fortunate to be able to make money; and there are those who by sheer luck and accident acquire wealth.

Many become full of themselves and arrogantly lose any humanity or sensitivity to others while they avidly chase possessions and status. It is noteworthy that those who have great wealth in our society often have favorable political/economic mechanisms to pay lower taxes, hide money in favorable accounts, and in general deceive the rest of the population because of their belief systems and legal loopholes. When I meet them my interest is in speaking out against them. They are and so is their wealth as transitory as the lives of the rest of us.

Just to be balanced, there are also those who are inordinately poor, down on their luck and rely on governmental subsidies and others forever that also do dishonest and illegal scams. Such practices are equally wrong. Tax evasion by some is unfairly transferred to the rest who then have to pay their own legitimate share plus the tax amounts being illegally evaded. Why must this be the way others function?

My "philosophy of life" focuses on seeking and identifying pleasure, comfort and awareness of Nature's beauty, and in the people I have gotten to know and love. Nature is subjected to a continual onslaught for profit, exploitation and personal abuse, as if it's here exclusively for human beings. What a tragic and foolish thought. Nature and all of its occupants must be respected and sustained. Nature gives us mental and physical appreciations and freedom and pleases our senses and lives. As for people, we are social animals and benefit from the diversity and behaviors of those we choose to spend time with. When I see another human being hurt or injured, I recognize how fortunate I am, and how such individuals need our attention and respect.

The concept of "loyalty" is an integral component of my philosophy of life. I take my friendships quite seriously. If for some reason I believe I have been treated "shabbily" or in a disloyal manner, I take this as a form of abandonment and rejection. My feelings are hurt and it takes a long time for me to recuperate and then to behave in a more balanced manner. Some friendships have not been continued, especially since Donald Trump came on the scene.

Since I was a young boy and thanks primarily to my mother's encouragement, I have read a great deal. All sorts of readings have given me thoughts to consider and give credence in my philosophy of life. For example, reading <u>Cry the Beloved Country</u> by Alan Paton made me sensitive to the horrors of prejudice and racial discrimination in South Africa. So too did <u>Black Boy</u> and <u>Native Son</u> by Richard Wright sensitize me to our American racism. I've read many books with Albert Einstein being the subject, including his writings. While being a genius and a brilliant thinker, he was a fine outspoken humanitarian, too. Thomas E. Wolfe

(1900-1938) is in my thinking a great American author, and I have read virtually all of his writings since being in college. As I still read and review books in the biological sciences, especially those focusing on human evolution, I have come to realize how much our lives are being shaped by our inherent history from eons ago. The past is with us.

Genetically, we are remarkably different, with each person truly unique. There remains much mystery about the roles and control of genetics in our development and our lives. We remain incomplete, still evolving, and with innumerable shortcomings in our thinking and abilities. Sure, there have been continual scientific and technological advances, and there have been great discoveries and improvements, but in many ways we remain primitive and less human than we are or would like to believe. Certain educational programs intentionally negate the scholarly and research tenets of evolution and push religious interpretations of the earth's formation and the evolution of plants and animals, including humans. Most of these focus on a commitment to "God" and faith and I reject them.

Although humans seem to be at war forever, I have a great hatred of war and what it does to most humans. I do not only mean wars between nations, but the kinds of wars and violence occurring every day throughout our society. How could anyone rape, or beat or kill another person? Our country is less than 5 percent of the world's population yet we house just about 25 percent of those globally incarcerated. Is this some indication of our success or failure as a society and nation?

Are there other traits that encompass my "philosophy of life?" Oh yes, there's a belief in speaking out on issues; holding fast to certain principles; being forthright with others; finding "success" in non materialistic things; and recognizing the frailties in others and certainly myself. I encourage those about me to stand up and be counted; avoid the ever-expanding emphasis on self-indulgence and entertainment in our society; and those narcissistic trivialities that take away precious time, energy and focus from quiet thought and, reflection.

When we evade serious discussions and self-reflection on difficult issues, the more we seek blatant, outright, empty pleasures, the more we will move towards becoming like the Roman Empire and its citizens. There's no doubt we have a world population exploding, now 7.4 billion of us and endless more on the way (estimates are between 70 and 90 billion people have ever been born). Too many in the world are in outright poverty, suffering from curable or preventable diseases, ill-health and considerable lifetime disadvantages.

There are other characteristics that could be included, but perhaps by expressing my thoughts, with further discussion there can be more clarification.

This effort to present my "philosophy of life" is quite long and even in some places long-winded. Many writers have the uncanny ability, the gift to be succinct and still accomplish their writing purposes. Even with this lengthy writing on my philosophy subject I've not covered other aspects of it, and for this I apologize.

References:

The reader might be interested in reading <u>Love People, Not Pleasure</u> by Arthur C. Brooks, president of the American Enterprise Institute in the July 20th <u>The New York Times</u> Sunday Review. It's directly related to a person's "philosophy of life," and certainly not predicated on fame, fortune, entertainment, sex or materialism.

Also of possible interest in <u>The New York Times</u>, July 17, 2014 is a cogent piece "Reclaiming Our (Real) Lives, How to wean yourself off social media, so your days can belong to you once more." It's by Nick Bolton, a columnist who regularly writes about disruptions in our lives.

2014

A LONG-AGO PHOTOGRAPH

C HINESE proverb: "One picture is worth ten thousand words." (Or is it?)

Several months ago Elise Ognibene Lentz the daughter of a deceased dear family friend sent me an old black-and-white photograph. On the back of it she wrote: "This is the picture I promised you ... perhaps Joan's wedding? Much happiness and good health in 2014."

Yes it was taken at the wedding of one of younger first cousins, Joan Naccarato on May 8, 1965. She was 18 years old.

Although Lois and I were at that wedding, I do not recall ever seeing the photograph before; nor have I thought about the event since then.

Let's identify each person from left to right, with their ages (in parentheses) at the time this photograph was taken:

My aunt Elizabeth Brancata Stramiello (70); first cousin Marge Stramiello Kushner (52); my mother Philomena (known throughout most of her life as "Billie") Brancata Muzio (62); my sister Maria Muzio Russell (35); my aunt Lucille Brancata DeWarde (60); Emma Armani Ognibene (58) the long-time friend of aunt Rose's; and my aunt Rose Brancata Naccarato (55), the mother of the bride, Joan.

What interests me is how the women are carefully and methodically lined up next to one another, almost in a formal reception line. It is uncanny they were positioned in such an intimate side-by-side family pattern, with no outsiders or other friends.

All 7 women in this photograph are obviously closely-related; they're attractive and formally dressed-up for Joan's wedding. They appear so full of life, all smiling, well-styled, looking healthy and comfortable within themselves and those about them. Each has a quiet elegance and sophistication to suggest they are possibly well-off, affluent individuals attending an important social event. They're as classy, self-assured and confident as any family portrait of the illustrious political Kennedy women of Massachusetts at one of their many publicized functions.

This photograph is just one instant, one captured millisecond in their life spans on that particular day in 1965. No matter how wonderful, gracious and comfortable they seem a more detailed in-depth analysis of their overall lives would be more revealing about their overall journeys. Remember Bob Murphy, our deceased dear friend and noted anthropologist's statement: "Things are never the way they seem."

I stared at the photograph for awhile. An old photograph can evoke long-ago memories saved up in those seemingly remote and seldom used storage regions within the brain. Examining a photograph can promote thoughts and feelings about the individuals shown in it and set off a wave of reactions.

Primarily because of what took place early in their collective lives, you will see shortly the Brancata sisters clung to one another for the rest of their lives. They were inside each other's lives forever after.

There's an Irish proverb that fits the Italian-American Brancata sisters perfectly:

"It is in the skeleton of each other that people live."

For these 4 Brancata sisters' their earlier role model and daily mentor was their mother Maria Tucci Brancata, a stern, competent and energetic head of the family. Maria ran several businesses simultaneously while also serving as the superintendant of the Baxter Street tenement where they lived. She was a no-nonsense, sound individual who found multiple ways to make money, including frequent bartering with neighbors and merchants. She even allowed a local bookmaker to keep a phone in her apartment for his sole use, with no one else to touch it. While doing so, she taught her daughters to sew, cook, clean, and do chores in the building, while keeping a careful eye on them, especially guarding them when the men who lived in the building were hanging around in the neighborhood. She worried about her daughters.

Maria had a particularly harsh relationship with my mother. It was within Billie's personality to disregard her mother's strict and tightly governing relationship over her. Billie insisted on doing do what she wanted; and she often was severely punished, sometimes for seemingly minor violations. But that didn't stop her from doing them again. The other sisters were more compliant or unwilling to take risks, or simply evaded getting caught and therefore not subject to their mother's heavy hand or stick. Years later, Billie would describe to my sister Maria and me some of her more memorable childhood experiences with her mother. Most were sad, some publicly humiliating and perhaps by today's standards possibly demonstrative of childhood abuse requiring outside investigation.*

In 1926, the 4 Brancata sisters, Elizabeth, Billie, Lucille and Rose and their brother, Dominick had a terrible, a most unusual sequence of sad experiences that came upon them. Billie, Lucille and Rose were relatively young (Rose was the youngest at 15); Billie and Lucille worked. These three still lived at home. The oldest, Elizabeth was already married at a young age, perhaps 17, and well on her way to produce 5 children and living in Brooklyn. Their brother Dominick was married living in Brooklyn. He and his wife had 9 children, and in 1947 had a separate tragic family incident. That might have also had severe repercussions on the 4 sisters. As I write this piece 88 years later, I believe these debilitating and shocking experiences were with them forever afterwards.

Their parents Maria Tucci Brancata and Egidio Brancata, my grandparents tragically died within 8 days of each other. Their deaths occurred in the tenement on Baxter Street in lower Manhattan. Maria fell out a high window while hanging clothes on a line. 8 days afterwards Egidio committed suicide by hanging himself in the basement of the same tenement.

At this late date my interpretation of Egidio's suicide is he was tired, drained, and despondent and overwhelmed by life. Right after his intensely powerful and controlling wife, the family's leader died, he found himself unable to rationally deal with this event and what he thought would follow. He'd been a quiet, overworked man who held two full-time jobs; seldom was he home or able to be involved in daily family matters. By his desperate and selfish exit, he thoughtlessly abandoned his already motherless children. Giving up one's life to suicide is a mysterious action poorly understood.

Now, the sisters, lonely and confused were totally parentless. Still grieving and abandoned the Brancata sisters were abruptly and callously dispossessed by the owners of the tenement building on Baxter Street. Billie, Lucille and Rose moved in with the oldest and also grieving sister Elizabeth and her husband Joe Stramiello in Brooklyn. On several occasions in recounting this matter, my mother Billie told me this was a quick, perhaps a week or so exit and a most traumatic move for all of them.

Two years after their parents' deaths and after living with sister Elizabeth and her tribe this living situation would come to a close for Billie, Lucille, and Rose Brancata. Life there was crowded and perhaps as chaotic as their tenement conditions on Baxter Street. It was hardly their own place. Another move would occur shortly.

This next location change was promoted because Billie was going to marry Frank Muzio. It is highly unlikely this marriage would have ever taken place if her parents had been alive. Billie's mother was an especially powerful force and it would not have been looked upon favorably. Frank had been married before and divorced from another local neighborhood woman after he returned from serving in France in the United States Army during World War I. Being a divorced man was hardly a strong selling point to traditional, more rigid Italian/Catholic immigrant parents. While it's pure belated speculation, if there'd not been any marriage I wouldn't be writing this right now. Nor would have all the other genetic events and experiences involving my parents, their children and their offspring thereafter have taken place either. But, that's belated speculation too.

Newlyweds Frank and Billie brought Lucille and Rose along in their marriage. This was a package deal. They were part of a commitment made by my mother to her two younger sisters; and my father Frank willingly accepted this arrangement. By today's standards such a marital arrangement is considered unusual. Even though Lucille and Rose were single, employed young women, there were family pressures, coupled with certain cultural restrictions to inhibit their having their own apartment. So, three sisters and newly-wed husband Frank moved to a different Brooklyn apartment. Still, it was close-by to their older sister Elizabeth's home in Bay Ridge. This marital group arrangement provided economic and social benefits. Later on, Rose and Lucille offered readily available baby-sitting services to Billie and Frank as their children were born. And a place to entertain dates when and if they developed. While living together, Lucille and Rose called Frank "Daddy" almost as an identifiable replacement for the father they lost so quickly.

Years later and with changing times, Lucille and Rose were able to get their own place. Yet, it's again noteworthy it was still close by to Elizabeth and to Billie and Frank in Brooklyn. It was within walking distance.

The 4 Brancata sisters continued to be deeply engaged with each other. Essentially they were inseparable, constantly in support of each other. They'd lived together as children, sleeping with one another in the cramped quarters in lower Manhattan; then together in Brooklyn; later on as married adults in Sunnyside Queens, Rose and Billie and their families lived in the same apartment house, separated by one floor. Then, Billie, Rose and Lucille and their husbands lived nearby to each other in Holliswood/Bayside Queens, and were joined by Emma and Sal Ognibene, their lifetime friends. As daily local buddies, they were inextricably bound together other as they exercised intense familial closeness from their early years.

They were habitually in one another's apartments and later on homes; sometimes you'd go to visit one of them and find another Brancata sister or two visiting there. The four of them arranged picnics, family outings, holiday dinners, vacations and just about every event for them.

Although their mother Maria had been dead for a long time, she was in many ways alive and well in the personalities of the 4 daughters. These women had strong, powerful personalities. They were smart, highly skilled, resourceful, and directly managed the major developmental events in their families. Similar to their mother they found multiple ways to earn money for their families. All wrote and spoke perfect English (their mother didn't), and solved all sorts of daily problems in their neighborhoods. They were excellent shoppers and cooks. All of them had sewing skills.

The sisters were extremely frugal, one might categorize them as "tight-fisted," and they handled each family's money matters, especially when their blue-collar husbands (all Italian-Americans) experienced unemployment or foolish business or gambling ventures on their own. Decisions about where they'd live, whether or not a home would be purchased, where the families would vacation and ongoing childrearing activities including where the children went to school, these were done exclusively by the women, and carefully thought out based on what funds could be allocated. They were in ongoing daily control of their families, making regular sacrifices for their children so there could b piano and dance lessons, and summer camp experiences, and school tutors.

Italian mothers and Italian-American mothers had a great deal of power and control within their family structures. Much has been written about such women by scholars, and there is a great deal of documentation to substantiate their authority, guidance and influence on the family. The mothers were the hub of family matters and exercised much influence often predicated on their self-sacrifices and deep commitments for the good of the family. Their husbands might have believed they were running things, but this was self-delusional. There was constant attention to the well-being of the family members; the Brancata sisters exemplified these qualities.

At different times, the Brancata women in the photograph carried out ongoing quasi-surrogate mother responsibilities for my sister and me. For varying periods of time, we lived with all of the Brancata sisters. Of course my mother and my older sister Maria were in my life virtually all of the time; as mentioned, Lucille and Rose lived with us for a number of years. As a youngster I spent weekends with Aunt Lucille while her husband Andrew was working in Trinidad. These visits revolved around going to a movie, having Chinese food, and attending church on Sunday before I returned home. When my father was a bookmaker at racetracks, and he and my mother would go to Florida to identify places of us to move to for the upcoming racing season, my sister and I stayed at Aunt Elizabeth's for weeks at a time. As a child, this periodic separation from my parents seemed like an eternity.

Throughout my childhood, these women were most kind, supportive and attentive to me. Lucille and Rose were especially generous and kind to me. They gave my sister and me many gifts over the years. My first Rollfast bicycle and my first leather first-basemen's glove came from these hardworking frugal aunts. They were forever encouraging me. They took me to visit many places and events and some of their friends in New York City; they bought subscriptions to the Saturday Evening Post and Collier's magazines I sold; listened politely (while hiding their laughter) when I sang as a child to imitate Frank Sinatra, that is, before my voice changed; and suffered through my piano-playing recitals and enthusiastically clapped when I finished even though many mistakes had been made.

My mother Billie was an excellent typist, an avid reader (Book of the Month Club and The New York Times), and always going somewhere to be actively involved with her larger family. She frequently encouraged me to read all sorts of books and to then chat with her about them. By stimulating my interest in reading, she promoted freedoms in so many areas. She taught me to type before I was a teenager and this skill also gave me skill and freedoms. She worked for many years for the federal government until she retired at 65 years of age. Even with a wide range of activities and interests, she still never learned to ride a bike, or use roller or ice skates. She had a variety of fears inhibiting her behavior, so she was always reluctant to try new things. Some of these fears were with her throughout her life; some were conveyed to her children.

Lucille worked at Macy's in their main office where cash throughout the store was sent to a secure facility where it was counted. This was until she stayed at home in Brooklyn permanently to make a strong repeated effort to have children. There were several miscarriages, but she and her husband Andrew eventually succeeded and had two daughters. Lucille and Andrew briefly ran a restaurant outside of Camp Dix, New Jersey. It was called "The Pig and Whistle."

Elizabeth spent the bulk of her life raising her family, do not know if she ever was employed in outside work. After my parents and Maria moved to Queens in 1941, I stayed and lived with Elizabeth and her family in Brooklyn to prepare for my confirmation at St. Ephrem's. It is only lately did I realize I lived or stayed at the same house on 85th street off of Third Avenue in Bay Ridge Brooklyn that the 4 Brancata sisters lived in together after their parents had died. That house has held much history for many of us.

Lucille and Elizabeth were the more serious of the 4 Brancata daughters; and they appeared to have more devout and narrow Roman Catholic perspectives about their lives and their families. They were also the most conservative in their thinking, attitudes and behavior. Billie and Rose seemed more simpatico with one another and they continued to be extremely close throughout their lives.

Aunt Rose was an outstanding seamstress and a person of much goodness. Rose worked 38 years in the union-permitted sweatshops of the New York City garment industry. Later on, she repaired and altered clothes for all her Bayside Queens neighbors, and also cared for their children as the younger mothers were more involved in social activities. Rose loved children and had an enthusiasm and understanding of them. Rose altered and mended my clothing, too. Afterwards, she was the "gatekeeper" at a private swimming pool/club where she attacked this job with energy and consistency: if you didn't have your issued entrance badge, no matter whom you were, you didn't get past diligent, persistent and good-natured Rose. She also energetically volunteered at St. Mary's Hospital for Children for about 10 years, requiring her to take 4 buses to get there. She had a continual willingness to help others, yet she was forever doubting herself and lacking self-confidence.

Dear friend Emma Armani Ognibene was a highly accomplished designer/seamstress who worked in the garment industry. When I was in various elementary school plays, she made several outfits for me that were so beautifully tailored. She was around our family so frequently I just thought she was a full-fledged member, she was Aunt Emma. Whenever she was there, she exemplified calmness and self-containment that was reassuring to me and those about us. She was quiet and with none of the explosiveness of the Brancata sisters.

None of them graduated high school (Billie did achieve a G.E.D. later); two of them never went beyond the elementary school level. Despite extremely limited formal educations, they knew how to get things done. Even so, we cannot ignore the stark reality whatever possible developmental opportunities these women might have had, they were stifled by their overall lack of formal education. Their career choices, their thinking processes and their abilities to cope with differing circumstances in their decision making were sharply defined by their schooling limitations. So too were the selections of their husbands influenced by such factors. (See <u>Women of the Shadows</u> by Ann Cornelisen; <u>Passage to Liberty</u> by Ken Ciongoli and Jay Parine.)

Sometimes when these families were together the husbands would joke or make sarcastic or cute remarks about being married to "these Brancata women," thereby faintly praising their uniqueness and solidarity. It seemed to be their collective defense as well as their attempt at comedy. This suggests they had at least a partial understanding and perhaps even hidden respect or irritation for their wives power and control. Such conditions are typical characteristics for Italian-American men and marriages.

The husbands would never acknowledge or perhaps were even aware of their less than leadership roles; they reflect more realistically the marital circumstances of those days and even today in certain cultures. Their respective wives would say little or nothing in public about such expressions, sometime smiling at one another. Perhaps when alone with each other they did.

Now that you've shared in the Brancata women's lives, or at least in my expository reflective explanation about them, are there any conclusions one can make about their journey?

It is my view the 1926 sequence of their parents' sudden joint deaths, along with their rushed removal into different living conditions and away from their original familiar surroundings as add-ons to their older sister's family forever shaped each Brancata woman throughout their lives. Their lifetime reliance and sister intimacy with one another were fostered by these events. In some respects, they were victims and prisoners of the combination of the tragic losses of their parents, their limited educational journeys, and decisions and choices that ruled their developments.

Their earlier tragic experiences markedly influenced and shaped the Brancata women. Yet, this is true for all of us, isn't it? There's no getting away or shedding those events and experiences impressed upon and woven into our personalities in our formative years. Later on conversations with their children, my first cousins along with my observations clearly support throughout their lives these women had certain fears and hesitancies to go beyond self-imposed restrictive margins. Such traits were at least partially transmitted to their offspring. Certainly this is so in my life, and efforts have been made to overcome them.

These long-range reflections about the 4 Brancata women's most consistent and noteworthy characteristics are: their kindness and gentleness; their lifetime ability to help others; living their lives without complaining or blaming others for any disruptions in them; and a lifetime vulnerability and hesitancy to embark on new activities or experiences. When and if they were dissatisfied or disappointed, there were no public pronouncements on these matters.

The times and their prevailing cultural forces in New York City that shaped these women cannot be ignored. For a whole variety of reasons their lives were ruled by those aspects of poverty along with limited opportunities for females, which did begin to change during the wartime period 1941-1945. They'd lived through World War I, the Great Depression and World War II. Their choices were governed or at least shaped by limited personal and familial resources further controlled by the superimposed cultural values.

Despite all of this, they did struggle and endure. There was an acceptance or compliance with their life situations, with little reaching out beyond what had taken place. Their lives were markedly influenced by unusual and debilitating events. There were other family tragedies and disappointments but they just keep moving on, and always without whining. The commonalities of these forces did induce their need to cling together, almost like puppy dogs holding on for the remainder of their lives.

In their own ways and together, they were all outstanding, hard working, persistent and unique persons. They all had a profound effect on my life. Could it have been otherwise? They accomplished a great deal, but exclusively within their immediate surroundings and mostly in familial relationships. Nevertheless, there seemed to be a prevalent sadness or hesitancy to all of their personalities, perhaps even varying levels of depression at different times for each of them. At different times in my life I have had sudden waves of sadness and wondered if there was some genetic pre-disposition connected to the Brancata sisters for it, or perhaps a metabolic/chemical disruption. When this happens, I engage in self-discussions and vigorously work at offsetting such unexpected mood shifts from remaining.

I am of the opinion each of them remained unfulfilled in their life's journey. In all our years together, I cannot recall one thought or discussion about their aspirations, their underlying beliefs about their lives, their feelings about their husbands or other events taking place in their communities and beyond. There were no discussions about "the future." Much remained forever unspoken or even given noteworthy comment. Perhaps they had established repressed margins to restrict them. They lived out their lives, loved, made mistakes and died.

Even so, seldom were the deaths of their parents ever mentioned; they were pushed back or repressed as if hidden, yet still ever present within them. Occasionally my mother Billie would describe her long-ago emotions related to these tragic experiences, and openly pace and sob about them.*

In this photograph above and in other photographs recently looked at, they are almost always smiling, proper and together. Such appearances were on the surface, hardly conveying their inner lives, feelings, thoughts or woe. If there were disappointments and there were, they were not publicly presented.

All of the women in the shown photograph are long deceased. The Brancata sisters, Billie, Lucille and Rose lived lengthy lives, with the exception of the oldest sister Elizabeth, who died in her late seventies; Billie went on to 82; Lucille well into her late 90's; and Rose just short of reaching 100 years. Cousin Marge, Elizabeth's oldest child lived into her 90's, as did two other Stramiello daughters Josephine and Viola. Dear friend Emma Armani Ognibene also lived well into her 90's. My wonderful sister Maria died much earlier at 70, due primarily to cancer from her incessant smoking since an early teenager. An additional contributory factor for Maria was excessive alcohol usage. Her early death is still with me.

Notations:

*Extensive details about my parents and sister as well as the Brancata sisters are provided in the memoir I wrote several years ago, <u>Buddy Remembers – Then and Now</u>.

Some early and what I thought were frank and helpful phone conversations were held with Elise Ognibene Lentz and Cousins Fran Naccarato and Joan NaccaratoAnastasio in my preparatory discussions, and I thank them for their assistance. Also, I express my appreciation to Elise for providing the cited photograph, which initiated this entire writing process months ago.

The reader will appreciate reading Alfred Lubrano's <u>Limbo, Blue-Collar Roots, White-Collar Dreams</u> (Hoboken, New Jersey, John Wiley and Sons, 2004.)

JUDGE JUDY SCHEINDLIN

THERE has been a proliferation of supposed "reality" television shows. Approximately 30 or more publicize themselves as featuring "reality" about individuals engaged in supposed "real life" experiences. Rather, they are fictitious creations meant to indulge and pre-occupy viewing audiences and are deceptive. Depending on their effects, they can make viewers less thoughtful and fill them with false mind-sets and interpretations about human behavior and life situations. The stark reality is these "reality" shows are hardly reality.

Here's just a partial list of the television subjects recently available to adults and children: marriage counseling; prison tattooing; sex advice; mob behavior; dating selection; "Mob Wives"; marital boot camps; survival teams on remote locations; familial disputes; potential investors for restaurants ; bad girls club; intervention; "Dance Moms" (a boot camp for concerned mothers and their daughters); husbands from Hollywood; "Tastes," (Best Cooks); and gossiping wives o f Atlanta, New York City and Beverly Hills. In addition, there are at least 5 court-subject programs competing with one another.

This might shock the reader but I have been regularly watching Judge Judy for the past 7 or 8 years. I am a loyal viewer and an expert able to offer analytical comments about her programs. Whenever friends find out I do watch Judge Judy, there are unusual facial expressions, quizzical comments, or sheer disbeliefs shown. How is it possible for this retired college professor to spend his valuable time watching Judge Judy? I'm often asked: "What makes her so special from all of the other types of 'reality' shows offered?

Judge Judy was a Family Court Judge and Supervising Judge in New York City for more than 25 years. Those experiences shape her strong beliefs regarding family conflicts, including child support; the importance of divorced or separated couples behaving with civility towards each other to benefit their offspring; and the importance of creating positive environments for their children. She urges those who appear before her to "do the right thing" and makes them aware of their "moral obligations." Judge Judy's missions are to assist individuals from being victims and to take responsibility for their actions. She uses many methods to do so.

Judge Judy is authentic reality TV. Typically she handles 4-5 cases in a one hour program format, five times a week. The people appearing before her are real; they have real complaints and disagreements. After listening to the plaintiffs and defendants and questioning them, Judge Judy's decisions are final. If the case does involve a monetary settlement she is limited to granting no more than $5000. Unlike traditional courts, the participants are relieved of paying up. The show's producer maintains a fund to carry out such decisions.

Important practical lessons can be learned from watching Judge Judy. These lessons are applicable and beneficial for all of us. Based on this program, there are frequent major disputes and confusion about parental responsibilities in child support cases, dog bites, car accidents, physical altercations, posting bail for another person, road rage incidents, disagreements between neighbors, tenants and landlords, property ownership, and non-married couples living together who are disengaging from one another.

Should we all know how to behave in these legal matters? As these matters unfold, we find out such an ideal seldom exists. It is puzzling how those who appear in Judge Judy's court have little understanding of court procedures, their rights in a court situation, or even how to present their side of a conflict matter. It might be helpful if a portion of our educational system could give more consideration to these frequently observed shortcomings by the litigants.

When someone is appearing for a case, it is vital to bring documentation (dates, times, locations and other facts) to support their position. For example, few plaintiffs or defendants recognize a written contract specifically spells out the conditions being agreed upon; and it can only be modified if the parties agree to do so in writing. Handshakes are wonderful in greetings and friendships, but clearly written documents are more legally valid. Landlords and tenants can avoid conflicts and confusion regarding their perceptions about the facilities when tenants are moving in or out, as well as the purposes of security deposits. Before and after occupancy photographs can be extremely helpful in resolving such a dispute.

Our formal courts are not designed to adjudicate "almost married" cohabitating couples. When you're cohabitating, there needs to be specific records kept and the avoidance of financial comingling if the relationship might dissolve.

Women appear to be quite generous in lending money to male partners, who prefer to erroneously believe these are "gifts." And if you do go before Judge Judy or any judge, be prepared to explain your sources of income if relevant to your case. She might ask "Are you on public assistance? Have you filed taxes recently? Judge Judy will certainly make you painfully aware of your possible illegal behavior. The almost 10-11 million daily viewers along with officials from Internal Revenue Service or assistance agencies will be observing too. Judge Judy is unforgiving of those who lie to her or she thinks lie.

Along with all of this, Judge Judy provides information about the law and legal procedures, and advises plaintiffs and defendants as to how to approach and improve situations. She has a low tolerance for vagueness and ambiguity and encourages clarification via orderly explanations; and despite's people's biases helps them to think more clearly. She works to get those appearing before her to be more accurate, focused and complete. Judge Judy goes about educating the participants and the viewing audience. Opinions are often presented rather than facts. Whenever plaintiffs and defendants make an effort to present "hearsay," she immediately cuts them off.

I learn a great deal about human behavior and life situations from these programs. I'm not suggesting Judge Judy is a perfect person on the bench. There are times when she calls someone "stupid" or "an idiot," and this bothers me. There are even occasions when she is unduly harsh; or she is brash; or she's humorous and sarcastic to those appearing before her. Sometimes she mentions her Brooklyn roots, her upbringing, her extended family and even her diminutive height.

As Judge Judy enters her 19th year of being on television, she is reportedly paid about 47 million dollars per year (that's right). Such amounts are given to professional athletes, movie and rock concert stars, fund operators, bank executives, and corporate titans. In our free society, it's what the marketplace provides. As long as Judge Judy's programs are watched by millions of viewers and satisfying those businesses who advertise on her program network she will function. Lately I notice an increased volume of commercials (to pay her salary), so her cases are given less time and development; if these distractions continue, I will regretfully leave Judge Judy.

As humans, we are imperfect and vulnerable, and can end up in situations where there are differences, disputes, outright arguments and even assaults. Such matters require resolution. Judge Judy frequently mentions that's what courts are for, to rationally resolve problems. In a democracy, we subscribe to effective resolutions done with civility and fairness. We need to respect our judicial system and our laws because they are vital to our existence and behavior. If we didn't there would only be greater chaos, confusion and animus.

You can find out a great deal more about her, her professional experiences and her life journey via a computer search, or by reading one of her books. I've read Judge Judy's most recent book, <u>What Would Judy Say, Be the Hero of Your Own Story</u>, sent by my sister-in-law Ellen Zulka in Florida. This concise volume offers Judy Scheindlin's 10 laws of success, along with her thoughts to improve one's behavior in legal matters and life.

2014

ESCALATOR EATS MOOSE

W HEN you look at the above title, you could easily think it doesn't make any sense. And in some ways, it doesn't. After all, how is it possible for a modern, often used technological transport device such as an escalator to devour such a huge animal as a moose? This couldn't happen, and while it sounds like some Sci-Fi tale, read on.

In late July and well into August Lois and I, accompanied by our dear friend Rose Mahoney spent three weeks in Ireland. It was a great voyage, full of natural beauty, history, friendly open citizens who were most willing to chat with us, and pleasantness all around. We learned a great deal about Ireland's culture, heritage and its historical "troubles" (that's what the Irish repetitively refer to them as) with England. The pervasive seemingly forever struggle for complete island-wide independence and freedom is very much present for the Irish population.

Never having been to Ireland before, we took cues from Rose who was born in Ireland and has relatives there, whom we visited. The journey throughout the entire island of

Ireland was a relaxed one, including an emotional visit to Belfast where Lois' grandmother had lived at 2 Joy Street and was baptized at nearby St. Malachy's Church in the late 1800's prior to coming to the United States. Walking on Joy Street and visiting the nearby church was a significant experience for us; Rose and I lit memorable votive candles; in the middle of the day in an almost empty beautiful church, three of us silently sat there awhile. We went to the superb museum at the shipyard where the Titanic had been built and where more than 100,000 workers once had jobs; this was another informative and moving experience.

Much thought and energy surround the experiences from this Ireland trip. Perhaps down the road I'll write about them, using some of the notes I made throughout our voyage.

At the end of our journey, Lois and I were back at Newark International Airport in New Jersey. We were going to catch a Jet Blue flight to Logan Airport, just outside of Boston. Pulling our luggage we got on a rather long escalator to take us to where the connecting tram is located. No one else was on the escalator. When we were about halfway up of it, somehow my piece of luggage slipped off the step directly behind me and I lunged reflexively backwards after it, trying to grab it as it accelerated further down the escalator steps. As the luggage tumbled down, I did too, bouncing down the sides and moving escalator steps. As I was tumbling, I made at least two attempts to get up, but I was completely out of control and couldn't right myself.

There was a man in a uniform; I think he was a pilot or at least looked like one about to get on the bottom of escalator. He had an awareness to quickly hit the escalator's safety/panic button where he was standing. The escalator stopped and an alarm rang out, as I continued downward. He asked me if I was all right. In my full embarrassment and confusion, I shouted out to him and a few others waiting to get on the escalator: "Yes, sure, I'm OK." Only this wasn't so. I remember being frightened because I didn't know how much damage there'd been to my body. There was a sickening sensation throughout my abdomen. Somehow, this abruptly reminded me of being in a football pileup with other bodies slamming against me and being at the bottom of the pileup, bearing much weight, confined and helpless. Suddenly, my breathing became difficult.

My trousers were torn and I was bleeding through from one knee; my sweater was torn, and blood was leaking through it from my arm; and my back seemed terribly bruised. There were gashed uniform stripes on my leg, arm and chest. On further examination I had the imprint of the escalator steps on my back. Lois lifted my shirt and looked at it and she commented: "You have a flag of stripes across your back, but no stars." My overall appearance was as if I had been mauled or clawed by some large animal. The escalator's steel steps had left major markings on me. One of the shoes I was wearing had several parallel claw marks imprinted on the top of the shoe; it must have gotten caught in a step as I tumbled.

With Lois now at my side, she gave me a surface physical examination. Formerly a registered nurse she understood the importance of carrying out a physical assessment after a trauma. She made me sit down on a bench and continued her evaluation. She noted no head wounds and no broken bones. According to her, I looked pale and disoriented. Then, a man in an official red jacket and wearing a badge came to us; he wanted information about the accident. He filled out some forms and I quickly signed them without reading them. He offered more help from airport services, but I insisted on not having any. A small crowd gathered, stared and then went about boarding the shuttle tram to other airport locations.

I wanted to just get out of there; publicly claiming we had to catch a plane, even though Lois kept emphasizing "Joe, we have three hours until our flight to Boston." This lengthy time span meant nothing to me, I just wanted to escape this scene where I had shown vulnerability. As an aging person, I gave thought to the possibility this was a manifestation of "slippage" in physical skills. By becoming less balanced and competent, it was my fault I'd tumbled down the escalator. Perhaps it was.

We decided I had to get out of my torn bloody clothes and clean up some of my surface cuts. A journey to a nearby crowded men's room was the next move. Have you ever tried to disrobe while taking clothing out of your luggage in a crowded public toilet where the commodes are specifically measured as "minimal?" While cleaning up some of the cuts and cloaking them with paper towels after I undressed down to my underwear, this was all done under public observations of men rushing into the facility. Having been in the USMC and in sports locker rooms it certainly wasn't unusual to change clothes in front of other men. Some just looked me, while others were asking what had happened. But with a bleeding arm, leg and back, and hesitancy to give even a brief explanation to inquiring strangers, in many ways this was disconcerting.

We purchased a first aid kit at a nearby newsstand. After passing several airport employees, they too inquired about me and offered to get further medical assistance. Despite the reality our flight wasn't leaving for hours, I stubbornly insisted on behaving independently and rejecting formal attention. After removing the paper towels I'd put on the cuts, Lois bandaged my wounds. Blood was already leaking through the new bandages. Once again we were in public and again there were those passing by and observing what we were doing. They'd look, and then continue on their hurried journeys.

The torn, blood stained outer clothing had been rolled up and discarded in the men's room; except for the sweater I'd been wearing. It's a long-time favorite and despite the blood-stains on the entire sleeve and several tears, it was being kept. Even though I was in pain and had cuts and scrapes, my thoughts went to salvage my sweater. It's an old one and I wanted to preserve it. There's a talented woman in Gloucester who has knitting skills and repairs sweaters. She's fixed some of mine. Once the blood was washed out in cold water before it could permanently set, she could repair the sweater. I did take the sweater to a special environmental cleaner who used enzymes on it; finally the blood discolorations were removed. When I wear the sweater or the damaged shoes from this experience, I reflect about what happened.

It's now 6 weeks after this incident. My cuts are healing and the stiffness throughout my body finally subsided; the escalator's "track marks" are still present but gradually fading away. There do not appear to be residual damages, but one's body can be deceiving. As a biologist I know how sometimes untoward effects on the body can show up long after the original provoking incident. Not all injuries are initially observable or detectable, especially those less visible.

During these past 6 weeks, many things have taken place in relation to this incident. After further probing I found out there are hundreds of thousands of escalators in our country along with many injuries, including occasional deaths. Older persons and children are particularly susceptible. Those unsure of foot; or those whose shoes or sandals get caught; or aren't paying attention can end up suffering. Many are unreported so it's difficult to realize the magnitude of injuries. My sister-in-law Ellen in Pompano Beach told her sister Lois a woman's scarf got caught in the escalator steps and she died. (This sounds similar to the great dancer Isadora Duncan's death, but her incident involved a flowing scarf caught in an automobile wheel.)

Newer missions have been identified for me. Recent activities have focused on informing anyone I know with children to caution them about issues related to escalators. Some parents thoughtlessly allow their children to go up and down escalators in malls for the pure fun of it. Escalators are not toys; they can be dangerous or lethal weapons. I'm encouraging others to pay attention as they board escalators to rate those escalator steps are moving and forming; and to definitely hold on to the handrails until they quickly and cautiously step on and off of the escalator. Or, better yet, to use an elevator instead of the escalator if one is available. Perhaps better warning signage near escalators will be helpful as less attentive passengers move about with their cumbersome luggage and children. I've written to the Newark International Airport authorities and told them of my experience, including announcing my responsibility for what did happen on their escalator.

Soon, maybe this weekend Lois and I will be going to a nearby shopping mall. I will go on an escalator for the first time since my disruptive accident. A long time ago I read if and when a person falls off or is thrown from a horse, the riding experts recommend for that person to quickly get back on the horse. This supposedly prevents undue lingering fear and future avoidance of horseback riding. That's my plan, to go up and down a mall escalator a bunch of times to see if I can successfully overcome this technological device in an attentive and balanced way. When I visit any malls I'm going to see if the escalators have proper warning signage and the emergency "Stop" controls are readily available and visually marked. If not, then I'll notify the authorities at that mall.

Now returning to the title of this piece, "Escalator Eats Moose," you might still be wondering about this bizarre title. You must have concluded there's no way a mechanical escalator could ever eat a moose. Then exactly what "Moose" is involved in this matter? Or is this just fiction?

Joe "Moose" Muzio

In my formative years in Sunnyside Queens, I hung out in the P.S. 150 schoolyard and spent many hours there. My buddies gave me the nickname "Moose" or "Bull Moose." I never knew how I got this title. Recently I checked with my dearest childhood friend since the 4th grade, Jerry Pagano and asked him how I got this slang name. He was pretty sure it had to do with my being a football player on the Sunnyside Robins, a local semi-pro team and the intensity I used to play the game; and the amount of time spent in the schoolyard doing conditioning exercises and staying in preparatory tip-top shape. I was a driven teenager. According to Jerry, schoolyard buddies supposedly decided I was strong like a real huge moose in nature, even though I'm pretty sure none of us had ever seen a real moose!!! That's how the "Moose" title happened to become. It's still with me amongst remaining older buddies.

So, it was Moose Muzio who was eaten by the vicious, unfeeling, moving escalator. Let's do what we can to make sure it doesn't happen to others, be they moose or not.

2015

THE SUNNYSIDE ROBINS FOOTBALL TEAM

Prologue:

THE Sunnyside Robins' athletic activities emanated from the Public School 150 schoolyard in Sunnyside Queens, located between most of 40th and 41st Streets, and between 43rd and Skillman Avenues. From the early 1940's on, this schoolyard was the epicenter for all seven-days-a-week athletic and social gatherings. If we weren't at school or carrying out chores assigned by our parents, or holding some part time local job, it was a safe bet we could be found in the schoolyard until the street lights went on, and then this was the communal unspoken signal to go back to our apartments, none of us lived in private houses. It was our neighborhood designated cement country club with its surrounding high fence, and marked off softball, handball and basketball courts. In addition to a football team, there also was a baseball team, a fast-pitch windmill softball team, and a basketball team wearing the Sunnyside Robins' name.

In the upper portion of the schoolyard the Sunnyside Robins football team held practices, walking and running through planned plays on cement. Anybody who came into the schoolyard got some sort of game there. Some walls in the schoolyard had whitened strike zones to distinguish whether a thrown ball would be either a strike or ball for the stickball matches. Any disputes taking place during the activities in the schoolyard were quickly resolved amongst us. A few of the older schoolyard participants had girlfriends and they too were regulars there. During World War II, a few of these older boys volunteered or were drafted for military service. Excluding the wintertime and in between schoolyard activities we would walk up 40th street to Seltzer's Candy Store, reach into a huge Coke Cola chest filled with ice on the sidewalk and pull out a bottle of Coke, Mission Orange, or Pepsi, and then pay Mr. or Mrs. Seltzer or their older son inside the candy store.

Significantly, this schoolyard territory was our exclusive ground without any parental controls or guidance. Our parents were too busy working to bother or to possibly immerse themselves in our schoolyard activities. We were devoid of any adults in the schoolyard.

Between 1946 and 1949 the Sunnyside Robins, a community football team won several league championships in the Queens Football Alliance and the Long Island Football

League. It was an exceptional team, well-coached and well-trained with extensive spring and summer practices each year. We even played an outstanding team from Philadelphia three times, the Venango Bears, champions of the Pop Warner Football League in that city. Potential players from about Queens and Long Island wanted to play on our team; at annual tryouts most of them didn't make it. As the Sunnyside Robins became better known, there were more teams wanting to play us and beat us. We developed a fine reputation throughout Queens and Long Island; and the local newspapers gave us much publicity.

Our Sunnyside Robins football uniforms were striking Kelly green and white, we had cheerleaders, a team song, a team photographer and trainer/manager. We even had a team physician whose medical practice was in Sunnyside; he looked after us gratis if and when a player was hurt; he offered suggestions about physical safety. The football fields were carefully laid out with limestone 10-yard markers; and there were competent, paid uniformed referees to control the game's pace.

Our head coach had gotten detailed, well-planned offensive plays from the University of Michigan and the Chicago Bears. Each player on the team had a play-book and the diagrammed plays were memorized. Each player knew what his particular assignment would be on every play and how to carry it out when that play was called by the quarterback or sent in by the coach.

This was a special time in our lives, full of anticipation, focus, and success in winning, and even occasional disappointment in losing games. On Sundays in the fall after church several of us would go to one player's basement of the apartment house his father was the building superintendent.

Long before the scheduled game we'd eat with his parents and brothers as an extended family. And then we'd get suited up in our football gear while we listened to recordings of popular college team marching songs. We got to know the words to these songs. Typically, some adult fans in Sunnyside would drive us to the games in their cars.

Several hundred fans for both teams and on special occasions more would come to see our games. At each game, the "hat" was passed around to the fans on the sidelines who'd contribute funds to support us. We also had annual dances and raffles to raise money for uniforms and other team expenses. The bulk of the players were from our Sunnyside neighborhood, with the rest from Jackson Heights, Elmhurst, Woodside, Long Island City and Astoria. There were a couple of players from the neighborhood who played only when home from military service on furlough.

The Sunnyside Robins players loved football, the team and the spirit of playing on our highly gifted and managed football team. My childhood buddies since the 4th grade Jerry Pagano and Larry Sullivan and I were the youngest players on the team, with Jerry having to eventually stop playing after a serious injury and his mother's vigorous intervention. All the other players were at least several years older. Even though I was comparatively quite young, I started at center on offense and on defense played linebacker. Most players on the team played just offense or only defense. Those about me thought I was an exceptional player; I did play with much enthusiasm and intensity. For me, it was an honor to be so young and able to play on this team for 4 football seasons.

My mother hated football and never came to one game. She worried about injuries. My father came to most of them, but he wasn't there to just watch the games. He was betting for us to win against supporters of the other teams. He'd seek out others to bet against them. As with other things about my father, I only found out about this after I stopped playing for the Sunnyside Robins.

In 1949, I was elected the team captain. After we won a major football game, it was another honor for me to be 17 and go to my local high school the next day wearing my shiny Kelly green Sunnyside Robins team jacket with the word "Capt" embroidered high up on the sleeve. But, wearing that jacket didn't help me to ask a young student in my English class out for a "date"; it took me almost two years to ask her. That's another story for some other day. Eventually I realized wearing the jacket wasn't so important to me or anybody else and I stopped wearing it to school. Our high school did not have a football team. Although I didn't play high school football I was good enough and had enough experience and training so later on in1950, I played on Columbia University's freshman football team. This was an even greater honor. The following year I was invited to attend the varsity football camp in Lakeside Connecticut, but decided not to go because I was a pre-med student and wanted to focus on my studies.

One of the hardest things for an offensive center (my position) is to accurately "snap" the football swiftly between his legs back to the person who is going to kick the ball just before it's going to be turned over to the opposing team. This is done when the offensive team hasn't been able to move the football in the plays it had the ball. Such kicking might only take place a half dozen times during the game. Yet from the standpoint of strategy and the ultimate outcome of the game itself, these kicks are terribly significant. Games can be and are won or lost on how effective this person's kicking was.

There's a lot going on at that instant. Why is this so? Because the kicker typically stands back about 12-14 yards behind the line of scrimmage. At the line of scrimmage the opposing team is lined up and actively trying to break through and prevent the kicker from kicking or cause him to fumble. If this happens, then the team that would have received the kick has a decided position advantage on the field. But, if the kick is a good one, the team receiving the ball will have a much longer distance to go to score a touchdown. If it doesn't, then it returns the ball by kicking it back. If you've ever watched a football game in person or seen one on television, or played football you might recall the details of this sequence of punting events.

Two players who joined our team were Marines on leave: one was the coach's son, the other his buddy who was supposedly an outstanding punter. He'd been playing on a Marine military football team. The team was told he would be helpful in a particularly difficult game we were scheduled to play. This Marine-on-leave punter, his name I will never forget was Ken Veselen and I practiced long before the game. He was kicking booming kicks going about 50 yards, which was more than we'd ever seen before. We seemed to hit it off quite well, I was centering the ball back to him accurately and swiftly and we were confident all would go well.

During this especially tough game, Ken Veselen was called upon to kick. Standing back from the scrimmage line about 14 yards, he awaited my "snapping" the ball to him through my legs. Despite our practicing session and the many times I'd centered the ball effectively in earlier games, this time I passed it erroneously way over his head. He had to chase it while the other team's players were rushing towards him. In a sense I'd created a disaster. Players from the opposing time had plenty of time to chase Ken and the aberrant football snapped by me. Several of them lunged on top of Ken and in this hurried forceful action severely damaged his ankle, so much so he had to go to the hospital. It turned out to be broken.

This was a terribly humiliating experience for me and our team. Not only had I directly caused a Marine to be seriously injured, but I had let our team down. No one said anything. I felt awful and since I was a devout practicing Roman Catholic at the time, I thought perhaps my individually bad behavior warranted some discussion with a priest in the confessional. In some illogical way I had let Ken down as well as God. In retrospect, this now all seems grossly immature, but that was how I was reacting to this situation. Ken was sent back to his Marine Corps base as a damaged person. He'd have to explain his injury and possibly face charges for his negligence (not mine) while on leave. What a mess I created.

This awful experience took place one Sunday in the early fall. The following Monday evening in despair I wrote a long letter on my trusty portable Royal typewriter to one of my football heroes, Charles "Chuck" Bednarik. He was an All American player at the University of Pennsylvania and played the same positions I did, center on offense and linebacker on defense and did so for the entire 60 minutes of the game. Bednarik was gifted and was being groomed to play professional football in the National Football League. Later on played 14 years for the Philadelphia Eagles; he was the last professional football player to play the entire 60 minutes/game in pro football. This was an incredible feat, certainly not done anymore. He eventually was elected to the College Football Hall of Fame and the Professional Hall of Fame, and was considered one of the greatest college and professional players in history, but this was long before those accolades.

I didn't tell anyone I wrote this letter. In it, I mentioned my jersey number was "59"; it was as close as I could get to Mr. Bednarik's jersey number "60" in our team numbering system. My letter explained the organization of the Sunnyside Robins team, my recent failure as a center, and how I damaged a Marine-on-leave having centered the ball way over his head. Then I asked Mr. Bednarik to give me any advice, any guidance, any tips so this situation would never happen again. After all, he was the outstanding center in the Ivy League. I did mention how some day it was my remote hope to also play in the Ivy League. I wasn't sure what teams made up this Ivy League, but did know Columbia was one of them and that Columbia's football coach was Mr. Lou Little.

Several weeks went by. I would check the mail every day; then a letter arrived at our home address. The return address on the envelope told me it was from Bednarik at the University of Pennsylvania. It was hand written on regular letter stationary. He offered several suggestions; he even drew some detailed pictures of a pair of hands on the football demonstrating his best way to hold the ball just prior to snapping it back to the kicker. His instructions were more than I had ever given thought. Mr. Bednarik signed his name "Charles 'Chuck' Bednarik" and he wished me luck.

At practice with the Sunnyside Robins the following week I did exactly what he'd written and drawn, again and again. The football was moving faster and more accurately through my legs to the punter. The punter wasn't Ken; he did not play for the Sunnyside Robins again. Now I was riding high, and with new information and confidence was on my way. Not once did I pass the ball over a punter's head, not that day or in any football game thereafter.

In appreciation to Bednarik, I sent him a "thank you" letter telling how much he helped me to improve, but never heard from him again. He made me a better center and he cared about me with his kind response and advice. Throughout his lengthy football career and beyond I followed his journey.

On March 22, 2015, <u>The New York Times</u> carried the detailed obituary of Charles "Chuck" Bednarik. He died the day before at 89 years. The obituary cited his years in the United States Air Force in World War Two, and many details about his extraordinary football days and his years beyond football. One of his five daughters reported he had Alzheimer's disease and how his prolonged dementia over the years was definitely connected to his intense football playing in college and professionally for so long.

For many years I'd kept Mr. Bednarik's letter written to me in1948, along with other letters from earlier years. (My mother did this too for her correspondence during her adult years.) In looking for Bednarik's letter amongst my long-ago saved correspondences, I couldn't find it. I'm going to keep looking, at least for a while.

EPILOGUE:

In May, 2000 there was a reunion of the Sunnyside Robins held at the Crowne Plaza Hotel near LaGuardia Airport in Elmhurst, Queens. Of the possibly 75 Sunnyside Robins, about 40 of us, all now "geezers" showed up with spouses and dates from around the country. We were unable to locate some members of our group. It was quite a weekend of friendship renewals and reminiscing. 50 years after the

Sunnyside Robins disbanded, but it seemed like yesterday in our conversations in the schoolyard. At the reunion we found out which Sunnyside Robins had died.

Perhaps the reader is curious as to what ever happened to many of us who eventually left Sunnyside, Queens. All of us came from working class parents, some who were immigrants. Because there was still a military draft, known as Selective Service, many of us served in various branches of the military, and then returned to schools and subsequent careers.

Here's a brief summary of career choices that had their origins in Sunnyside and P.S.150 schoolyard via the local New York City public and parochial educational systems:

Advertising Executive
Artists
Bartender
Banking Executives
College Professors
Commercial Airline Pilots
Commercial Artist
Computer Company Executive
Department Store Executive
Financial Broker
New York City Firemen
Food Firm Executive
High School Teachers
Industrial Engineer/Sales
Lawyers
Market Researcher
New York State Trooper
Owner of Jewelry Business
New York City Police Officers

High School/College Sports Official/Coach
School District Superintendent
U.S. State Department Official
U.S. Marine Corps Career Officer
University Vice President
Writer

2015

KILL THE KILLERS

" **T**HOSE who cannot learn from history are doomed to repeat it." George Santanyana, philosopher/writer

The more I find out about the Islamic terrorists, AKA Jihadist terrorists, Al-Qaeda and its affiliates, any other militant Islamist organizations, even Boko Haram in West Africa along with other fundamentalist cells throughout the world, I simply prefer to call all of them "The Killers," the more I do not understand how the rest of the world tolerates their existence and proliferation. Are populations throughout the world again waiting for the United States of America to clean up their problems, sacrifice our men and women's lives, use our resources, and then have us rebuild their destroyed and ravaged nations? Do native populations ever come forward and give full evidence they care about their own countries?

Or, by sheer madness, will our country be lured into more endless wars and an unsuccessful journey? We probably have the greatest and most powerful military force in the world. And yet as has been pointed out in a recent article in <u>The</u>

<u>Atlantic</u>, January/February 2015, "The Tragic Decline of the American Military" by James Fallows, asks the question "Why Do the Best Soldiers in the World Keep Losing?" (Page 72.)

There are little data to support ever again sending United States troops back into the insanity of Syria, Iraq, Israel, Afghanistan, Lebanon, Iran, Turkey and the other Middle East nations we've subsidized and propped up over the years because of their oil resources to feed our oil addiction. We cannot cure this pervasive, long-standing, historical madness. With our advanced technology and our strength we must stay out of these battles for as long as we are committed to our own democracy rather than superimposing ourselves in their outright craziness. And, new approaches and more intense efforts must be identified to protect America and Americans.

By no means am I suggesting any form of American isolationism. A few weeks ago I purchased and am reading NikolausWachsmann's "kl" (German abbreviation for the concentration camps.) The book's full title is <u>KL - A History of the Nazi Concentration Camps</u>. This book can be quite instructive to all who are concerned with "The Killers" and other maniacs. The concentration camps existed long before the beginnings of World War II, except they were being formed and operated under a different name; they were referred to as "detention centers." These centers were functioning throughout Germany early during Hitler's reign, as early as the spring, 1933; and with Nazi conquests were spread throughout Europe.

"In all, the SS set up twenty-seven main camps and over 1,100 attached satellite camps over the course of the Third Reich, though numbers fluctuated greatly, as old camps closed down and new ones opened; only Dachau lasted for the entire Nazi period." (From Wachsmann's book.)

World War II total deaths are at least 50-60 million, maybe more. Millions of others were maimed and battered for the rest of their existences after the war. Nor should we ignore or exercise amnesia regarding the wanton brutality of the Japanese military throughout World War II, either.

It isn't much of a stretch to observe what has been occurring in the Middle East for the past 15 years or so: Invasions; full exploitation of captured females including young children females to sexually pleasure the killers under the guise of some obscure interpretation of their religious tenets; slaughtering those who dissent, mostly males who are not pledged to the killers. They behead, rape, sell women into slavery, seek ransoms for hostages, destroy irreplaceable centuries-old antiquities and carry out other evil acts in their pursuits. They might even be using mustard gas. What might happen if they ever get a hold of atomic weapons or more poisonous materials?

It is noteworthy that no world scholars of any balanced minds agree with such bizarre religious interpretations presented by these "Killers." The sum of "The killers'" actions is the devastation of countries and people to support their madness, quite similar to the Nazi onslaught long before and during World War II, and Japanese imperialistic activities, too.

So now what? There must be a world-wide commitment to engage and crush these killers before they become even more powerful. Of course the United States and its powers will be involved in providing technical advice, military equipment and armament, but first those countries most proximal to "The Killers" must get the action rolling, and they must be aside their differences and coalesce their energies, too. If we ignore "The Killers," if we delay confronting them, as historians point out did happen with the Nazis almost 70-80 years ago, then there will be utter chaos and destruction of the most severe types. Their malignancy will endure.

No Chamberlains (Great Britain official just before the start of World War II), no weaknesses, no negotiations. No matter what their organizational names, their supposed religious beliefs, their stated intentions, "The Killers" and their supporters are detrimental to civilization, rationale behavior and sanity. We will need long-term consistent political will and strong moral commitments. Kill "The Killers," and do it now.....Do it for humanity...Semper Fidelis.

EULOGY

THOMAS E. FORD
DELIVERED ON JULY 30, 2015
FORT LEE, NEW JERSEY

Good morning.

Thomas E. Ford was born on July 9, 1931. He died on July 25, 2015.

To Tom's loving wife Diane Jankowski Ford; to their three daughters, Chris, Caryn and Kim; to their 5 grandchildren, Jillian, Brad, Ryan, Sean, and Jack, the youngest; to Vic, Diane's brother and his wife Pat and their daughter Susan; to family friends Danny, Rick, John and Jim; to next door neighbors Debbie and Matt; to all others here, the dedicated hospice people, and to all others here and beyond who ever knew Tom.

Let me begin this eulogy by reading an insightful, encouraging poem. And if you're attentive and awake and patient I will conclude this eulogy with another poem that Tom liked. It's titled: The Dash by Linda Ellis.

Tom Ford's early childhood years were hardly pleasant, comfortable, or traditional. Like all of us, he was forever shaped by those early childhood forces imprinted within him. The extent of their influences remain mysterious. Nor can they be disregarded, denied or minimized.

Tom was raised in upstate New York during the height of the Great Depression, with his mother, brother Mike and sister Pat. His father abandoned them early on, and was never in their lives again. No one knows what happened to him.

During this Great Depression and poverty, each of the Ford children spent time separately infoster homes and orphanages. In some of these places, Tom was beaten and there was no appeal. Tom's recollection of these experiences were deep, traumatic, and lonely.

After college in Buffalo, and after Tom and Diane were supposed to get married but didn't, by sheer accident they reconnected in California: she was teaching in Long Beach, California with some of her buddies from the East Coast; he was in the Marine Corps as a Second Lieutenant at Camp Pendleton. From there their lives moved on to again dating, an engagement, and eventually marriage in 1956. As the cliché goes, "the rest is history."

Despite the chaos and discomfort of his childhood years and possibly some in Diane's too, Tom in concert with Diane devoted their entire lives to each other, their daughters and their grandchildren. Their efforts have been to offer love and stability to their family, even those who were only there for awhile.

Family was and is everything to Tom. His unyielding commitment and belief was in the strength, love and sustainability of family. His earlier fragmented experiences prepared him intuitively to value and strive for family and community.

When there were lifetime difficulties as there always are, sometimes he'd become so quietthere was only his silence.

He would hold fast. He was wounded but would say nothing or littleuntil that matter passed or was resolved. Tom's unannounced mantra could be found in the words Winston Churchill told the students at Harrow in 1941 about never giving up.

Like the long-distance runner he was in college, he sure was a persistent, enduring human being.

It was in the early spring of 1971, a meager 44 plus years ago that Diane and Tom invited Lois and me to their home for dinner, to discuss whether Tom and I, along with others would like to team up and be part of a local political campaign in Leonia.

From early on we knew we were instinctively compatible. We seemed to like one another right away. Some people you brush against and move on. But then there are those you sense a closeness, an affinity, and you want to be with them and know them better and longer.

There were substantial initial reasons this might be. We both had been raised as Roman Catholics; and both had either fallen away from the church over time, or been shoved out the door. We both had been United States Marine Corps Officers, (although later on when I jokingly kidded Tom about never having served, he came over with his honorable discharge paper and a photo of himself in full uniform, which is here today). We both had run for elected offices in Leonia and had lost; and we both were forthright, judgmental, and intense. Others might have suggested we were stubborn young men loathe to compromise.

Added to this mixture we were both fortunately married to strong, highly competent, patient and determined women.

It was to become a perfect secondary simulated marriage between Tom and me; forged by inexplicable circumstances. So began our joint journey that is still going on until today.

After an intensive door-to-door campaign and with our colleagues Peg Muenstermann, Dick Dean, Marty Hayes and George Tomaro, and involving dedicated volunteers like Don Wynn and Anita and Manfred Gans and Ginny Brown and Bob and Yolanda Murphy, and some others still around in Leonia, we won that election. We were now in the majority and served for 4 years. It was a wonderful experience to serve with Tom as mayor and the other active, caring and attentive democrats.

With Tom leading the charge, this was an exciting time In Leonia. We were energetic and full of positive missions. Because of Tom's administrative leadership and persistence we were able to accomplish a great deal that has impacted the history and development of our Leonia community:

- Dedicating 14 ½ acres of Highwood Hills in perpetuity as a nature preserve and buffer;
- Forming the still active Leonia Environmental Commission for recycling and education;
- Bringing about Leonia senior housing to completion;
- Studying tax assessments to ensure fairness for all property owners;
- Instituting policies to professionalize and educate Leonia police department officers;
- Involving more concerned Leonians who had long been excluded;
- and with Tom's insistence, treating the old guard minority with civility and respect.

Other than our immediate families, Tom and I have spent more time in these 44 plus years with one another: Car pooling for 12 years several hours, each day; morning breakfasts all over NYC and Brooklyn where we studied the quality of oatmeal in hundreds of restaurants. After all, Tom was a fine expert as to whether there were any worms in the oatmeal, based on his wonderful and extensive experiences in foster homes and orphanages. Together in Brooklyn at Kingsborough Community College; talking; sharing books; ideas; thoughts; many letters; going to plays and movies; Junior Mance jazz concerts; visiting on vacations.

We were involved in all sorts of personal and professional causes, and making efforts to try to shape the community about us.

And of course, attending the three weddings of their lovely daughters.

We'd make frequent reference to the paradoxes, the inconsistencies, the enigmas, the mysteries throughout our society, and the unresolved long-standing personal, corporate, educational, environmental and global issues.

As for those car pooling experiences, offspring Chris Ford and Frank Muzio were occasionally with us and can attest to those unique and adventurous, sometimes harrowing experiences. These were indeed wild rides!!!!

In the mid-19th century, Ralph Waldo Emerson, once wrote: "The world is his (I added "or hers") who can see through its pretentions." Tom Ford lived Emerson's statement. He was uncomfortable with anything phony, insincere, manipulative, anything that smacked of taking advantage of another human being. He understood suffering and unfairness, and never forgot those who continued to suffer or were disadvantaged.

Nor did he understand those who because of good luck and advantage, behaved as if they thought they were genetically better, who had amnesia and insensitively forgot. They were unfeeling and arrogant. They neglect the variables that contribute or detract from a person's development and their ultimate success.

When Tom was confronted with such situations he often spoke out. You always knew where Tom stood. And sometimes to maintain civility and harmony, he would remain silent. Later on, we'd talk about such matters in our many meetings, phone calls and carpooling sessions.

Tom consistently felt deeply for others. Since he barely had a father only briefly, he mentored other young men and women, including our three sons Frank, Edward and Matthew. At the college, he spent much time and patience in advising students, mostly males, about the Marine Technology Program and their future lives. He understood how we all need assistance and guidance. If I were psychologically trained, I might suggest Tom served as a self-appointed surrogate father to many of the students he helped, the father he never had in his life.

When he was at the Alfred P. Sloan Foundation before coming to Kingsborough, he had responsibilities to offset some of the discrepancies he saw in our society. He was involved in minority programs to improve the educations and upward mobility of downtrodden groups that were long neglected. He served as a trustee of a black college, Tugaloo and was a major force in that place and its students forever after.

At meetings in Leonia when Tom was the Mayor, and at the college where we worked Tom had the uncanny ability to see through the jargon, the excuses, the trivia, and the selfishness. And when this went on too long, he'd abruptly speak out to make clarity and to promote decision-making. He would ask questions, methodically seek data, want to look at written reports and better understand the issues. Then he'd make notes. And at a subsequent meeting he'd inquire: What had been accomplished since we last met? This unnerved and bothered those reluctant to do positive things.

He made me a better and more thoughtful person and a more effective leader at the college and in life. For a few years I was Tom's "boss," but Tom never had a "boss" nor needed one. He was always my colleague.

Afterwards when Tom and I had retired from our missions at the college, we continued to be in close contact.

Tom absolutely refused to use a computer; but always analytical and concerned, he had oneof his highly competent support staff members: wife Diane, granddaughter Ryan or daughter Kim send his detailed thoughts and comments, and questions on all sorts of topics.

I used to kid him that with his interest in poetry, especially William Wordsworth and other authors, along with his writing of many letters to his 5 grandchildren and his daughters over their years of development, he'd have been a fine English professor. Tom's writing is direct, clear, uncluttered and insightful. He once wrote a detailed paper on Wordsworth, "Poet of Solitude, Nature and the Universal Feelings of the Human Heart." Much of Tom's life was spent in solitude and in privacy, along with his books; his discs; his poetry; and his travels with Diane.

To have known Tom, and to have worked with him, and to continually socialize with him so intensely was a rare privilege still with me to this day. He let me in; and allowed me to be his friend. What an honor this has been.

As soon as one thinks you know another person, no matter how long and what whatever intimate depth and breadth, do you think you ever knew that person completely? Can anybody get inside another person's mind and spirit? Or are there always components, fragments and particles remaining forever unknown and unknowable and locked up within all of us? There were dimensions of Tom that were hidden, sometimes almost mysterious, unspoken, inexplicable.

Like all of us, he was complex; like all of us, he was sometimes confusing; and like all of us he was flawed.

By now it must be patently clear it is impossible to encapsulate our long, loving, lasting friendship. Our lives have been inextricably and accidentally entwined.

And, by now, it must be patently obvious that Tom lived his life with purpose, integrity and sincerity. He accomplished so much beyond any personal accolades and he's done so quietly, modestly, never seeking praise. His many accomplishments transcend time, space, glory. While on his journey he has cared and loved many of us.

His journey is over and yet in so many ways it is still underway and flourishing for all of us. Just look around.

Now, with your patience, I would like to conclude and read one briefer poem appropriate for Tom. He liked this poem.

> It's: <u>Like the River</u>
> Thomas Wolfe, author*(here's its first eight lines)*
> Why are you absent in the night, my love?
> Where are you when the bells ring in the night?
> Now, there are bells again,
> How strange to hear the bells

In this vast, sleeping city!
Now, in a million little towns,
Now in the dark and lonely places of this earth,
Small bells are ringing out the time!

And now for all of us still here: Let's keep thinking and working on our dashes from our beginnings to our ends!!!!!
Thank you Tom, with love and Semper Fidelis.

2015

BEING AN ITALIAN-AMERICAN
– THE BATTLE GOES ON

W E'VE been living in Rockport, Massachusetts since May 2008.

It's a beautiful New England coastal town about 40 miles north of Boston, 4 miles beyond Gloucester, which is the oldest seaport in America. During this time Lois and I have found new friends, new activities, and peace and comfort amongst the people here. There is warmth and goodness amongst almost all of them, and virtually no pretenses.

Since getting here I have a particular pattern of going to a wonderful place, the Cape Ann Coffees in Gloucester where each morning I get my New York Times, say hello to the owners and the young staff, order a coffee and usually a bagel or pastry. This place is a well-run, pleasant local community business with much character and history. When I first went there I would sit alone and mind my business. Eventually several other customers asked me to join them. I think they were initially curious as to who I was, most of them have been going there for years. They're long time residents of

Gloucester; some have lived there all their lives. Most of them are old, but not as old as I am.

The conversations revolve around local politics, concerns about America's future, and always the Boston Red Sox, the Boston Bruins, the Boston Celtics and the New England Patriots. Depending on the season, one of these sports franchises is an almost exclusive topic. I don't think some of these residents have yet recovered from my lack of enthusiasm for the teams they live and die by. Once in awhile one of their lifetime buddies dies, they talk about the person, remember incidents when they were young, and mention their children. Then, at the end of each day's main discussion, the group disperses to wherever they go, a doctor's appointment, shopping, cutting their lawns or taking care of grandchildren. Most no longer work.

In the past few years I've sat in the coffee shop with a veteran who served in the Marine Corps in Korea and has a Purple Heart. He's one of the fewer men there who's older than me. We get along quite well, and I believe he believes our USMC backgrounds are similar, even though I've never been in combat and he knows this. Somehow, we connect, it might be the commonality of the Marine Corps. He's had a bunch of health problems and recalls how one time I visited him in the hospital. He was an enlisted Marine and knows I was an officer, and he tells anyone willing to listen at our meetings, they must always respect an officer from the Marine Corps. I listen and say nothing, smiling internally.

There's another person who sits with us regularly. He too has many health problems, some from a long time ago and others more recent. This person knows my Marine buddy from early childhood. He's somewhat unpredictable in his remarks; they could easily be classified as inappropriate, sometimes not connected to the conversation going on. If there are several of us sitting together, most don't say anything and the conversation keeps right on rolling along, again mostly about local Boston sports, gossip about those in Gloucester or local politics, once in awhile the changing seasons.

A few times this person has made some hurried statements about Italian-Americans, but he doesn't call them this. He refers to them as "guineas." In case the reader doesn't know this, this term is considered highly offensive slang to any Italian-American. There are several others equally offensive: they're "wop" (means without passport), "grease ball," "dago," and "ginzo." There might be others but these about cover the more derogatory ones.

When I was a child I heard all of them in the neighborhood I grew up in, and used to get into fights, physical confrontations with those who used them in the schoolyards in Sunnyside and Woodside, Queens, New York. I just wasn't going to let others call me these words. But that was so long ago. In recent years and long away from those early days, I thought we were long past such negative and unkind labeling. This was my mistake.

I'll spare the reader some of the details, except to point out this individual mentioned above did use the slang term several times after I politely urged him not to do so. I told him I am an Italian-American and calmly gave him a brief lesson in our heritage and why saying this was not the way to treat anybody or any group. Just to be accurate, he did find it possible to make a couple of remarks about Jews and I again told him this wasn't right. Despite warnings, he continued to make these remarks. Occasionally he's make statements about other behaviors he believes Italian-Americans exhibit. His stereotypes are sweeping and erroneous.

The last incident that took place was when he spoke vaguely about wanting to get to Mass General Hospital in Boston but he's in much pain when he drives. I then offered to drive him there. He asked me what I would do while waiting for him at the hospital. This was easy for me, I told him I'd read a book or go to a museum, or perhaps even go to the North End and have lunch there until he was ready to come back.

The North End in Boston for those unfamiliar with this location is a wonderful ethnic section of many Italian restaurants, shops and residents where Lois and I have gone many times since moving to Rockport. Lately, a growing number of college students live there, but still it maintains a strong Italian, Italian-American identity. It's similar to Arthur Avenue in the Bronx and the Mulberry Street area in New York City, but much larger and more populated. This person then said to me "Oh, that's where all the guineas are." I stared at him, again told him he was out of order and walked out of my favorite coffee place. This did it for me. It was the last time I spoke to him, and I haven't seen him since.

There's more to this unpleasant story. The various others I used to meet with and enjoyed listening to and talking with have called me at home, they understand I've not been in the coffee shop these mornings and they're upset about the situation. My wife Lois' view is I'm allowing this insensitive old man who can't control his thoughts and mouth to control my life, he prevents me from enjoying my friends. This is not my view.

He's an incorrigible bigot and doesn't know what else to do about his behavior. On the other hand, I simply will not allow him to make any further derogatory remarks to me about Italian-Americans or any other group. There's something pathetically sad about this person. He lingers in his distortions and thus is possessed and owned by them. I am not a psychiatrist, or a neurologist, or a child development psychologist. Whatever made this person this way is well beyond my comprehension.

Down the road he somehow just might get the message and stop coming to the coffee shop. That's my hope. Since my absence has also been noted by the owners of the place, I spoke with them and they regretfully understand my position. Now, I go in there when I'm just about sure he won't be there. And I've arranged to talk with my other friends beyond the coffee place.

To someone not involved in this seemly trivial perhaps meaningless situation, my final comment is this: Each of us is motivated by different forces that shape us in our daily lives. I have chosen this particular route because it's integral to my family's Italian-American journey. In so many ways I am more an American than any residual influences of being Italian. While I defended myself more vigorously as a child and young teen-ager, my method at this age is still intense but driven without physical forces. The battle is still on, it's just more subtle. And, I will not yield.

Notation: The references for an earlier essay "Chronic Misrepresentation of Italian-Americans" are applicable for this essay, too.

2016

REMEMBRANCES; VIEWNAM
WAR MEMORIAL VISIT

MANY years ago, maybe 20 or so, Lois and I visited the Vietnam Memorial in Washington, D.C. The Wall, as it became known, was dedicated on Veteran's Day, 1982. Some names had inadvertently been omitted and had to be added in 2010. An American woman, Maya Lin is the designer/architect of this unforgettable memorial. Shortly afterwards, it resulted in my writing an essay about this visit.

Even though I was never in combat in the Marine Corps, I think of all those who were. Whenever we go through Washington, D.C., we stop and visit The Wall.

Here's the essay written so long ago with revisions:

Yesterday, we saw the Vietnam Memorial in Washington. The day was crystal clear, the kind that simultaneously reminds one of the recent hot summer and upcoming cool, refreshing fall. The memorial is located between the Capital and the Washington Monument, two prominent and easily recognized structures. At first, if there weren't signs indicating directions and location, you wouldn't know about it or see anything. It still isn't completed, so duck walks, ropes, some piles of earth are around the area, along with neatly printed signs of apology from the agency in charge.

As you walk along, the memorial isn't easily visible because it's set in the lower end of a slope, almost as if it was hidden, or because it was thought that the monument belonged in a trench to signify some remnant of old war tactics, or to serve as some sort of mass grave for the 58,267 names that appear on the black marble slabs, shiny and polished enough to see one's reflection in them.

The names are arranged in gradually increasing lists from the edge of the trench, ultimately meeting in a bent-L configuration, and cut in the marble according to the time during the prolonged and ugly war that the individual man died. As one walks deeper into the pit or trench and the lists get longer, there's a feeling of dread that so many went to their end for who knows what.

Along the path, some people touch names, others have left small bunches of flowers near the bottom of the slab containing the friend, relative, comrade. Some times at the base of the slabs there's a pair of combat boots, a bottle of Jack

Daniels. All of these items are for remembrances of those gone. If you're looking for a particular person's name, there's a directory to identify the larger numbered slab on which it appears.

One woman, who was obviously of Mediterranean ancestry, stood pointing to an Italian name while her daughter repeatedly adjusted her camera for the right setting, only to fail each time. The woman was quite short and had to stretch high up to be near the name. She waited with grief (it turned out that she was the mother of the name she reached for), but extended patience until her daughter could use the modern devices successfully. The daughter mumbled something about the camera's dead battery or some other problem that was probably interfering with the photo-taking. The old woman stood quietly, but by her gesture telling everyone that his was her name, her boy, her sorrow and death. Finally, the daughter told her mother it was hopeless, the mother touched the name with a folder being given out by the Park Service employees, and together, they slowly left with the older woman holding her daughter's arm.

Other people brought their children, some with balloons and others with toys they'd been playing with in the park. Most everyone was quiet, some cried, others stood back trying to view all the names in one panoramic sight, perhaps trying to comprehend how many names were there and how many had died. Many children looked, ran off, came back, wondering what was going on.

Despite the warmth in the air, there was a coolness and growing shadow as the afternoon moved towards early evening. Small groups kept coming as the sun set, but there was the ever present silence of those who remained coupled, sometimes holding one another, with the quietness of those arriving. Occasionally one could hear sobbing in the trench. Everything seemed muted and remote, each person reflecting wondering about death, the inevitability of deep silence, thousands of names without faces.

This same day on our way home, we traveled to Atlantic City for a brief encounter with the gaming tables, to the city of sleaziness and shoddiness, false promise, abandoned buildings and ultra modern, grotesque casinos. Solemn time at the memorial where there were so many names without faces to be followed by noise, glitter, glazed over looks, faces without names vigorously and intensely focused on slot machines. Virtually no one spoke, only periodic yells when the light on top of the machine flashed off and on and coins were coughed out into waiting hands, unused plastic coffee containers, or carefully placed cloth bags so that the coins were channeled from the machines to the purses. But, eventually those coins and more would be put back into the machines.

EPILOGUE:

Perhaps it will be instructive to summarize raw figures concerning those Americans whose names are forever on the Vietnam Memorial Wall. It will remind us all of the senseless losses and sorrow that result forever.

THE RAW FIGURES ABOUT THE VIETNAM MEMORIAL WALL:

- *Of the 58,267 names on the Wall, 39,996 were just 22 years old or younger.
- *The largest age group, 33,103 were just 18 years old.
- *8,283 were just 19 years old; a few 17 years old, 1 was 16 years old.

- *997 soldiers were killed on their first day in Vietnam.
- *1,448 soldiers were killed on their last day in Vietnam.
- *31 sets of brothers are on the Wall.
- 31 sets of parents lost two of their sons.
- *West Virginia had the highest casualty rate per capita in the nation;
- there are 711 West Virginians on the Wall.
- *8 Women are on The Wall, they were nurses who cared for the wounded or dying.

If somehow you've not viewed The Wall, it will be enlightening to do so. And then go to see the Korean War Memorial nearby; and the more recent World War II Memorial. Then visit the Arlington National Cemetery and the Iwo Jima Memorial, both in nearby Virginia. There's a quotation on one of the Washington, D.C. monuments, I believe it's on the one commemorating the Korean War. The statement is: "Freedom is never free."

Unless you visit these sites and others, unless you lost someone, there is the tendency to forget. We forget these deaths just as we forget all those adults and children who die due to violence from guns in our country each year, about 30,000 deaths (including firearms suicides). This figure is approaching the annual number of those who died from automobile accidents.

FURTHER REFLECTIONS ON THIS DATE, 2016:

In more recent years our country has been engaged in a wide variety of ongoing battles, some call these "undeclared wars." This is especially so after the World Trade Center Towers came down in late 2001, although there were global incidents prior to this one in which Americans were attacked at embassies and elsewhere, mostly in the Middle East. America has been in many wars and battles in the twentieth and twenty-first centuries. The casualties, the costs, the wastes and the pre-occupations keep piling up, but somehow they didn't get the attention they deserve.

There are countries, cultures and people throughout the world that have hatred or distrust for America and our principles. And other long-standing cultural and religious disputes are continually and violently erupting. Some of these are predicated on hundreds of years of on-going conflicts. The dynamics of these ill-feelings are beyond comprehension in the traditional studies of international relations, history, or human behavior, but they do exist.

Perhaps it will serve some purposes if instead of America's leaders and its citizens enumerating the fine roles our country has served in the past, we make a sincere, clear effort to understand the rationales for our being disliked by those around the world. We've taken certain actions that have not been viewed as beneficial to other nations; we've made mistakes in our actions; and these actions have occurred for decades under a variety of governing administrations. Such events will be with us for a long time. Perhaps part of any healing process is to acknowledge mistakes. While this isn't easy such actions can be given more serious consideration. Throughout all of this, civilians and children die, cities and villages are destroyed, and millions live in massive sadness and deprivation. And these disruptions appear to be intensifying.

America has about 850 military bases throughout the world. Many are in dangerous places and subject to constant vigilance. Our nation has expended thousands of American men's (and some women's) lives in these battles; many others return home maimed and damaged forever; and millions of others in those other countries have lost their lives, including children and infants. It is difficult to accurately total American dollars spent doing all of this, but it is certainly in the many trillions.

Lately, there have been some citizens frantically advocating we need to go back to all of these places where there are disturbances and "finish the job," put more American boots on the ground, do more bombings and destroy all these radical infidels and their evil intentions. (They never mention thousands of innocent adults and children will die, too.) Some presidential candidates spew out even tougher and as vague words than these. I refer to this as the incessant "war cry." They occasionally quote retired career military personnel who endorse more military interventions. Military promotions, medals and heroes are the normally expected and obvious results of wars, along with casualties, including the recent increases in combat veterans committing suicides. The total costs for war are seldom calculated or easily available.

Fortunately, there are still sane voices that have a deeper understanding of history and these never-before complex global disruptions and brutalities. They seek resolutions at conference tables, in patient, difficult negotiations with those of remarkably different cultural goals. We need calmness rather than cage-rattling and screaming. Our hope is our leaders and our representatives exercise sound, thoughtful caution without foolishly unleashing America's unquestionable military superiority that just might initiate a cataclysmic Third World War.

Then, what if this does happen because of bad behaviors and misunderstandings between the leaders of powerful nations? How quickly we forget. We ignore our history. We're barely out of the twentieth century with its two World Wars during which an estimated 110 million military personnel and civilians died. This figure includes the Armenian slaughters of 1915; the 11-14 million citizens who died in the 1,100 concentration camps in Europe from the early 1930's until 1945 (even though someone occasionally grabs the temporary limelight and bizarrely pronounces there never was a holocaust); and the more than 500,000 citizens who died from the two atomic bombs on Hiroshima and Nagasaki, Japan, half within days, the rest afterwards due to radiation and related illnesses. Added to these figures are those civilians killed during the Korean and Vietnam Wars, the genocide in Rwanda, the killings in Syria, along with casualties in other parts of the Middle East, Africa and Crimea. Around the globe right through yesterday, there have been so many battles, wars and killings.

Some politicians and others ignorant of history keep beating the drums and are so willing to ship everybody else's sons and now more recently daughters off into combat, death, or permanent injuries. Do those screaming for more battles ever enlist and go themselves? How about their offspring, do they go? Why are they so anxious to spill other people's blood?

REFERENCES TO PROMOTE CLEARER UNDERSTANDING:

+ <u>A Rumor of War</u>, Philip Caputo.
+ <u>Secrets: A Memoir of Vietnam and The Pentagon Papers</u>, Daniel Ellsberg.
+ <u>Fire In The Lake – The Vietnamese and the Americans in Vietnam</u>, Frances Fitzgerald.
+ <u>Hiroshima</u>, John Hersey.
+ <u>Vietnam, A History</u>, Stanley Karnow.
+ <u>All Quiet on the Western Front</u>, Erich Maria Remarque.
+ <u>A Bright Shining Lie and America in Vietnam</u>," Neil Sheehan and John Paul Vann.
+ <u>The Wall – Images and Offerings from the Vietnam Veterans Memorial</u>.
+ <u>KL: A History of the Nazi Concentration Camps</u>, Nikolaus Wachsmann.

2016

THE WORST JOBS IN AMERICA

S EVERAL days ago, CareerCast.com published its 28th year ranking-report of 200 Jobs in America. From this compilation, CareerCast.com presented the "10 Worst Jobs in America," as well as the "10 Best Jobs in America." (The complete 200 Jobs in America list can be viewed electronically on CareerCast.com.)

The criteria used to determine such "worst jobs" are: environment (emotional, physical and hours worked); income (growth potential and salary); outlook; and 11 stress factors. Also given consideration are travel, deadlines, interaction with the public and average hours of work.

Here are the worst jobs according to CareerCast.com:

+ Logger
+ Newspaper Reporter
+ Broadcaster
+ Disc Jockey
+ Enlisted Military Personnel
+ Pest Control Worker
+ Retail Sales Person

- Advertising Sales Person
- Taxi Driver
- Firefighter

Are CareerCast's stated criteria for this list of "worst jobs" valid? The CareerCast's choices of a Logger, Pest Control Worker and Firefighter certainly can satisfy the "worst category" designation. In these 3 cases, difficult or deplorable work conditions, possibly danger, poor health and death are forever about them. But, it seems highly questionable for CareerCast to include "Disc Jockey," "Retail Sales Person," "Advertising Sales Person," "Broadcaster, and "Newspaper Reporter." These jobs are typically carried out in comfortable, pleasant, "white collar" surroundings. There have to be "worse" ones than these on CareerCast's 200 job list.

Did those who prepared this list give any consideration to jobs involving "hard-work," or "at the end of the line," or simply "unpleasant" or "unrewarding" jobs with minimal chance for any sort of career advancement and development? How could they overlook such factors?

With further thought, based on many years of observations and experiences, I decided to develop my list of "worst jobs." The criteria for my list are different than CareerCast's. My presentation of "worst jobs" focuses on "hard physical and mental labor" positions; where workers are in frequent danger of injury or possibly losing their lives (some do); and doing jobs considered unattractive ones, with little opportunity for long-range personal growth. Some might even be considered demeaning.

A few of these positions are high paying, as well as they should be considering the dimensions of the jobs. In developing my list, I could have included many other jobs fitting this description. For example, a stonemason, servicing and emptying septic systems and a cemetery gravedigger are easily categorized "worst jobs" possibilities.

Here's my list of "worst jobs." In addition to job titles, brief comments regarding each job are provided (as was done in <u>CareerCasts</u> 200-job list).

- Scavenger. Digging through garbage receptacles and trash bins to salvage refundable deposit bottles and cans for income; then transporting them to recycling centers.
- Sandhog. Building tunnels; working deep underground while breathing contaminated air; enduring excessive noise and possible injuries; sometimes involving adverse work conditions (the bends-decompression sickness).
- Coalminer. Working hundreds of feet below the surface, relying on singing canaries to determine when the pollutant gases could kill, or if the miner is subjected to being trapped due to mine cave-in. Black lung disease and chronic back problems are frequent lifetime afflictions.

4) Sanitation worker in urban environment. Having to haul and handle all sorts of garbage and waste, lifting heavy containers and experiencing harsh work conditions that often promote injuries, some from ongoing street traffic. Envision functioning without regular, reliable garbage and trash pickups for any extended period.

5) Health care practitioner – nurses, physicians, aides in urban hospital emergency rooms. Staff carries out life-saving efforts to offset chronic violence, accidents and strange

circumstances; along with needy and irrational patients and families. Chronic stress.

6) Industrial deep-sea fisherman (or woman). Harsh weather conditions; away at sea; dangers and hazards aboard ship. There are strong possibilities for onboard accidents and injury or going into ocean. Highly unreliable catches.

7) Inner city public elementary or high school teacher. Each day the teacher confronts social, economic, personal student/ family issues; student assertive behaviors; while professionally making efforts to fulfill educational missions with layers of bureaucracy.

8) Slaughter house employee in an industrial meat/poultry-food facility. Animals serially prepared for human/pet consumption; amidst disturbing conditions of killing/ brutality, putrid waste materials; unsafe working facilities; workplace injuries.

9) Steel worker (ironworker) on bridge and skyscraper construction site. Assembling and guiding massive steel components into positions from heights, and then in securing them, riveting, etc., while the worker "walks the steel." Stress, danger, inclement weather.

10) Custodial toilet cleaner. Public toilet facilities in restaurants, colleges, schools, sporting arenas, offices/ factories, train/plane stations. Those who use them often leave them in filthy, unsanitary conditions; nor do they make efforts to clean-up their misplaced toilet bodily fluids and products.

So, now you have two lists, the <u>CareerCast</u> list and mine. You might want to produce your own list of "worst jobs in America." Conceivably, it could be quite different from either of these. And it could be an enlightening experience for you to identify them.

My list of "worst jobs" serves our society and our lives directly and indirectly in vital and personally necessary ways. They are significant jobs done for the rest of us; ones most would avoid, and seldom if ever give thought to doing. The women and men who do carry out these jobs must be determined and courageous to do them, and in some cases quite desperate to earn a living. People need work, and work is intrinsic to being human. The reader can ask one simple question: "Would I be interested in having any job for my employment from this list?"

Perhaps the next time you see someone doing one of these "worst jobs," or any other tedious job, you might want to acknowledge that person's existence by simply saying "hello," or "thank you for what you do, you are important to me and others." No matter what the "job," there's a certain dignity to it in behalf of the rest us and our collective lives. Everybody serves a role.

2016

THE VOLKSWAGEN CORPORATION AND ITS SELF-CREATED DECEITFUL FIASCO-A DANGEROUS BUSINESS MODEL

A FTER almost 15 years of corporate internal secrecy, Volkswagen Corporation officials reluctantly admitted having installed a specific cunning engineering device termed a "defeat device" in 11 million diesel vehicles in Europe and around the globe. Added to this are 500,000 more diesel vehicles in the United States with these same devices." Diesel car/truck engines notoriously emit toxic pollutants that create smog and unhealthy conditions. They are subject to strict, clearly understood regulations accompanied by authorized testing procedures to minimize overall damages to the environment. Volkswagen Corporation is the parent company for Audi and Porsche, two premium auto producers; the diesel engines for these companies were also modified with these "defeat devices."

The reader has to understand what this cheating or "defeat device" can covertly achieve. Only when these outfitted vehicles' diesel engines are undergoing emission inspections in a testing facility, the installed mechanism renders them to be falsely classified "clean." False measurement data are provided. Paradoxically under typical on-the-road operating conditions, the illegal software doesn't function, and when not being inspected, these same supposedly "clean" vehicles are chronically spewing out major emissions. The environmental pollutant known as "nitrogen oxides" (nitrogen oxide and nitrogen dioxide) are consistently 40 times higher contaminating figures than falsely reported in any "clean" testing procedures. (The reader is invited to Google the topic for more related writings, including detailed diagrams of the installed "deceit devices.")

The recent discovery of these deceitful corporate practices resulted only after a small independent research group at the University of West Virginia (Center for Alternative Fuels Engines and Emissions) tested several Volkswagen diesel vehicles and reported earlier submitted emission tests data were completely false. Again, these vehicles were emitting major toxic environmental pollutants. How could this be? How come no one found these "cheating devices" had been continuously functioning in millions of vehicles since at least 2009? Where were the authorized testing organizations over the years? What agencies in Europe and the United States were protecting unknowing consumers?

After the falsehoods were uncovered by this outside and unbiased group, then the Volkswagen Corporation executives initially denied, minimized or attempted to "cover-up" what had been going on. They went on to scapegoat possible lower- level employees; or remained silent and unresponsive for months. Finally, there were vague corporate acknowledgements and apologies about the distribution of the "defeat devices." Subsequently, with vacuous statements such as "we're sorry and we take full responsibility," a few key Volkswagen officials resigned, retired, or were transferred. Others remain in place.

Recently, major investigations and lawsuits have been initiated on a global basis, and particularly in the United States. Federal agencies and California, Massachusetts, Maryland, New York and Texas states are pursuing investigations and legal actions, as are European officials where most of the diesel vehicles are used. Volkswagen Corporation officials and their lawyers have been in extended negotiations with various federal and state representatives and lawyers. The appointed negotiator federal judge Justice Charles R.Breyer has been diligently moving these matters along to bring about resolutions, compliances, and possible punitive actions. Criminal, civil and class-action litigations are expanding and will take years to resolve.

The overall long-term economic damage to the Volkswagen Corporation, its dealerships, investors, and customers is incalculable. The price of its stock has dropped 25 percent; negative publicity has discouraged potential Volkswagen car buyers from purchasing its non-diesel vehicles; the organization's reputation is severely tarnished. The ultimate impact on future vehicle sales, even if the organization can survive this prolonged fiasco is yet to be measured.

It is extremely difficult to calculate the overall magnitude of damaging pollution effects on the environment and individuals. (Countless tons of toxic materials have been spewed out for 15 years by millions of diesel vehicles.) This will eventually be a component of the settlement. The still-to-be determined economic punitive penalties for this long-term deceit will be in the billions of dollars, as much as 40 billion-60 billion, perhaps even more. Still to be adjudicated will be prosecution for the involved corporate officials, and the possibility of jail terms. Such punishments could deter similar future corporate behaviors.

It is noteworthy how in the cited articles, public discussions and corporate officials' pronouncements and statements, there is the absence of any focus on corporate or individual moral/ethical responsibilities and ramifications.

Now that this debacle has been uncovered, my focus will be on moral/ethical issues involved in this "defeating device" deceit as they affect the organization, individuals in it, and the millions of deceived citizens who purchased or leased the diesel vehicles.

Moral/Ethical Issue One: Fortune Magazine (August 2016) states Volkswagen in 2015 was the 8th largest world's corporation and in 2016, is the 7th largest. It employs almost 600,000 people; and historically is a highly successful organization and one of the world's largest auto manufacturers, if not the largest. Why then did this successful corporate organization covertly design and install in11 million vehicles worldwide and 500,000 vehicles in the United States an engineering device meant purely to deceive and cheat the emission standards, and consumers buying their diesel vehicles? (If you're curious about the breadth and depth of this outrageous cheating matter, try counting to 11 million and then add another 500,000.)

Second Moral/Ethical Issue: Within the Volkswagen Corporate boardroom and in the specific decision-making process what took place to promote this illegal concept to deceive consumers, the testing agencies, the dealers, investors and those in the broader community about the massive amounts of toxic materials detrimentally spewed out into the environment for so many years? Why was this done? Who specifically bears responsibility for this? The investigatory and settlement issues will have to decipher who within the massive corporate structure knew what, where, when and how.

Third Moral/Ethical Issue: Did any board members, engineers, supervisors, assembly line personnel, salespersons, or advertising staff, in the Volkswagen Corporate organization ever question this ill-fated decision? Out of all of the thousands of Volkswagen employees, did somebody, anybody stand up and say "Excuse me; I don't think we should be doing this."? And, if so, what were the reactions to such a position?

Fourth Moral/Ethical Issue: What logic drove Volkswagen Corporate officials to deny their involvement; then to blame lower level employees; and subsequently minimize the magnitude of this deceit? Did they seriously believe they could ultimately evade corporate and individual responsibility once more intense scrutiny and exposure revealed Volkswagen's fiasco?

Fifth Moral/Ethical Issue: Did corporate officials sincerely believe their peculiar initial offer to those millions of deceived diesel car owners they would readily accept a small inconsequential monetary gift card from Volkswagen (essentially a "bribe")?

Concluding Moral/Ethical Issue: Germany and its people have a long history of scientific, engineering and technical creativity and productivity. Its universities have international respect; it has produced significant discoveries and innovations in various disciplines; and it has been a society with "attention to details" in medicine, the auto industry and other fields such as microscopy, photography, chemistry, aviation and even armaments development. So, why didn't the Volkswagen Corporation leaders just carry out these traditional and endowed positive qualities and legitimately go about resolving the original underlying vehicular diesel emission problems rather than engage in producing a "cheating device" as a manifestation of deceitful, dishonest and damaging practices?

If only the Volkswagen organization and its officials had behaved with integrity and carried out its missions properly and ethically, this deceitful fiasco, the wasted energy, along with the cumulative deleterious environmental outcomes could have been avoided. And dangerous and potentially criminal behavior would never have occurred.

We might want to look deeper into the psyches and the culture of those involved individuals, and the corporate mentality that fostered such widespread outrageous behavior. Perhaps studying Goethe, Schopenhauer, Nietzsche and other German philosophers, even composers Wagner and Schuman will promote some clarification.

Is there a connection between the silence of so many during the holocaust and the covert operations of the concentration camps before and during World War II, and the silence of so many in this covert corporate fiasco over many years? When humans avoid immersing themselves in matters that require moral outrage and taking a stand, will they somehow instead find moral/ethical solace and resolution in selfish and self-interest behaviors? This is the dilemma.

Perhaps this matter will become a classic case study for graduate school programs that focus on business enterprises, corporate decision-making and individual/corporate ethics in our society. Certainly included in this are the topics of greed, excessive profits, disregarding the environment and health, and winning at all costs.

Rev. William Sloane Coffin (1924-2006):

> "If you don't stand for something, you're apt to fall for anything."

References:

(For a list of books and articles about Corporate Corruption, please go to: https://www.questa.com.)

For the past two years, print, electronic and broadcast media have provided outstanding coverage on this matter. In the The American Prospect, spring 2016 there is a lengthy comprehensive analytical article (pages 78-83) titled "Volkswagen's Big Lie." The New York Times has given extensive detailed coverage. At least 14 major articles since December 2015 and right on through July 28th, 2016.* (The headlines from just a few of the most recent The New York Times articles are: "Lawsuits Trace VW's Cheating All the Way to the Top," and "Latest Attacks on VW Aim at Its Top Leaders.") The Christian Science Monitor, The Wall Street Journal, Forbes, and The Guardian had feature articles.

*My appreciation to Anthony Dunleavy, a friend and former USMC buddy for providing some references and our conversations on this subject.

2016

FREDDIE LIKES THE CHAINS

IT was mid-August, 1945. World War II had just ended. The Japanese government finally surrendered after our military forces dropped an atomic bomb on the cities Hiroshima and another on Nagasaki; Germany had already surrendered in May, 1945. This war had been going on since the late 1930's, although in some ways much longer. Some historians believe it was a delayed continuation of unresolved World War I matters, which had ended in 1918 and was supposedly "the war to end wars." The United States didn't officially get involved in World War II until the Japanese bombed the naval base at Pearl Harbor, Hawaii on December 7, 1941, but had been providing substantial material assistance to Great Britain before then.

When World War II was finally declared over, there was widespread joy, relief and anticipation. The joy was global elation and relief because after years of killings, maiming, and destruction stopped; the optimistic anticipation was for the men and women coming home and what was going to happen now into peacetime. How would they react after being away in war? How would those at home treat them once they came home? Everything exuded energy and activity; hope, goodness and smiles were in the air. As victors, there was no stopping America and its allies now. We were on a national role of boundlessness and hopeful confidence; anything could be accomplished.

Amidst all of this, there was uncertainty and concern; a new era was upon us. It would require much energy and commitment to transform nations and individuals after those war years. Huge numbers of military personnel returned with serious physical and psychological damages that maimed them forever. Military influences would gradually subside. With time more and more service personnel would be home to their families and get back their civilian jobs; some would return to school and begin to live out the dreams they had been storing up and hadn't been able to realize for awhile.

At this time, my parents, sister and I lived in a 4-room apartment in Sunnyside Queens; this was the same for all our friends and family, too. No one we knew lived in a private home. My father suddenly announced my parents purchased a summer home in Greenwood Lake, an 8 or 9 mile-lake straddling between New York and New Jersey. This decision to acquire a summer cottage for family vacation purposes was a completely new one for all of us. It wasn't that we were rich, but we somehow had enough money to have a home in the country, a place distant from where we normally lived. My father had presented it to my mother as an investment. We'd own it. It would be so much better than going to places where you'd have to pay rent. Since it was about 60 miles from Sunnyside and we had a car, it was going to be a relatively easy trip for weekends and ongoing family use. I suspect my mother reluctantly and quietly went along with his ability to move quickly, but in her mind this was foolishly spending money. My mother guarded money as vigorously as she protected and loved her children.

This house in Greenwood Lake wasn't directly on the lake itself. It was about a mile away from the New York side of the lake. We would have to walk down a long hill to get to the lake; going down the hill was fine; but afterwards coming back after swimming and climbing that hill later in the day on a hot summer day wasn't much fun. The house was somewhat small, it had a porch where family and friends could sit, talk, and play cards. The rooms were dark, covered with knotty pine wood that gave off a stale wooden odor; the kitchen was small and so was the bathroom, where two people couldn't fit in it at the same time; there was a brick fireplace in the small living room. There were two small bedrooms, and stairs to the attic which was unfinished. My parents would frequently have to sleep in this hot attic when too many relatives visited, which seemed to happen right after we had the house and just about every weekend.

There were other houses in the area spread out on similar pieces of property, and you could see some from our house. A short time after we were there our family met some of the neighbors around us. They were mostly Italian-American and Irish-American families from Brooklyn and Queens, blue-collar folks who'd made recent investments in getting a home. It was a spreading exhibition of possible upward mobility, and a new experience for many moving beyond just their apartment rentals.

The property itself was about an acre or so, with many older mature trees on it. At that time, I didn't know what this acre size meant, but my father gave me a quick lesson in its arithmetic dimensions, drawing a sketch of a measured acre. Now I could understand this size. Shortly after we were there, my father decided it was important to have a nice, open, uncluttered lawn. This involved the two of us methodically cutting down a number of the trees, laboriously working side-by-side to do this. We had the daily help of a local farmer who had a wagon and two mules that pulled the massive tree roots out with chains. Why he wanted a level pristine lawn without any trees on it so deep in the country was never clear. I didn't question him. Perhaps it was his way of achieving some new middle-class status, a longing to move upward beyond his earlier years of being on the streets and tenements of New York City. Throughout his life he was working at moving up.

One of these nearby neighbors was a man named "Freddie." He had served in the United States Navy for about 4 years aboard a ship during the war. You could see Freddie's house from where our house was located, and where he lived with his wife and a couple of children about 10 and 12 years of age. He was somewhat of a loner, but he'd talked with my father on several occasions. My father had that way about him; he could talk with anybody on any subject, even those he knew little about, but he was an inquisitive person forever seeking clarification. Usually, if I was around I stood there and listened to their back and forth chatter.

During the first summer we were there, while my father and I were clearing trees on our property for the lawn my father wanted so desperately, Freddie was busy with his own project on his property. He wanted to mark the border of his entire piece of property with a continuous heavy anchor chain all around it. Where Freddie got this amount of anchor chain, piled up in a heap on his property was never clarified. Probably it had been excessed by the Navy as its vessels were being decommissioned and stored. Such an anchor chain is quite bulky and thick; it would have to be to secure the heavy weight of a naval ship's anchor.

As his project took more definitive shape, it did seem a little unusual for Freddie's country home way off in the woods to be entirely demarked by a surplus ship's anchor chain. Anchor chains are frequently seen at entrances of naval shipyards and naval bases. It might have been better or more appropriate if it had been at some seashore house or even a boatyard or yacht club right by the ocean where it made more natural nautical connections. It was as different and equally unexplainable as my father wanting a perfect lawn with no trees on it.

Week after week there was progress on Freddie's work, he was lugging sections of the bulky anchor chain, positioning them, securing them to the posts and moving along his chain-fence project. Every 5-6 feet this anchor chain had to have some sort of supportive column or bulky metal post to help keep it partially elevated off the ground. It was what Freddie wanted and he was making it happen. This was heavy work and he kept at it without any help. After many weeks of vigorous, persistent work, Freddie was finally finished. He walked around the enclosing massive anchor chain fence, and checked it to see if was properly aligned and secure. I wish I had a picture to show so you could better understand how different, how this property with its surrounding anchor chain fence seemed. Its uniqueness made it entirely stand out from every other property in the area.

Once word got out about Freddie's completed anchor chain fence, neighbors came by and stared at it; then a few cars drove by, too. When some of us went down by the lake for a swim and while sitting on the narrow beach, residents made passing comments about his fence. It became the topic of gossip, remarks, jokes and judgmental statements. Since I was a child, I said nothing but listened; although it was clear even to me this created anchor chain fence was causing a certain amount of inexplicable widespread upheaval for others.

One day a few neighbors were standing around and so were several of our family members who were visiting us for the weekend from Brooklyn. Again the topic about Freddie's heavy anchor chain fence suddenly was being discussed by both the neighbors, along with our visiting relatives contributing their comments. Again, all the comments were negative, disparaging and non-productive. Our visiting family members were equally judgmental and adamant, even though they were neither property owners nor even Freddie's neighbors, nor had they done any work on the anchor fence.

These protestations gave anyone listening the distinct impression there was a gang or mob mentality of consistent opposition building on this topic, and the participants weren't going to let go. I just listened. The typical comments were: "Why did he have to do this?" "Did he have to bring his Navy memorabilia to this place?" "Wasn't there something that could be done to have him remove it?" "Maybe some of us should go and talk to him about this matter." "Isn't there a regulation or rule or code against this sort of thing?" Nobody seemed to like what Freddie was doing, but Freddie liked his anchor chain fence.

During all this time and amidst the back and forth repeated chatter, my father said absolutely nothing. While my father had limited formal education, never going past the 6th grade, his intense varied life experiences gave him at least a Ph.D. in acquired knowledge and analytical abilities. He'd served in the army in France during World War I and understood the horrors of war; only seldom did he ever speak about that journey. He had the ability and directness to approach anybody and converse with them, regardless of their titles, positions in life, or the topic going to be considered. He was unpretentious and natural, and had a confidence that allowed him to do this; he was a strong advocate of "be yourself," a believer of "live and let live." Also, he had a tolerance for all; that is, I never heard an unkind or bigoted remark from him about any person, race, religion or nationality. Throughout his lifetime he was consistently fair. This didn't mean he was some sort of pushover; he quickly reacted if someone offended him or did something he believed was dishonest towards him or another person. It was ill-advised to cross him.

There were times my father could be explosive, loud, forceful. Often, it was unpredictable. Sometimes if you knew him well you could predict when this was going to happen. His face got more serious, his jaw would tighten and sometimes his eyebrows would narrow around his hazel eyes, giving him a focused, tense look. But, despite all his preparatory reflexive activity, and my expectations since I'd witnessed his temper in the past, instead he spoke in a controlled, quiet voice, almost inaudibly. In his distinct lower East Side of New York City accent, he spoke simply, saying "Why don't all of you just mind your business and accept that Freddie likes the chains, he likes chains." Then he repeated, "Freddie likes the chains." Nothing else was said; there was silence, no one reacted or commented any further. The simplicity of his words put a sudden verbal blanket on the situation, at least for then. The conversation shifted to newer areas about sports, the weather, and the noises some motor boats were making out on the lake.

Why then, did Freddie's anchor chain fence seemingly become this continual topic of discussion, intense criticism and concern amongst these people? The anchor chain fence was Freddie's manifestation for individuality and independence. This was what Freddie was doing, expressing his privileges to freedom, self-direction and choice. It was his demonstrative right to "be" in a democracy that he and others went off to war to defend. Since he came back alive, certainly he was entitled to some sort of special personal dispensation and latitude, some end-of-the-war leeway to compensate for his war efforts.

From then on, whenever some controversial topic was brought up, some judgmental remark, some inconsequential but hurtful comment about someone else's behavior, beliefs or attitudes, none of these having absolutely anything to do with Freddie or his anchor chain fence, my father would simply say, "Freddie likes the chains." This became familial code synonymous for "cease and desist;" "let matters be," and "let it go." Sometimes once he said this, others laughed and possibly thought about Freddie's rights to do just as he pleased. They had these same rights.

As I recall this matter and write this almost 70 plus years later, it still puzzles me why supposedly reasonable well-meaning individuals could have been so concerned about what Freddie was doing on his property with his anchor chains. We'd just survived the most devastating war in our history; places, cities throughout the world had been totally destroyed; an estimated 90 million civilians and military dead casualties; the horrors and evil of the German concentration camps and their Aryan "purification goals" were made visible;

and we'd just dropped two atomic bombs killing hundreds of thousands of Japanese civilians. At last, we were moving into a peaceful, hopeful phase of humanity, we could believe for awhile. Couldn't we just enjoy this new found luxury of peace and quiet at least for awhile, even a brief period?

This "Freddie likes the chains" expression has had an extended life. Now, it's used to offset or counter balance all sorts of totally unrelated matters. If you were a newcomer and hadn't heard these four words before, someone more knowing about its original usage could give a quick explanation about Freddie's the massive anchor chain around the border of his property. Even to this day this day if a new or unusual situation comes up, I'll think back on this story and might even blurt out "Freddie likes the chains." Those around me who have heard the story understand its original meaning.

After several years and eventually after my parents tired of having to sleep in the hot attic because so many relatives showed up on weekends, they did sell the cottage. When we left, Freddie's property was still marked off with his massive anchor-chain fence. "Freddie still likes the chains." And as we drove away for the last time, my father's pristine, carefully manicured lawn devoid of trees was still there, too.

TRUMP THE THUG

P LEASE Note: This essay is being written shortly before
our 2016 presidential election. The term "thug" is
indeed a harsh one. In my lifetime I've known and observed
thugs in neighborhood schoolyards, the military, workplaces,
sporting events and other social settings. It is a term one uses
rarely. If somehow Trump wins and is sworn in as our next
president in late January 2017, I will again be respectful of the
office and its occupant. But is there any doubt in the reader's
thoughts what my beliefs are about Trump?

It's two days before our nation's voters will pick the
next president of the United States. In two days we will be
finished with the ugliest, the most disjointed, illogical and
unkind presidential election process we've ever witnessed.
Even reasonable political analysts and long-experienced
pundits have been overwhelmed by its historical harshness,
viciousness, brutality, and lies repeatedly circulated through
easily accessible electronic transmission as truths. Both
political campaigns have put forth lies and distortions;

objective fact-checking sources report far more on Trump's side than Clinton's.

What has driven our nation of almost 315 million to be two days before this election where Trump is still a strong choice? Are the voters drinking his "elixir"? Are they seeking a Savior? If Trump were to win, will he transform his rhetoric into our nation's new reality? Will the proposals he wants to bring about make us better citizens and more respected and responsible humans in a complex world?

Two days before the election on the front page of <u>The New York Times</u> there is a double-column centrally placed photograph of Donald Trump awkwardly holding a baby. The caption on the picture is "Pretty Baby Mr. Trump plucked a baby from the crowd in Tampa, Fla., on Saturday, calling the child 'so cute'." Politicians always pose with babies. The picture shows Trump with his jaw tense and non-smiling, careful the baby doesn't touch his cufflinks, red tie or perfect custom-made dark blue suit, or starched white dress shirt. Other than his hands around the baby's sides, there is no other physical contact. He keeps the baby a safe distance from himself. Perhaps holding a baby is an unfamiliar process for him; does he even know the beauty of a baby, what a baby smells like and how soft its skin feels?

He comes into towns and cities, appearing suave and knowing, and then proceeds to speak almost in riddles and chatter. He may have known his three wives, and those he abused, but demonstrates little understanding of human relations and humanness. In some ways he is a creation of himself, surrounded by passive, complying and adoring relatives who are equally unknowing about what life in America is about. One of his past dearest friends and former lawyer was a brutal person, Roy M. Cohn who lived a life of disruption and unkindness. (Didn't our mothers teach us you can tell a great deal by the people a person hangs around with?) He brings to the election process crudeness and rudeness, while he lashes out at others throughout our society.

The prestigious and respected journal <u>Scientific American</u> and noted scientists declare he is scientifically ignorant. He denies "climate changes" as a hoax. Outstanding Economists inform us he will be damaging to the economy. He has repeatedly demonstrated he is unknowing about foreign affairs, national issues, our history and Constitution. He makes statements about abandoning NATO, using nuclear bombs, and rejecting Muslims into our country. He promises to build walls; and deport those he declares must go, or put them in "detention camps." (This same term was used to intern thousands of American-Japanese citizens during World War II and thousands of German citizens in the formative years of Nazi Germany.) Are these logical, analytical, democratic statements? They might be attractive to some who have a wide variety of angers and disappointments, but especially provocative and brutal to sound reasoning and decency.

Are we to ignore his Atlantic City casinos past; his business failures and avoidance of taxes; his distorted statements about women; his reluctance to allow public viewing of his submitted income tax forms; his avoidance of military service because of bone spurs, yet stating he knows more about ISIS "than the generals;" his scams at defunct Trump University; and his documented abuses of employees and contractors?

Two specific areas Trump is most egregious are 1) how he portrays women, and 2) how he uses language. No matter how much he reassures the world he respects women, his statement: "more than anyone else in the world," this is just a fraudulent, empty comment. He claims women who have abortions should be punished. (The Supreme Court ruling, <u>Roe v. Wade</u> that allows abortions nationwide has been in effect more than 40 years.) He sees women as playful, thoughtless beauty objects, believes in their specific physical shapes to satisfy his narcissistic needs, and then belittles women who do not conform to his bias about beauty and intelligence. He degrades women not measuring up to his superimposed measurement standards. To him, women are trophies, similar to his branding name and his construction towers. Has anyone noticed how similar the women around him are to Barbee Dolls or perhaps the programmed Stepford wives? He is a macho show-business creation.

As for his language and speech patterns, he speaks in brief, unthoughtful phrases, and substitutes vague provocative terms to express his shortcomings in knowledge with self-praise and adoration. He constantly diverges from any more logical, well-presented thoughts and ideas. Whenever he speaks, he riles up crowds with emotional and erroneous statements, never enlightenment nor clarity. He encourages thoughtless mob mentality and reactions.

Throughout this campaign he has spoken of how the system was "rigged." He calls his opponent "cheating," "corrupt," "lying," and "crooked" along with other disparaging and destructive terms. While his crowds yell "lock her up," does he do anything to discourage such brutal dissonance? For 5 years he spoke of President Obama as not being born in America, thereby perpetuating this lie, along with "the worst president we ever had." Perhaps his teacher was Joseph Goebbels, head of propaganda for the German Third Reich.

Goebbels believed and vigorously practiced if you tell a lie often enough, it eventually becomes the truth.

Can he truly define the meaning of his ambitious but ambiguous slogan to "make America great again?" What does it mean when he talks about "draining the swamp?" Trump uses language to obfuscate, to tear down and destroy. By doing so, he keeps us off-guard and accusatory. Aren't there complex global issues involving more than 7 plus billion people in the world that have multicausational bearings on his slogan?

The two candidates have been studied and presented their perspectives about America and the world. Some analysts have commented how the female candidate is educationally, intellectually, and experientially highly qualified for presidential office, while the male candidate is particularly unqualified in these same realms. Throughout the world, about 70 nations have had a female head-of-state. Will America finally have one?

As I've observed and paid attention these past couple of years to assess the various presidential candidates and specifically heard Trump's repeated remarks, my mind wandered back to 1954 when Senator Joseph McCarthy and his prosecutorial assistant Roy M. Cohn (the same one) were involved in the Army/McCarthy hearings in Washington, D.C. At one point in those hearings, the prominent attorney Joseph N. Welch spoke out in defense of a young colleague as he addressed Senator McCarthy with the following statement:

> "Have you no sense of decency, sir? At long last,
> have you no sense of decency, sir?"

Has he no sense of decency? Have the rest of us gone mad? No matter what the election outcome in two days, will there ever be a return to civility, comity and rational behavior by our future candidates and their supporters or have we devolved into more brutal and unforgiving practices and habits?

2017

PRESIDENT TRUMP

T HE last writing presented on the www.joemuzio.com website was on November 6, 2016. That was two days before our recent presidential election, and after a most peculiar, vicious and disruptive campaign process. The title of that writing is Trump the Thug. It's about the person who's been granted our national leadership under the most historically bizarre circumstances.

Writing during this election disruption has been difficult. There was a downward, empty gnaw, an unexplainable sorrow. And it has little to do with Hillary Clinton having lost the election, even though she did receive almost 3 million more votes than Trump. She was a more qualified candidate, but conditions fostered the opposite outcome thanks to distortions, deceit, and widespread misplaced anger.

During the election campaign and since, I longed for traditional and reasonable civility, presentation of thoughts and ideas coherently, and mutual respect for legitimate disagreement via sound dialogue. Whatever happened to serious, open debates where the voters could be exposed to varying views on serious issues beyond empty words that appeal to our emotions and biases? Because we have lost these ingredients and other respectable behaviors, I have been in mourning about these losses and unsure they will ever return.

To measure any person's lifetime, you look at the totality of it, upbringing, his/her family, education/ occupational developments, interpersonal relationships, how that individual treats others, along with a variety of other observable factors. It's the person's journey. Looking at Trump holistically, as an educator for more than 50 years and having served for several years as a United States Marine Corps officer, I do not think he is especially smart, analytical or capable of critical thinking. I am hardly qualified to evaluate or judge Trump's psychological conditions; but, by categorizing and analyzing his repeated public statements cause me to worry about his qualities, abilities, motives, and his underlying philosophy as well as his limited comprehension of our national problems and their resolution.

There is little or nothing in Donald Trump's lifetime experiences that verify he is intelligent or a caring human being. Are we to believe he is smart because he does unusual, often unpredictable, nasty things, or because he tells us he's smart? He is a creation of the pretentious theatrical world playing with us as if we're in one of his shows, or watching some carnival event. Does his show business/casino/sports/ real estate background and celebrity make him a clear thinker who understands leadership, history, decision-making, and how to govern our diverse nation? Being president is much more complex than building buildings bearing his name, running casinos and beauty contests, or developing golf courses.

Trump's presence and his representations expand my distrust of him. He is a marginal and in some ways an enigmatic person. What and how he enunciates, and his disjointed plans for America, along with those around him who spew out falsehoods, unkind remarks and hateful statements. He does not exemplify our country's underlying historical values and beliefs; nor does he articulate those perspectives demonstrative of logic, truth and decency.

His use of language is especially vague, sometimes thoughtless and disorganized. Can there be such things as "alternative facts" the equivalent of verifiable identifiable consistent ones? Why would anyone enunciate false statements on many significant matters? Besides Trump stringing 140 characters together in Tweets, there's more to effective language pronouncements. "Tweeting" might be convenient, fast and based on brevity, but it doesn't assure clarity, thoughtfulness or understanding. In some situations it's simply whining, or screaming, sometimes name calling. In this world of global electronic transmission and accessibility, doesn't he recognize his words can be checked and refuted?

He rails about the media and refers to them as untrustworthy, "the enemy of the American people." Democracies insist and embrace a "free and unencumbered press" in contrast with those authoritarian nations that rigorously control the press. What is it within a "free press" he's afraid of? Perhaps Trump would like a Ministry of Truth as in George Orwell's <u>1984</u>. He seeks to ban Muslims coming from specific countries, but claims that's not his purpose; he insults leaders of countries (Russia's V. Putin excluded); he believes our nation needs increased nuclear bomb capabilities, justifying this with terms like "top dog." He threatens to bypass longstanding negotiated global agreements. Trump wants confining walls on our borders; to do away with regulations for the common good; and to belittle environmental, energy, health and economic policies as restrictive while ignoring their identified benefits. He keeps referring to "deals" he'll make, without details, as if he's negotiating real estate or resort/golf propositions. Amidst all of this, he reassures us he's "running a smooth functioning machine."

Some of his statements are provocative and frightening: To round-up, detain and remove massive numbers of the undocumented, AKA illegal persons. Recently I read KL: A History of the Nazi Concentration Camps by NikolausWachsmann. No doubt the reader will be alarmed by my comparison of these "detention" camps' original history in the late 1920's and early 1930's with his frequent statements to put "bad dudes" and others in jails, including the continued use of the military confinement operation in Guantanamo, Cuba. Where is due process in Trump's world?

We are in the dark about possible roles Russian officials played to influence our national election process and to affect our nation's sovereignty. At least four ranking Trump officials had direct communications with Russian officials during/ after the campaign. Trump still hasn't released his Income Tax Forms, despite prior statements he would. What's in these documents he's afraid we'll see? (Until this situation, presidential candidates provided such information for public scrutiny for more than 40 years.)

Will Trump magically transform into a more sensitive and caring moral leader? Will he be more thoughtful? Time will tell. We can expect Trump to behave more "Trumpian." As the expression goes, "past is prologue." His positions create unneeded anxiety, stress and sadness. He fosters loneliness, separateness and despair. He promotes, almost thrives on confusion, diversions and selfish anger towards others. Does he comprehend terms such as "empathy," "compassion," and "sense of community?" Does he respect comity and civility? Can he feel for those in poverty, ill-health, and with educational disadvantages?

We are in a concerted battle for the constitutional democratic history of our country. Will we become an authoritarian nation wrapped in the pretense and cloak of a democratic society? Our nation could be lost and become a gross insensitive horror show. We must hold Trump and his cohorts accountable and with no exceptions. Based on Trump's "track record" as well as those surrounding him, they require close scrutiny. Participation and activism are the key words. We have to be involved at various levels: rebutting falsehoods, supporting candidates offering logical and reasonable solutions, and engaging our elected officials who serve us. Other suggested energetic roles are: speaking out on issues; having open, direct and calm conversations with other citizens; writing letters to media editors will serve positive purposes; and perhaps running for local and statewide offices. The battle is already underway.

Footnotes:

Conservative, well respected analytical writers such as George Will, David Brooks and Thomas Friedman along with others present all sorts of critical questions about Trump. Frank Bruni, Maureen Dowd. Nicholas Kristof, Paul Krugman and Gail Collins are consistently critical. (Yes, most of them write in The New York Times.)

For an encapsulation of Trump's recent behavior, see David Brooks' Op Ed pieces in <u>The NY Times</u>, February 17, 2017, "What a Failed Trump Administration Looks Like," and on February 21, 2017, "This Century is Ruined." Also, read related articles in <u>The New Yorker</u>, February 27, 2017: "The Talk of the Town, "The Political Scene," and "Letter from Washington.") It is suggested Trump read David H. Freedman's book, <u>Corps Business – The 30 Management Principles of the U.S. Marines.</u> Another reading is <u>The Road to Character</u> by David Brooks. These might benefit him, improve how he leads and treats others, and possibly our nation while he's performing as president.

REFLECTIONS OF A PROFESSOR EMERITUS

INTRODUCTION:

To be able to work within the college community and environment is a fine privilege and a noble career location. It is the designated societal center of freedom and intellectual opportunities and discourse within our democracy. The culture, history, organizational concepts, and principles of a college are to enhance positive developmental qualities: collegiality, open exchange of ideas, discussion and transmission of knowledge, research to enhance bodies of knowledge, supportive relationships, integrity, and rational, civil behavior.

This writing is through the long lens of time, distance and thought processes. One might wonder why 15 years after retirement in 2002 it is even being presented. Let me offer some explanation. The almost 33 years spent at Kingsborough in the Department of Biological Sciences was essentially the bulk my professional career. The college is a viable community of faculty and students, and also involves the energy and commitment of the building and grounds and cafeteria workers, and administrative assistants, security staff, and office cleaners. Reflecting on these years, half of which were as chairman, and well after I exited from the college helped me to better understand the college and the prime reasons we are there for the students. My thinking and beliefs have been belatedly clarified. Just because a person is no longer at a particular institution doesn't necessarily mean he no longer has thoughts and interests about the college's missions and its evolving challenges.

In 1969, I came to Kingsborough as an assistant professor; and from 1971-1972 served as the "acting chairman." While there, I taught a variety of courses, received tenure and eventually was promoted to professor. For 15 years, from 1983-1998 served as the elected department chairman; and from 1994-2002 was Director of Marine Technology. Other assignments: College-wide Personnel and Budget Committee; CUNY Faculty Senator; representative to CUNY Marine and Fresh Water Institute (CUMFI); Program Director – NYC Louis Stokes Alliance for Minority Participation in Science, Technology, Engineering and Mathematics; Grievance Officer, Kingsborough's Professional Staff Congress (PSC) unit; and involvement with the college's Women's Studies Committee and Italian-American Committee. With colleagues, we developed the audio-tutorial approach to human anatomy and physiology; the Physical Therapy Assistant Program; and continual course revisions and new courses in the department over the years.

This presentation can possibly assist Kingsborough's current administration and faculty to serve diverse students and help others regarding collegiate leadership. Perhaps someone who's a chairperson or aspiring to become one; or a higher ranking administrator could benefit from it.

The main topics are: 1) a department chairman's functions in relation to other faculty members in support of students' educational experiences; 2) Kingsborough Community College's unique academic calendar and its impact on faculty members, students and ongoing educational processes; 3) proposals for future consideration; and 4) some concluding reflections after being away from the college.

DEPARTMENT CHAIRPERSON'S FUNCTIONS:

The City University of New York (CUNY) By-Laws provide brief descriptions about chairpersons' responsibilities. Beyond these, there is little definitive written information on a chairperson's overall functions and ongoing responsibilities. Much is shaped by a chairperson's personality, their character and energy levels and how they identify their roles within the college's milieu.

One learns to be a chairperson by being a chairperson. It's "on job training." Much of what occurs will be based on compromise, consensus, good will, collegiality and comity. Being a leader offers opportunities to influence an organization, to help those within it, especially students and faculty, and to have a positive impact. This requires focus, often long hours, and a willingness to be out front to promote changes. A chairperson needs to recognize and appreciate she/he is "first among equals." Mistakes in judgments and decision-making will be made; this sometimes results in unsatisfactory outcomes and temporary setbacks.

While faculty members are educated in specific subject disciplines and trained in related research activities, typically they have no preparation in the operational subjects of leadership, organizational structure, personnel management, employment practices, or budget preparations. These areas are vital as to how the college meets its missions and to any chairperson's work.

A chairperson's roles represent an unusual combination of administrative and educational responsibilities. Some of the prime missions a chairperson has are: To make the department's personnel more diverse; receptive to newer curriculum programs and management approaches; to involve faculty actively in the department/college; and improve interactions with students.

Kingsborough chairpersons continue to hold faculty rank, although their functions deem them as members of the college's administration. Does a chairperson serve the faculty she/he represents or the administration instead? Or perhaps serve both on equal terms? In this dual capacity, how is such an individual perceived by one's colleagues? It is a straddling relationship.

The Chairperson's Extensive Activities, although there are undoubtedly others:

+ Conduct scheduled department meetings with agendas/minutes, and follow-up.
+ Seek & recommend with personnel committee qualified faculty, includes CUNY designated Affirmative Action candidates.
+ Carry out observations with personnel committee of faculty. Be readily available for students to guide and resolve problems.
+ Support curriculum revisions and institute new programs.
+ Engage departmental committees in subject area changes.

- Assist faculty to prepare for tenure, advancement, doctoral dissertations, grant proposals, research and teaching efforts.
- Inform colleagues on educational materials and developments.
- Serve on college-wide committees and ad hoc groups.
- Prepare detailed annual evaluations of faculty and technicians.
- Design faculty teaching schedules, assign faculty observations.
- Lead faculty in new educational realms, course revisions.
- Inspect and improve department's equipment and facilities.
- Write internal and external communications.
- Inform administration on budget and facility requests.
- Arrange periodic guest speakers for staff development, and
- then identify funds from administration or other sources.
- Periodically meet individually with faculty, staff members, and students.
- Prepare reports, grant proposals and other requested documents.
- Carry out assignments via administrative requests by the president and/or dean of faculty.
- Encourage faculty in broader college/community projects.
- Meet with public, university and community officials.
- Maintain and improve the college's aquaria facilities via staff and budget requests to administration. (Biological Sciences' assignment.)
- Serve on special committees as requested by college officials.

These chairman's responsibilities concomitantly interfere with that same individual's ability to carry out the more traditional roles as an academic. Being an effective chairman can involve inordinate time, energy and mental processes. Some faculty members avoid ever being considered for chairperson, they want no part of this responsibility or its functions, including a lack of desire to attain leadership and its burdens. Instead, they prefer their freedom to focus on scholarly interests and independence, to focus on their teaching, research and writing, or possibly interests beyond the college.

CHAIRPERSONS – TENURE / NON-TENURE FACULTY

Tenure is the long-established principle within educational settings. It provides faculty members guaranteed continuous employment after having completed a "trial" or non-tenure period. At CUNY it's a 5-year period. Sometimes "early tenure" can be administratively authorized. Substantive academic/budgetary crises or gross malfeasance by a tenured individual are potential exceptions to tenure continuance.

There are substantial benefits to tenure. It enhances the individual's freedom in scholarly writing and research pursuits, without objections or implied punitive authoritarian actions; protects individuals from being dismissed on whim, or being quirky or unspoken discrimination; can encourage faculty efforts in controversial topic realms; and provides job security nonexistent in most professions and careers. Tenure also prevents administrations from arbitrarily removing personnel to achieve a desired reduction in overall personnel costs.

Possible tenure disadvantages are: allows faculty member to "slack off" in academic commitments and productivity once tenure is achieved; creates difficulties if a faculty member is persistently unsatisfactory or incompetent; limits opportunities for newer appointments in newer academic areas; and has no upper age limitations, or evaluations of mental and/or physical capacities, including those involving drug/alcohol addictions.

Most academics that pursue tenure are highly motivated and actively engaged in satisfying stated criteria. Academically prepared younger enthusiastic faculty often put forth new approaches that enrich curriculum developments and the college to better serve student populations. By providing guidance and positive leadership, a chairperson can be quite helpful to non-tenured faculty as they seek to become more competent. With the chairperson serving as a mentor, periodic meetings with these individuals can be supportive to their goals.

There are incidents when an individual is hired and disappoints, and performs poorly. This can result in interpersonal discomforts. Even so, difficult decisions must be made. Leadership by the chairperson and others involved in personnel decisions must focus and serve the best interests of the department, the institution and the students, and maybe even that individual not being reappointed.

As for tenured faculty, there are limited evaluative processes to support effective performances. Faculty can be perceived as independent contractors given a wide swath of professional freedom. Without self-directed commitment, or corrective measures, a tenured person can languish. Still, a chairperson can make efforts to assist such individuals by meeting with them and discussing their behavior. With persuasion, encouragement and trust they can become more responsive professionals. There were rare occasions when a tenured faculty member did not carry out expected responsibilities. Despite repeated efforts to promote change and without positive responses, I gave up on such an individual.

At Kingsborough, faculty evaluation procedures revolved around unchanging stated criteria with standardized administrative evaluation forms. With cursory periodic faculty observations accurate evaluations are difficult to achieve. The departmental Annual Evaluations (tenured faculty not seeking promotions were exempt) could be more informative and instructive to the chairperson and individual faculty member having this evaluation.

Some academic institutions prefer multiple 3-5 year contracts instead of tenure. This permits individual faculty and the institution to conduct on-going evaluations to determine if the parties mutually choose to renew their contracts for another time period. There are times it is advantageous for a faculty member to move on to a different environment; and sometimes an individual desires to do so.

The tenure concept and multiple year contracts require more open discussion and analysis. Along the thousands of colleges and universities in our nation, some have sound tenure or contractual processes. Sample contracts can be studied as positive examples from other administrations. Academic professional organizations could be helpful by promoting accurate communications and information on these topics.

THE COLLEGE'S ACADEMIC CALENDAR AND RESULTING EXTRA OR 'OVERLOAD' TEACHING HOURS:

Kingsborough Community College has had an unusual academic calendar, known as the: "12-6-12-6" system for many years. The academic year is divided into 4 distinct periods: a 12 week fall semester; a created 6 week winter semester; a 12 week spring semester; and a 6 week summer semester.

Full time faculty instruct about 13 hours in the fall and about the same amount in the spring, for the combined total of 27 hours for these two semesters. These instructional hours are carried out 4 days each week, the 5th day is designated for "professional development," although not necessarily at the college.

During any or all of the 4 fall, winter, spring and summer semesters, faculty can volunteer to teach readily available additional "overload" hours. When this voluntary "overload hours" teaching is coupled with the required fall and spring teaching hours, it can amount to a high level of teaching hours. In some departments, the "overload" total for a faculty member could almost equal the total for the fall and spring assigned hours. For example, by teaching 6 hours additional for each of the 4 academic periods, the result is an additional 24 teaching hours, which are just a few hours short of the expected fall/spring 27 hours. By allowing faculty to teach so many combined hours, it can cause them to become dull and stagnant instructors. It could be analogous to working in a factory.

Significantly, because full time faculty engaged in "overload" teaching assignments have less unencumbered time and attention for other critical and expected professional responsibilities faculty normally carry out. Beyond classroom hours, faculty are expected to hold regular office hours for students; serve on departmental and college committees; promote curriculum revisions; assist in ongoing departmental/college matters; pursue additional academic credentials; carry out research projects and scholarly writing. (It is noteworthy some faculty involved in chronic "overload" teaching also sacrifice other scholarly developments, including the pursuit of advanced degrees and then were not able to be considered for promotion and advancement. It may also explain why comparatively so few faculty take sabbatical leaves.)

In addition, for full-time faculty who do carry these "overloads" covertly deprive other emerging prepared professionals to have career opportunities. Newcomers, recent doctoral graduate students, or more staff beyond the college are prevented from having full time and adjunct positions. Such an arrangement can be contrary to a comprehensive intellectual commitment for the on-going development of the college, including innovative and flexible learning/teaching systems.

For faculty already paid an annual salary to simultaneously and conveniently have additional earnings within the same structure during overlapping time periods does seem highly irregular and undemocratic. It is antithetical to the college's missions. Our salaries were respectable and comparatively high, yet seemingly inadequate for those who sought further compensation for their personal economic patterns. The extra compensations from "overload" became expected as "largesse" for some full-time faculty, who argued this "overload" teaching was needed so they "could put bread on the table." (Their words.) Simply stated, some faculty members could view the continual "overload" supply as their "cash cow."

The "12-6-12-6" system translates into the faculty who do not teach "overloads" only being required to be at the college from late August until just before the winter holidays (fall semester); and then from mid February through the early part of June until Commencement (spring semester).

Under such programmatic conditions, the mandated total days faculty are present are approximately 105-110 days for each full year. This calculation is based on the 2-12 week semesters, with 4 days each week for teaching and related activities, plus those days for scheduled proctoring of examinations, registration assignments and yearly Commencement exercises. (Please note: This is not the expected schedule for administrators or chairpersons, whose responsibilities are ongoing throughout the year.)Thus, faculty are free, that is, not expected to be at the college for almost two months during the winter interval, and about 3 months during the summer, while on an annual salary.

Kingsborough's "12-6-12-6" academic arrangement clearly advantages the faculty, even though it purportedly allows students to accelerate or repeat failed courses. Faculty are able to make a choice between having highly desirable schedules with ample blocks of uncommitted time, or to make exceptional amounts of extra pay by teaching "overloads" so readily available at the college.

The above description focuses on the faculty's relationship within the "12-6-12-6" academic. But, the critical pedagogical issue is its potential impact on students' operational learning experiences. In this format, the amount of classroom time is supposedly the same as those time allocations in more traditional classroom schedules. Examination of the distribution of hours as well as the depth and breadth of learning experiences, particularly courses involving laboratories do not support such contention. To compress community college students' learning into these briefer periods while they have concomitant personal and occupational responsibilities does them an intellectual disservice. Typically, community college students require more thorough learning/teaching experiences in appropriate configurations rather than not less.

My belief is without definitive objective and verifiable supportive research data to the contrary, this long operational "12-6-12-6" pattern at Kingsborough needs to be restricted. It is deleterious to sound educational principles and the ability of students and faculty to effectively carry out detailed comprehensive learning/teaching within a community college.

This entire "overload" topic should have been made more public, analyzed and subject to regulation via the broader CUNY legal system. With more open discussions and review, "overload" might have been ruled illegal. Nevertheless, the college's administration, our professional union, and apparently CUNY's policies did allow it without correction. Certainly, this warrants re-examination to clarify its origins and purposes in relation to the needs of today's more diverse student populations in our society, especially those at a community college. There is much we still do not know or understand about teaching/learning, and these processes require more analysis and study.**

** Please note: During my earlier years at KCC I also did volunteer and took advantage of "overload hours" for additional compensation.

PROPOSALS FOR FUTURE CONSIDERATION:

1) Fall and spring semesters will be converted into 15-16 week standard academic semesters. There will not be the artificially-structured 6-week winter module.

2) Full-time faculty members will no longer carry "overload" or extra teaching assignments for additional compensation beyond their allocated annual salaries and committed time periods. The 6-week summer module can be available for students and extra faculty compensation will be available.

3) Kingsborough and CUNY administrators will hire more full time faculty in accordance with CUNY's state Affirmative Action designations. The professional organization (PSC/CUNY) officials will encourage this because with more membership its revenues and influence increase. When unexpected registration figures warrant it, qualified adjunct faculty members from beyond the college will be hired.

4) Leadership manuals and workshops will be developed for those who aspire to become department chairpersons. Faculty and administrators are encouraged to enroll in relevant preparatory programs in leadership and management at graduate schools of education.

5) The college's administration will provide ample Release Time for faculty members to assist in identified departmental administrative responsibilities as determined by the chairperson. This is important as departments and registration expands and administrative loads at the department levels are more burdensome.

6) The college's administration will programmatically and economically support faculty development and curriculum revisions to better prepare students for technological/educational advances and careers in our changing society.

7) Chairpersons and other faculty members will provide innovative methods to enhance learning/teaching based on emerging educational research findings. Kingsborough will be more educationally flexible for diverse students' needs and interests.

8) For intellectual renewal and restoration, faculty members will be encouraged to take regular sabbatical leaves. This enriches them, and ultimately their professional activities.

9) Term-limits for department chairpersons will be considered. The possibility tenured faculty will serve on a rotating basis might be innovative and beneficial. Chairpersons will have annual conferences and written evaluations from the dean of the faculty.

10) When a faculty member retires from Kingsborough, there will be a comprehensive "exit interview." The president or the dean of the faculty will conduct this interview. Information obtained could be helpful to the college's leadership for future activities. Perhaps those leaving if they desire could be invited to present a concluding address to their colleagues.

REFLECTIONS SUMMARY:

The faculty and the administration are there for the ultimate consumers, the diverse students. Many students including older adults who attend a community college for the first time know little as to how to cope with problems they encounter at the college. Prior educational experiences, unfamiliarity with college procedures, perhaps being the first members of their family to attend college can make them believe they are confused and powerless. Those in leadership positions can pay attention to their needs; and when students are exposed to guidance and possible successful resolutions, they express relief and appreciation. These are freedom-rendering experiences that intuitively promote hope and sensitivity for them.

As chairman, I was able to directly help students. Students met with the chairman, were treated fairly, and hopefully matters could be made better for them. Sometimes this involved a supportive phone call, a letter of recommendation, advice about colleges and programs, a change in schedules or major, books being loaned to them, or assistance to get them part time work. On other occasions it meant words of encouragement and guidance.

In retrospect, having been a chairman for 15 years was ill-advised. In 1998 and after refection, I realized the department would benefit from new leadership and a fresh approach. President Leon M. Goldstein and our colleagues were informed I would not be a candidate for the chairmanship again.

So, after almost 33 years at the college, this was not an easy process to disconnect from those I knew, worked with and cared about. During my journey, certain colleagues remained enigmatic, and seemed to lack the kinds of commitments considered important to our profession. There were periods of uneasiness at Kingsborough when I was unable to understand certain college and university administrative decisions. Some aspirations had unrealistic aspects, as did expectations of others. Earlier disappointments and lingering irritations to promote changes at the college have given way to quieter acceptance and newer interests.

Finally, my apologies for the length of this document, but these are serious, complicated matters and they require detailed explanations to promote a greater understanding and possible change. At this point, some of this document is controversial, and might not be in keeping with prevalent views of some at the college. If it would be helpful, I would welcome the opportunity to talk with appropriate college officials.

Addendum: Over time, this document was shared with several Kingsborough Community College presidents, including those who were acting and interim ones, along with several former Kingsborough colleagues.

2017

COLLEGE FRATERNITIES IN
THE UNITED STATES

P EOPLE are communal social animals. We choose to be
with other humans in many different social groupings
under differing circumstances and changing motives.
When we do join a special group, it gives us an identity
to be part of a unique body or institution for an espoused
cause or function we might think is important. When
joining, people tend to believe and feel they are designated,
chosen and different, perhaps even better than others. Most
organizational groups have mission statements to present
their underlying purposes or goals. This information
stimulates interest in being involved with that group. An
underlying aspiration of these formed associations in our
society is to perpetuate their declared functional uniqueness
and to promote their existence in perpetuity. To consider
dissolution would imply failure, and loss of power and
influence.

Early in our American history, male students at colleges
and universities began to form selective clubs within these

institutions. They were titled "fraternities." In 1776, the first scholarly fraternity was formed, Phi Beta Kappa. This prestigious group solely honors academic excellence, and it still continues to exist for that positive purpose. Virtually all fraternities formed since then with the exclusion of Phi Beta Kappa have extensive initiation procedures termed "hazing." Hazing experiences are meant to enhance potential members' spirits, promote their sense of belonging and solidarity to that particular group. But, seemingly amusing initiating activities evolved into thoughtlessly dangerous, sometimes even life threatening processes for the unknowing and enthusiastic newcomers.

Groups especially designated for female college students titled "sororities" were formed. (It would have been peculiar and inappropriate to call female aggregations members of a "fraternal" body.) Based on reported data, sororities have minimal or virtually no dangerous or destructive hazing incidents for those who pledge their sororities. Females appear to treat other joining females with reasonableness and civility. Maybe females are mentally and genetically more sensitive to empathetic and cooperative experiences in sharp contrast to their male fraternity counterparts.

Beyond fraternities and sororities, professional and amateur sports teams including male high school sports and even military organizations carry out widespread initiation hazing activities. Some activities are amusing and simple; others can have unanticipated serious negative repercussions.

The prime subject for this writing will be on collegiate fraternities and the highly questionable hazing practices repetitively used on the newcomers to these organizations.

For those who choose to join a collegiate fraternity there are specific initiation procedures devised by those already within that group. These usually begin during the early portion of each fall semester when incoming students are observed, and subjected to scrutiny and cursory comments as if they were in a horse auction or beauty contest. Politely and ingratiatingly, current members of these organizations make efforts to superficially bond with selected newcomers and make anecdotal gossip observations to verify if they will be given any further attention that leads to a more formal consideration process.

The first phase of these invitational or initiating procedures is known as the "pledge period." It's when critical decisions will be made as to who will be "welcomed" and "invited" to join particular groups. Then, each organization's membership decides by a voting process, often secretive, which persons will be invited to "pledge" their group. Some of the more highly desirable candidates might even be "wooed" by several fraternities simultaneously. Some have parents who at one time did belong to a particular fraternity, and they encourage their offspring to become part of such a supposed proud familial legacy. For those who anxiously await such the decision making and curiously want to be accepted, to belong, this can be a stressful as well as disappointing or exhilarating time period. Some of the newer students don't get invited to join any group. Such obvious public rejection during this highly anticipatory period can be quite disconcerting.

Once a person does pledge a particular fraternity the devised initiation "fun" and the engaging "rites of passage" ritual take hold. In reality, many initiation projects specifically assigned to pledges by fraternity members are insensitive, potentially life-threatening, and are clearly examples of underlying dangerous "machismo" motives. All of this occurs while still emerging students are becoming

333

familiar with new college life, campus living, often being away from their families for the first time, and getting involved in serious academic studies. As they quest for identity, these are fresh and unknown experiences.

The stated purposes of fraternities are seemingly well intentioned. Some are purely positive service or religious organizations. Whatever their purposes, they need to respect those who want to join them. Otherwise, they are just exhibiting some of the worst traits in our society. Bad, hurtful behavior is never more than just bad, hurtful behavior, no matter whatever one wants to call it. There are planned social events; some are actively involved in social, environmental and campus causes. When there are established residential buildings or houses, they are convenient, even luxurious places to live while attending college as alternatives to dormitory rooms or off campus living. They can also be unfettered social havens for widespread alcohol and other drug usage within their exclusive environments, and possible facile sexual encounters.

Besides these roles, they are repositories of members' already submitted term papers on course subjects and copies of prior course examinations, anecdotal comments about professors, and other information to benefit those anointed into that fraternity or sorority. Some groups maintain lists of prior chapter and national members who've achieved notoriety or "succeeded" in various careers. They serve as contact persons to network with for assistance in future career/employment positions.

In the early 1950s while a student at Columbia, I did pledge and join Sigma Nu, a national fraternity. It did not have a massive fraternity house, but rather a suite of rooms proximal to the main campus. The membership was a diverse mixture of out-of-town and New York City area male students, selected from public and private schools, and of reasonable personalities and interests. Along with my designated pledge partner, our prime and obviously innocuous pledge activity was to go to New York's Central Park Zoo, talk to a designated animal attendant and convince that person to give us a portion of lion feces (that's right). After persuading this person, who thought it was a ridiculous but amusing request, we did get a portion of lion droppings. As we sat on a rock in Central Park, our next task was to force some of it into a narrow opening at the top of an empty glass Vitalis Hair Tonic bottle provided by the fraternity brothers. This miniscule bottle opening could barely accommodate the tip of a toothpick. It hardly satisfied the advertised concept of a "dab" that could come out of it. For those of you old enough to recall, Vitalis Hair Tonic's well-known advertising slogan was "a little dab will do you."

We needed all our problem-solving skills of young freshmen college minds. Despite repeated efforts and much patience, we continuously failed to get one lion feces particle into the barely visible opening. We thought about cutting off the bottom of the empty Vitalis bottle with a glass cutter, stuffing some droppings in, and then buying colorless glue to carefully secure the bottom back on. Our hope was the fraternity brothers wouldn't see what we'd done. This idea was disregarded.

We initially treated our fail efforts seriously. We brought the empty Vitalis bottle and a small amount of lion droppings in a covered pan back to our buddies to prove we'd at least gotten something done, and explained our lack of success to those we hoped would still become our fraternity brothers. We were naïve and still capable of being worried about our failure. We didn't know what would happen and this was a major concern. The brothers were hysterical at our described failing efforts. We then laughed too. That was the end of this silly zoo experience. We did get admitted into Sigma Nu; and got back to attending classes and studies and developing new friendships. Surprisingly, this was an unusual learning process.

Why almost 66 years later do I relate this seemingly innocuous adventure tale? Because there are no logical comparisons with what two innocent pledges were asked to do then and any of the more recent documented and disturbing pledge activities. The reader is invited to do a computer search of the term "Hazing Deaths in the United States." Another vital reference will be found at the National Collaborative for Hazing Research and Prevention at the University of Maine. The results are quite shocking. There are frequent incidents that involve alcohol and other drugs, physical abuses, sometimes rape and assaults of campus females, and patterns of dangerous and lethal behavior. There are even incidents of suicides by hazed pledges.

Here's a list excerpted from a NBC News Report as to hazing activities pledges carried out so they could join fraternities. This compilation is a meager smattering of literally hundreds if not thousands of similar incidents throughout our nation's collegiate environments. Many experiences are clearly violations of law. Other reported hazing experiences are highly sadistic and dehumanizing.

* Several weeks ago in Spring 2017 Boston police were called to the Phi Delta Theta house at MIT and reportedly found <u>a party to rival a scene from the movie "Animal House"</u> — the first floor transformed into

an illegal nightclub, a waterfall cascading down the center marble staircase, a crowd almost three times the maximum occupancy, and underage teens boozing.

(Muzio comment insert: "Animal House" was an influential fraternity house comedy-farce film put out by National Lampoon in 1968 starring John Belushi. Later on, Belushi died of a drug overdose.)

*   In February 2017, one Phi Delta Theta brother was allegedly <u>choked to death</u> by another during a fight at Indiana University of Pennsylvania.

*   The chapter at the University of Central Florida was put under review in February after hazing allegations, <u>according to the campus newspaper.</u>

*   A fraternity member was <u>kicked out </u>after being arrested for an alleged sexual assault not connected to any fraternity event at the University of Wisconsin-Madison last October.

*   A chapter at Middle Tennessee State University was put on probation in August 2016 amid allegations of hazing, that included blindfolding pledges in the woods, and use of hard drugs, <u>according to NBC affiliate WSMV.</u>

*   In April 2016, the fraternity disclosed that a member at Kansas State has been <u>accused of a sexual assault </u>at the frat house a year earlier in what it called an "isolated incident."

* The Washington State University chapter was reportedly suspended in April 2016 during an investigation into whether two <u>students were drugged</u> at a party.

* The <u>president of the Baylor University chapter</u> was charged with sexually assaulting a woman outside a party in March 2016.

* A chapter at the Georgia Institute of Technology was sanctioned by the school in October 2015 after white members were accused of yelling racial slurs at a black student, but the <u>suspension was lifted</u> after a third-party review.

* The Washburn University chapter was suspended in April 2015 because of <u>"inappropriate" text messages</u> including one that reportedly said, "Remember, women are objects."

* An Ole Miss brother was removed from the frat after he appeared to bite the head off a hamster in a spring break video that circulated in 2015.

* The Loyola Marymount University chapter was suspended in February 2015 during an <u>investigation of hazing violations,</u> according to the campus newspaper.

* The University of Pennsylvania chapter was suspended in December 2014 for a <u>holiday card</u> that showed mostly white members posing with a dark-skinned blowup doll, the campus newspaper reported.

* The national organization suspended operations at the Texas Tech chapter in September 2014 after an uproar over a banner that read: "No Means Yes, Yes Means Anal."

* In July 2014, Oklahoma State University suspended a Phi Delta Theta chapter for hazing and alcohol violations, including paddling of pledges, the Daily Oklahoman reported.

* The Emory University chapter was suspended for four years in July 2013 because of hazing that included a "fight club," and forced feeding and alcohol, the campus newspaper reported.

This list does not include a recent highly publicized tragic incident in Beta Theta Pi fraternity house at Pennsylvania State University. There a young student pledge died while intoxicated after falling down a flight of stairs. His fraternity brothers did nothing for many hours while he lingered in a coma until someone eventually called 911. Currently 8 of them are under indictment for ignoring his deteriorating conditions, his death and then trying to cover up this matter. This fraternity house is now closed. Then in September 2017 at Louisiana State University a student pledging the fraternity Phi Delta Theta died, with excessive alcohol consumption involved. 10 of the fraternity brothers have been indicted. Significantly, the college's president stated such incidents are rare and most fraternities serve many positive relationships, including "lifetime friendships." The word "rare" or justifiable because of benefits cannot mask the magnitude of this.

It is extremely difficult to consistently obtain accurate figures on the number of fraternity pledges at colleges and universities who die each year because of humiliating life-threatening hazing experiences, or those left permanently disabled. On a nationwide basis there are many incidents never reported; and others remain unknown due to cover-ups or denials by academic institutions, fraternities, or even pledges themselves. If these revelations were accurately reported and readily available they might unfavorably influence student recruitment efforts and the potential marketing of an institution.

So, here we are in the early fall of another new academic collegiate year, when fraternities seek new members. College and university administrators need to do a much better job to protect their students, and to do so right away. Enforcement of "zero tolerance" for any destructive or dangerous pledge experiences would be a fine start. (Most fraternities and some academic institutions in recent years have such stated "zero tolerance" policies about hazing regularly disregarded.) Markedly improved oversight of fraternities could be helpful; having reputable senior advisors to monitor them; orientation sessions to educate incoming females and males about these organizations and how alcohol and other drugs can be lethal, and often lead to sexual assaults and violations of females.

Those who choose to pledge a fraternity can be sensitized to avoid anything they perceive might harm them physically and/or mentally. Parents can be more fully engaged and questioning too, alerting in advance their offspring to potential negative experiences in their newer environments amongst supposedly well-intentioned newer buddies. And, when these fraternity chapters are part of national societies, leadership on the national levels could be more adamant and instructive to prevent untoward activities occurring in their chapters.

Events that result in student hazing deaths are historically followed by memorial services. There are expressions of grief, along with transitory explanations to identify supposed causative factors, that is, motives for their history and predictability. Strong calls for corrective steps from political leaders and occasional enlightened institutional administrators soon follow. Shocked and grieving parents seek answers while they call for investigations and remedies. But, earlier reactions give way to a long-term limbo cliché of "kicking the can down the road." Eventually seemingly isolated events are forgotten, there's amnesia about them, but hardly so for parents of their dead or maimed children. Sadness forever persists long after the tragedies. Static, uneventful complacency is preferred. These disturbing matters remain unresolved; they keep on happening with the same horrible outcomes. The following year the same pattern goes on to repeat it. Is this some form of madness? Why does it continue to happen again and again?

Each fall, emerging enthusiastic and unknowing children go off to colleges, their brains not fully mature and their decision-making abilities questionable. They are subjected to experiences supposedly done to promote commitment to fraternities and other positive principles. But, each academic year pledges die, with now unfulfilled lives, and leave forever despondent and grieving parents and families. Some chapter fraternity houses have been suspended, temporarily shut down, or occasionally permanently closed, yet the negative incidents persist almost forever.

Beyond all of this, two vital questions to be considered: 1) Why would any reasonable person be so desperate to join any group knowing its members might potentially damage or cause tragic consequences to their very being? 2) What drives another person or persons to carefully plan and then irrationally promote bizarre activities or supposed pledge rituals to humiliate or even accidently harm or kill another human being?

Thoughtful analyses might give us insights and understanding about human behavior and potential violence in our society well beyond college and university realms. Like other aspects of our modern society, violent acts are all about us: rapes, group sexual assaults, mass slaughters, racial confrontations, sexual abuses of children, riots at sporting events, suicides and yes, fraternity hazing experiences that result in deaths. They are manifestations of outrage, anger and abuse. Are they part of a national collective pathology?

Despite extensive research much remains unclear as to the etiology, contributory motives and effective preventions of violence. Isn't there a deplorable inconsistency for students in fraternities to pursue higher education and intellectual development yet simultaneously engage in violent acts towards others who will become their "brothers"? Do these earlier cited examples of violence persist beyond college years in a modified and subtle form? Are violent acts remnants of our earlier evolutionary stages, or is this too simplistic?

What prevents us from being kinder and gentler towards one another? So long ago, the late Robert Kennedy wrote and spoke about our need to become "gentler."

References:

The New York Times, Op-Ed, September 26, 2017: "Get the Keg Out of the Frat House" by John Hechinger, who also wrote the book True Gentlemen: The Broken Pledge of America's Fraternities.

Secrets of the Tomb ...Skull and Bones, The Ivy League, and The Hidden Paths of Power, Alexandra Robbins, is an investigative focus on this Yale University secret society.

"A Death at Penn State" by Caitlin Flanagan, November 2017, The Atlantic, pages 92-105.

2017

RAPE, SEXUAL HARASSMENT
AND ABUSE IN AMERICA

I N the past few weeks there has been considerable media
coverage about mostly women and occasionally men
revealing their long-ago incidents of rapes and sexual assaults.
In an avalanche of pent-up feelings hundreds of women have
brought forth the abuses they suffered from celebrities;
motion picture notables; political figures; Catholic clergy;
office and corporate colleagues; sports coaches; academics;
military staff including the military academies; medical
personnel; prominent media persons; and apparently within
every occupational and social realm where women and men
interact.

Although there are expanding lists of prominent others
(to date so far, more than 63 celebrity persons), the most
identified example is President Donald J. Trump. He publicly
bragged about sexually assaulting women in last year's
election campaign and then referred to it simply as "locker
room" talk. His newest approach is he denies this, and claims
it isn't his voice in the video tape shown! Trump also denies

the more than 15 women who've accused him of sexual transgressions, calling them "all liars," and how he planned to sue them.

(This author's comment: I have been in many private and public athletic locker rooms in my lifetime and in various USMC facilities where men gathered and changed clothes, and in all these experiences I never heard any comparable degrading or vile remark or language about women, their bodies, or their behavior, and I am not deaf.)

You might be interested in reading December 4th, 2017 The New York Times Op-Ed piece by Billy Bush, who was one of the "stars" on the bus with Trump "Yes, Donald Trump, You Said That." In that same article, Bush points out there were 8 men on that bus who heard him, and goes on to provide a quotation attributed to Trump: "People will believe you. You just tell them and they believe you." Also, Lindy West's "Our Harasser in Chief," The New York Times Op-Ed, December 14, 2017, and Gail Collins' writing "Donald Trump's Gift to Women," Op-Ed, December 14, 2017.

Trump had endorsed Roy Moore for a Senate seat in Alabama. Roy Moore has been accused by multiple females, including younger teenagers; but Trump claims that Moore "denies these allegations," and he's "needed" in the Senate. One must wonder why else Trump defends Moore? He wanted politics ahead of morality. Fortunately, Moore lost; it's citizens' pushback on bad behavior.

Opponents and deniers of those who make these revelations, which are possibly criminal acts, claim such information should have been presented sooner whenever these incidents supposedly happened. In a number of reported cases, those who were victims and then silent with non-disclosure settlements as part of monetary settlements were obviously forced to keep these matters to themselves. Another accusatory reaction is maybe they're made-up stories and now are only coming out for potential monetary compensation reasons.

Such perspectives smack of the long used and erroneous "blaming the victim" rationale thrown about by those seeking cheap explanations. These responses are hardly new ones for women who've been chronically humiliated in everyday work and social situations, and then told they caused them, so they better remain silent and forget about them. This comment is sometimes accompanied by "they wanted it." Some who've been openly "accused" have vehemently denied the charges; others have amnesia about the years gone by. A growing number of sexual abusers including elected political figures have contritely acknowledged their abusive and unauthorized behaviors, offered sobering apologies and claim to "take full responsibility," whatever that means. Some have resigned their positions.

There are countless others we do not know about; thus the uncertainty as to reliable figures regarding overall rapes and sexual assaults. In this relatively new age of electronic transmissions females are subjected to verbal and sexual abuses this way, too. A reasonable somewhat simplistic source of information is to just ask women and young females "Have you ever been subjected to physical and verbal sexual abuse and harassment to degrade or threaten you?" This will yield additional data. For anyone who attended grade school, there's a cliché typically presented in early general science classes about "icebergs." The cliché is "it's the tip of the iceberg." This translates into further awareness 9/10's of the iceberg's mass is below the water's surface and therefore not readily visible.

Those mostly women who've been personally violated have pervasive, emotional and rational reasons for being reluctant to come forward when they were originally exploited and abused. Fear of losing a job, not being believed in their statements, or believing in their abilities to take on powerful and financially advantaged males can control another person's decision-making. Unless a person has directly experienced such an intimate and disturbing mental and physical violation of rape and/or sexual assault, one cannot speak fluently, casually, or critically on this subject.

Even after coming forward and publicly revealing these most private intimate matters, both women and men still need to have their bodies and lives respected, protected and believed. (See <u>The New Yorker,</u> October 23, 2017, Ronan Farrow's "Abuses of Power," pages 42-49.) Why can't members of our society believe and accept these behaviors to women are verbal and physical acts of violence against them? Then, they can be treated as criminal events and will require law enforcement interventions followed by follow-up legal processes to adjudicate them openly.

These horrendous rapes and assaults cannot be excused away. If they are, it only empowers such violators and future ones to pursue their serial bad behavior. Then, it becomes the "norm" for such irregular behaviors. Do we have any measurements of the long-term destruction to females in addition to these sexual violations, into relevant areas of depression, self-worth, and impacts on their future relationships beyond the assaults? Resolving these questions could educate all of us as to how to become more sensitive and empathetic organisms and avoid the havoc and brutality thrust on others. For example, Socrates once said: "Define your terms." Perhaps we can benefit from more accurate and clear definitions and distinctions between "rape" and "consensual sex." Such clarifications would yield better understanding of these definitive differences.

The underlying problem isn't with women, it's with men who have power and control, and developed belief systems they can do this and get away with it unscathed. In 1975 Susan Brownmiller wrote an enlightening book, <u>Against Our Will – Men, Women and Rape</u> in which she also historically details rape of women, men in prison, in war and in slavery and child molestation.

Early in her book Brownmiller offers her speculation:

> "Man's discovery that his genitalia could serve as a weapon to generate fear must rank as one of the most important discoveries of prehistoric times, along with the use of fire and the first crude axe. From prehistoric times to the present, I believe rape has played a critical function. It is nothing more or less than a conscious process of intimidation by which all men keep all women in a state of fear." (Page 15.)

While some find this sweeping generalization demeaning to both women and men, we need to calmly explore such a definitive belief or statement. Until we uncover underlying reasons males carry out these unwanted violent and heinous attacks on women (or other men), only then will data and analysis provide potential preventative resolutions. Why does abuse of women seem so prevalent for so long? Are their distinct biological characteristics in males, at least some of them that allow them to believe, engage and encourage destructive acts on females? And if there are such traits, why don't all males exhibit them but others never demonstrate them? What reliable data have been found since Brownmiller's pronouncements more than 40 years ago?

Some men have made anecdotal statements symptomatic of "rebound phenomena." Because of this recent notoriety and concern for being classified as potentially dangerous to women, a share of men have openly commented they will have the least communication with women in the workplace and in social settings. By avoiding legitimate and sincere communications with women does nothing to cope with the historical and documented humiliations of women based on the reported data. Such a blanket defense seems silly. It implies punitive action to ostracize or further punish women, almost as if they are a contagion. This also implies men are victims too. That's hardly the situation. Nor does it resolve the underlying issues. Humans are intellectually capable animals with more problem solving and thoughtful processes and certainly capable of rational behavior.

One realm that might help in matters of rape and sexual abuse is related to legislation and laws relevant to the statute of limitations. There are varying time limitations on the federal, state and international levels to pursue legal actions. There are no limitations on seeking those who've committed murder, kidnapping and other heinous crimes. This means no matter when these events occurred they can be pursued by law enforcement agencies and the legal system without regard to the calendar. While there are justifications for placing reasonable time limits on certain alleged crimes endlessly to protect possible defendants, a newer concept regarding rape, sexual assaults and abuses would be their specific exclusion from any statute of limitations.

Comprehensive legislation with accompanying changes in attitudes would be necessary to remove statute barriers that currently prevent prosecution of these destructive human abuses. Advances in data gathering techniques directly related to forensic science now permit evidence to be scientifically gathered, stored and accurately maintained beyond an arbitrary time barrier. These evidentiary data could then serve positive purposes in long-ago incidents regarding rape and sexual abuses.

Progress, respect and civility can result. Behavior can be changed. It is a long, historical battle for women. Attention Must Be Paid.

Please Note: "The Patriarchy Isn't Going Anywhere" by Susan Faludi, The New York Times Sunday Review, December 31, 2017, pages 1 and 3.

While the focus of this writing until now has been on the rape and sexual harassment and abuses of individual humans, can there be logical and reasonable comparisons between what women are subjected to in rape by men, and what governments, powerful organizations and individuals are doing in the rape of the planet? Beyond individual rapes and sexual assaults going on for what seems forever there can also be the "rape" of a nation, an environment, even a community or perhaps the entire planet.

More and more there are expanding examples of nations that have been plundered, areas in the world where there have been global damages, and other geographical situations where plants, animals and other life forms have been destroyed to extinction. Some humans believe the planet is for their consumption and benefit, and it is perfectly all right to excavate all of its minerals and non-renewable natural products for themselves.

Serious, objective observations only confirm what humans have been doing to this planet for centuries, but more so in recent years when there is expanding human population and increased materialism: its warming, massive pollution, chemical degradation of the land and bodies of water, especially the oceans, and our atmosphere give much data. In long range analyses, these are essentially "rape," wanton and selfish destruction without regard for the overall imbalance and damage caused. Such behavior disregards any human connections to all of the other life forms on the planet, or the belief humans have a "stewardship" or reverence for it.

Addendum References:

Curriculum Development: "Transforming a Biology of Women Course to Include Feminist Perspectives," Loretta Taras and Joseph N. Muzio. Transformations – A Resource for Curriculum Transformation and Scholarship. The New Jersey Project Journal, Volume 10, Spring 1999.

Feminist Approaches to Science. Ruth Bleier (ed.), Pergamon Press, The Athene Series, New York, 1986.

The second X – The Biology of Women, 2nd Ed., Colleen M. Belk and Virginia M. Borden, Brooks Cole, CA, 2002.

2018

THE SLAUGHERING OF
SCHOOL CHILDREN

SINCE April 1999 (Columbine High School, Colorado) through February 2018 (Marjory Stoneham Douglas High School, Florida) across our country there have been 24 reported incidents of school children being slaughtered, the result of violence and armed weapons. The number of dead children is 170 from these incidents, although others were wounded and still bear damages of gun shots. The impact on families and friends of those slaughtered is also upon thousands of others. The resulting sadness will not cease.

There have been other massive shooting incidents in Las Vegas, in houses of worship, movie theaters, and other public places. Families and friends of these victims mourn forever these slaughters, too.

Recent reactions and supposed remedies to the most recent matter in Florida have been all over the place. It would be senseless to cite all of them; they've been in the media and are being considered by public officials and law enforcement persons as well as citizens' groups and outspoken intelligent students activists who soon will be voters.

The focus of this response is on the subject of arming designated teachers in our nation's schools systems as a defense against these potential acts of violence. If carried out, it would result in about 718,000 teachers being armed, training them, supplying proper weapons, securing them and investing in huge amounts of money for a highly questionable, possibly chaotic procedure. In essence, our schools would become armed camps with some educationally-prepared professional staff members who in addition to their ever-expanding learning/teaching responsibilities might be willing to also carry out these war-like burdens. There are approximately <u>300,000,000</u> known weapons already out there in our nation (that's right). Will it be beneficial to add to this enormous number?

To date, the bulk of law enforcement officials, those highly knowledgeable about weapons including veterans and military personnel, the majority of teachers polled and many parent/citizens are dubious and unimpressed with such ill-conceived reflexive proposals. Reasonable, practical and psychological objections are being raised, including the unknown deleterious impact on students, the learning environments, and teachers and staff.

Then, why, oh why is President Trump pushing this concept in his daily presentations? His pronouncements are quite similar to those of NRA leaders. In <u>The NY Times</u> front page report on February 27, 2018, he comments how even without a weapon "he'd storm in to stop a killer." President Trump never served in the military and had 5 deferments for alleged bone spurs, thereby avoiding service during the Vietnam War. This translates into someone else randomly having gone in his privileged place, and perhaps having been killed instead. His knowledge and experience with weapons is minimal and untested. He sounds quite brazenly heroic from afar. Authentic heroes never brag about their future and unknown intentions to behave heroically.

Although it was long ago, I was trained as a USMC officer and had extensive experiences with various weapons including assault ones. Weapons require continual maintenance and strict safety procedures, ongoing training and repetitive passing of qualifications tests. Even in the most controlled circumstances weapons can be unpredictable; and because of unanticipated accidental events lethal to proximal innocent individuals. Those professionally trained and experienced make mistakes, too. You can check out another former Marine's views in the February 25th The NY Times Sunday Review, page 4, "I Don't Want a Gun in My Classroom" by Anthony Swofford.

If your believe arming teachers in schools is not a sound idea, you are urged to communicate via e-mails or phone calls to our elected and school officials so they have a clearer understanding of reasonable opposition to this concept. Perhaps more rational public discussions and debates will result in sound prevention of future slaughters or at least their sharp curtailment.

Stay informed and be an active citizen. Otherwise there is no democracy.

2018

THOUGHTS ABOUT AN 86TH BIRTHDAY

A COUPLE of days ago and surrounded by our family to celebrate, I had a birthday. Now, I'm an 86 year old geezer, even though I don't feel or act that old. Birthdays are a fine time to reflect and wonder about one's life and what's going on out there.

It was just about this time in June 1944 when Dwight D. Eisenhower led the Allies in the invasion of Normandy France. This was the major turning point towards victory and peace in World War II. In 1968 this date, Robert F. Kennedy was killed; a few months before in April so was Martin Luther King. These assassinations along with John Kennedy's in November 1963 and other civil rights leaders have impacted so much of our lives. During the 1960s in at least 125 cities across America there were riots related to civil rights and protests against the continuing and highly questionable war in Vietnam. Our country experienced violent tragedies that make us wonder what could have been.

There have been other memorable events around the world and within our country. No doubt each of us can provide major additions to these four cited events, the list would be a comprehensive list of historical events that have shaped our individual and collective lives along with the rest of the planet. The list could go on and on.

Have we witnessed significant worldwide improvement changes since the end of World War II and beyond? Certainly. Have scientific and technological discoveries and innovations brought forth considerable benefits to many throughout the world? In many cases, yes, but still in others, no. Despite continuing complex global issues have we not witnessed innumerable advantages for segments of the world's population? Because of civil rights legislation and changing attitudes, minorities have far more rights than in the past; and women have, in many situations, achieved rights and privileges long denied to them so they might have full and equal development. There still is much more to do in both of these historically long-neglected realms.

After his brother John died, Robert F. Kennedy had a clinical depression. He became involved in reading the Greek poets and philosophers as he sought a modicum of solace and understanding. Eventually he recovered but was different in many ways. He supposedly had a couple of epiphanies and renewal in his faith with energy. As someone seeking to become president, he advocated peace, justice and compassion for those who were suffering. His travels around our country made him fully aware of poverty and the disadvantages of many children. He was a voice of reason, wonder and sensitivity, but he was destroyed.

This is a quotation from a Robert Kennedy speech:

"My favorite poet was Aeschylus: 'In our sleep, pain which cannot forget falls drop by drop upon the heart until, in our own despair, against our will, comes wisdom through the awful grace of God.'"

Kennedy went on to say:

"What we need in the United States is not division; what we need in the United States is not hatred; what we need in the United States is not violence or lawlessness; but love and wisdom, and compassion toward one another, and a feeling of justice toward those who still suffer within our country, whether they be white or they be black."

Why am I writing to you at this time, or even providing this selected identification of certain events? Partially because any reasonable review of events in the past few years are equally overwhelming as those earlier events. Our country is in the midst of chaotic leadership, a great deal of corruption of our political system, and world events seriously endangering the environment and the planet itself.

The current direction of our national political system is troublesome, it lacks compassion and civility, and is often predicated on lies and efforts to disrupt and destroy any sort of harmonious rationales. We are in deep trouble. The created disharmony is intentional; it prevents us from seeking reasonable solutions to long-standing national and global problems.

America is an experiment and like all other experiments there can be mistakes, unforeseen events and failures. Angers, disputes and deceit seem to be chronic right now. 50 years plus have gone by from the explosive and revolutionary 1960s and we're still wrestling with the same underlying issues along with newer complex ones. There are no guarantees our nation can succeed and that our democracy will prevail.

You might be interested in reading a book, <u>RFK His Words for Our Times</u>, edited and introduced by Edwin O. Guthman& C. Richard Allen. Robert Kennedy believed our nation's finest days could be ahead of us. The book is a compilation of Kennedy's writings and his aspirations, with comments by influential historians and others. It is a far cry from what has been going on these past couple of years and because of the most vicious, uncaring and irrational person in the White House right now. You are urged to be informed and to be involved before it's too late.

2018

T HESE Next Few Essays Are Interrelated And Are
Presented Together:

Yes, it's almost the end of 2018; and yes it's been a rough
year for citizens and families. There have been various
"Family and Friends" letters sent to you these past few years.

In today's The New York Times, there is a special report
titled: "This is our reality now." The subtitle of this report is:

> "President Trump has systematically undone
> protections of the environment over the past
> two years. He says they have cost jobs and hurt
> the economy. But undoing them also comes at a
> cost. Here is how the profound shift in federal
> policy is affecting communities across the
> country"

<u>Here are the major section titles of this twelve page report:</u>

Dismissing Science
Easing a "War on Coal'
Sidestepping Protections
Profiting, at a Cost

The last page of the report focuses on the <u>78 Environmental Rules on the Way Out Under Trump </u>(And 11 Rules Reinstated After Challenges).

Based on related research from Harvard and Columbia Law Schools and other sources, according to The Times' analysis:

> "All told, the Trump administration's environmental rollbacks could lead to at least 80,000 extra deaths per decade and cause respiratory problems for more than one million people, according to a separate analysis conducted by researchers from Harvard."

We have experienced two years of the Trump-led administration. Trump and the Republican legislators have repeatedly focused on removing a wide variety of federal regulations that have positive effects on citizens' health and well being. He is sacrificing human lives and an overall positive environment in exchange for his business-mentality beliefs for supposed jobs and profits. He does not understand environmental issues, American history, or the complexities of global damages that could potentially destroy this planet and living organisms. Often, he disregards more qualified advisors and makes decisions on capricious conceptual judgments. He lacks knowledge and sensitivity. In addition, he consistently lies. According to reputable <u>Fact Checks</u>, in his two years in office he's lied more than 7 thousand times!!

<u>Family and Friends</u>, what can you do about these disturbing matters? First of all, read the report and be informed. Then, consider communicating with your elected officials via e-mails, phone calls, community meetings. A third possibility is you can inform your neighbors and friends and encourage them to know more about environmental issues and what is going on.

Historically, we've had Theodore Roosevelt, Ralph Waldo Emerson, Henry David Thoreau, John Muir, Aldo Leopold, Rachel Carson, John McPhee, Lewis Thomas, Sylvia Earle, and Elizabeth Kobert along with many other informed and sensitive activists/writers and citizen groups to lead the charge.

Maybe you have the talent, ability and energy to make a similar commitment. Or, at least raise your voice and be heard if you care about the future of the planet and its residents. We still live in a democracy.

<u>Hello Family and Friends</u>:

Over time, on some 10-12 occasions I have communicated with you. There are times in life when we need to be reminded of certain underlying issues taking place in our country and our neighborhoods, and they have to be brought forth openly. In my opinion, this matter is certainly one of them. It's by Paul Krugman and appeared in <u>The New York Times</u> on July 15th. Here's the Krugman Reference:

"Racism Comes Out of the Closet
The Dog Whistle Days are Apparently Over"

"Send her back," "If you don't like it here go back," "love it or leave it." These same kinds of statements were made, and worse to my grandparents and some of their children from Italy including my mother long after they were here as citizens. When does this stop?? Hatred and anger do little to resolve long standing matters, and they are terrible examples of discrimination.

In today's The New York Times, Op-Ed section are two additional pieces, one by Charles M. Blow: "The Rot You Smell Is a Racist Potus; and another by Kevin M. Kruse: "How Trump Is Worse Than Wallace." Both of these provide clear-cut examples of Trump's harsh racist remarks against those who are black or brown. Why does he specifically denigrate them?

There are too many examples of hatred, unkindness and discrimination that dominate our society. We have a president who thrives on stirring up these matters and frequently lies. For the nation's leader, this is disgraceful. If we tend to ignore them as commonplace, then somehow we are accepting them. How much more of his attitudes, words and behaviors will we accept? Does he seek impeachment so he can even rile up his troops to create even more chaos and confusion? Why is the Republican party and its elected officials so silent? Will we eventually lose our democracy to hatred and distortions?

Over the years, I have used a quotation by the Reverend William Sloane Coffin: "If you don't stand for something, you're apt to fall for anything." Please pay attention and yes, do stand up. Recently there was a bumper sticker that said: "Being a citizen in a democracy is not a spectator sport."

Each day we are subjected to more pronouncements about "fake news." Sometimes we're told there are also "alternative facts." If writer George Orwell were alive, he'd have a field day with such terms. And so would Senator Daniel

Moynihan who advocated "people are entitled to their own opinions but not their own facts."

Those interested in accuracy have found President Trump making statements that are purely inaccurate and often outright untruths. Then, when asked about them he waltzes around and denies having said them. The hope is we're all too busy to keep up with his statements and to dissect them. And the next day, more of his comments. How does one gather reliable verifiable facts on which to think clearly and to make sound decisions? This is extremely difficult because of the incessant barrage, especially from the national leader and his minions who put out all sorts of blatantly false information, confusing statements, and harmful remarks about others in our nation and elsewhere. What are his motives in doing this? Is he even aware of his disruptive bizarre linguistic comments?

We need to recognize it is President Trump who specializes in daily putting out "fake news" and "alternative facts." He constantly creates foolishness. He creates his own reality, spews it out, and then wants the rest of the nation to follow him. Or is he just playing us?

Here are just a few examples of his most recent distortions, crude and inexplicable behavior; each day he provides more examples:

1) Recently you received an e-mail from me documenting in detail 10 ways the current administration attacks civil rights, especially the most vulnerable and those needy citizens in our society. It was published by the Southern Poverty Law Center. Let's cite them again to refresh our memories: Promoting White Nationalism; Slashing Civil Rights Enforcement;

Reving Up the Deportation Machine; Banning Muslims; Attacking Voting Rights; Shredding LGBT Protections; Encouraging Police Abuses; Reviving Debtors' Prisons; Undermining Public Education; Eroding the Rights of Students with Disabilities. Are these indications of positive traditional democratic principles in our nation?

2) During the recent Senate hearings on Justice Brett Kavanaugh, President Trump repeatedly made statements to distort, confuse and defame the sensitive female individual who presented her remembrances of a traumatic experience involving this person. After the hearings and in his public speeches around the country he made fun of her and belittled her. How cruel and inappropriate. Equally puzzling are his public audiences who reflexively laughed and mocked her too, thereby endorsing further unkindness and silly comments from the president. Over the years, he has made all sorts of dehumanizing comments about women, and then he brags about how much he loves women. This is the President of the United States who behaves like a show business huckster comic and then denies he made fun of her (Interview with Leslie Stahl on Sunday, October 14th).

3) During the last Presidential campaign, then candidate Trump spoke about his income tax returns and told us they'd be released once the IRS audit was completed. Two years later and still there is no promulgation of his returns. Will he ever release them? See <u>The NY Times</u>, October 3rd and October 7th, 2018 "Trump Engaged in Suspect Tax Schemes As He Reaped Riches From His Father." There's available tax

procedures to legitimately reduce taxes; and then there's outright tax evasion and lying. Why is he so secretive and guarded about these returns? Is he afraid we'll find out more falsehoods about him and his behavior?

4) Since the years of Presidents Franklin D. Roosevelt and Harry Truman, even earlier presidents, American citizens have been promised a national health care system. We finally got one with President Obama, even though it has many flaws. Since then the Republicans have creatively worked to destroy it. President Trump has promised to get rid of it and continues to do so.

Where are we, <u>Family and Friends</u>? Do we become immune to the <u>incessant barrage of lies and hurts President Trump spreads around</u>? Are we so preoccupied with our individual lives we neglect our critical roles as citizens in our democracy and avoid involvement? If this happens on a broader scale, our democracy is in jeopardy, it can slip away and eventually it will be gone. There are no guarantees democracies prevail; to date, ours remains because it has been guarded and nurtured, even with its faults. The historical tendency is for autocracies and dictatorships to survive. There might be differences between these two, but ultimately they destroy us. Why does President Trump expend so much energy criticizing and degrading our allies' leadership while remaining silent or condescending to global dictators? You must speak up; you must vote; you must be an active and informed citizen who cares about others. And strive to identify reputable sources of information so you can evaluate the material being presented. We all need to pay attention.

References:

How Democracies Die, Steven Levitsky and Daniel Ziblatt

Fear - Trump in the White House, Bob Woodward

These Truths - A History of the United States, Jill Lepore

LETTER TO THE MUZIO FAMILY

Hello Muzios:

Today it is raining and cold and we're all indoors because of a pandemic in which the world and our lives have been changed. I decided to write a piece about my parents and my sister and wanted to share it with you all. Here it is:

Please review these following dates. As you might see, there are a couple of relationships between them.

My father, Frank (no middle name) Muzio was born on February 28, 1891 and died on April 27, 1958; my mother, Phyllis Brancata Muzio was born on January 21, 1903 and died on May 29, 1985; and my sister, Maria Delores Muzio (later on Russell) was born on January 29, 1930 and died on May 22, 2000.

You'll note all three individuals were born in the winter; and all died in the spring.

On April 27, 1958, I was with my father Frank at the Veteran's Hospital in New York City. It was raining and cold and I rushed over there from the New York Naval Shipyard in Brooklyn, where I was stationed as a USMC First

Lieutenant. When I got there he was barely alive, he was in a coma; he died while I held his hand. I stayed with him in the silence of the room for what seemed like a long time, and then went outside and told a nurse he was dead. It's just 62 years ago, yet I remember it as if it occurred this morning.

When my mother died on May 29, 1985, I'd received this information from Aunt Rose while I was at the college in Brooklyn. Immediately I drove to her apartment in Holliswood, Queens. In her apartment there was Aunt Rose in tears, a physician, and a police officer. Rose told me my mother was on the floor of her small bathroom, she was about to take a bath and had collapsed on the floor; and when Rose found her she had discreetly put some clothes on her. I went in the bathroom, closed the door and got on the floor and held my mother in my arms for awhile. That was just about 35 years ago, yet I remember it as if it took place early this morning.

When my sister Maria died on May 22, 2000, I was driving through the Brooklyn Battery Tunnel on my way to the college and got a phone call from Bernie Russell, my sister's husband of almost 50 years telling me she'd died. Then, I asked him to put David Owen Russell on the phone because Bernie told me David had taken pictures of my sister and I couldn't understand why he would do this. I recall screaming at him, while driving through the tunnel, veering across the double line in the middle of it. That was just almost 20 years ago, yet I remember it as if it was just taking place today.

These three individuals were the essence of my life from birth and childhood on. Most of my remembered childhood experiences involved them, along with others long forgotten or unnoticed. Each one of them loved me, gave me support and energy, and in so many ways shaped me and contributed to the person I became and have become. All three are obviously gone a long time; but they are still with me. They are within me, and I think about them each day if only for a fleeting moment.

Why am I telling you this? Someone once said "your memories are your life." (I don't recall who said this.) I wanted you to know about these memories too. My life memories continue to be formed along with each of you as I journey along. You give me love, concern, attention, even humor and bring positive dimensions to me; I am so blessed by all you do for me.

Thank you on this cold and rainy April day. Be safe.

2020

STATE OF THE UNION ADDRESS

L AST week, President Trump gave his third State of the Union Address. At this address Trump in a showboat way had the Presidential Medal of Freedom put around columnist Rush Limbaugh's neck by Milania Trump. Earlier recipients of this prestigious medal: Mother Teresa, Rosa Parks and Elie Wiesel. For some of Limbaugh's outrageous, inflammatory and inaccurate comments on a variety of topics, please see <u>The New York Times Review</u>, February 9, 2020, page 2.

No matter which president delivers these addresses, it is important to check them out for their truthfulness and accuracy. Since according to various reputable sources fact-checking his public statements, President Trump has told 16,000 (that's right) lies, misrepresentations and outright distortions since being in office. Keep in mind it was Josef Goebbels, Hitler's Minister of Propaganda who once stated: "If you tell a lie big enough and keep repeating it, people will eventually come to believe it."

PolitiFact - Fact-checking Donald Trump's 2020 State of the Union address –

https://www.politifact.com/article/2020/feb/05/fact-checking-2020-state-union-address/

https://www.psychologytoday.com/us/blog/mind-in-the-machine/201812/complete-psychological-analysis-trumps-support?fbclid=IwAR3Sed8-oYyibvbIelqU4zcV4-GsUVyBU_UTowtqX-ZPye-DnZBt4mbArZ0

While these are the beliefs of only one psychologist, other groups of psychiatrists and therapists have provided their interpretations of President Trump's traits and behaviors.

Please note it was before The Mueller Report was released or the more recent Impeachment process that occurred in Trump's "acquittal":

On late Friday, February 7th, Trump began to force removal of any who testified against him under oath in the Impeachment Hearings, with others having already resigned or retired, too. He believes in superimposed punishment delivered quickly and without explanation. He is a strong advocate of destroying those about him, and thus imparts fear, spite and danger to the non-adoring. Historically, one wonders why anyone with integrity and strong character would work with him or for him, no less disregard his continually aberrant behaviors as he goes about lying and hurting others.

Is there any reasonable explanation for voters who continue to support him? Do they honestly believe he is a sound, intelligent, caring leader for our country? Why does he beguile some voters? Are they too, just as Trump seeking a less compassionate, preferably more White, and environmentally ignorant society that focus simply on money, materialism, and show business qualities? Will somebody, anybody, please provide a cogent explanation of what is going on in America?

Just before the 2016 presidential election, I wrote an essay for my website www.joemuzio.com. It's titled Trump the Thug. In February, 2017 a second piece President Trump was also provided. Now into the third year of Trump's term we are continually exposed to his gross examples of inappropriate leadership, massive resignations or removals of officials, statements defiling individuals and groups, lies and highly questionable policy decisions. There were 7 days in January 2020 where the United States was almost drawn into an ill-conceived war in the Middle East, potentially causing the losses of many of our military service personnel's lives along with other individuals. We've been in military combat in Afghanistan for 18 years without resolution. How much more chaos, deceit and poor performances do we need? It is entirely possible our democracy cannot endure and we will become an authoritarian state.

In the February 3, 2020 The New Yorker, Jill Lepore, a professor of history and author has written a fine piece, "In Every Dark Hour - In the thirties, democracy's survival was in question. What was our answer?" (pages 20 - 24). Here is an excerpt of her writing:

> "American democracy in the twenty-first century is withering. The Democracy Index rates a hundred and sixty-seven countries, every year, on a scale that ranges from 'full democracy' to 'authoritarian regime.' In 2006, the U.S. was a 'full democracy, the seventeenth

most democratic nation in the world. In 2016, the index for the first time rated the United States a 'flawed democracy,' and since then American democracy has gotten only more flawed. True, the United States still doesn't have Rome or a Berlin to march on. That hasn't saved the nation from misinformation, tribalization, domestic terrorism, human-rights abuses, political intolerance, social-media mob rule, white nationalism, a criminal President, the hobbling of Congress, a corrupt Presidential administration, assaults on the press, crippling polarization, the undermining of elections, and an epistemological chaos that is the only air that totalitarianism can breathe."

You are encouraged to read the entire article.

This is a mighty powerful and telling statement. Is this the kind of country we want to live on? I hope not. Be involved, be active, pay attention and stand up.

2020

TRIP TO THE FLORIDA KEYS

I N February, Lois and I flew to Florida. We rented a car and drove from Fort Lauderdale down a portion of the Florida Keys to Marathon, halfway to the southern end of Key West to attend a surprise 80th birthday party for her sister Ellen. Relatives and close friends journeyed there from around the country to honor Ellen. With a few exceptions, most of the relatives and friends were essentially unknown to us, although Lois had met with some of them on her trips to Florida and another time to Wisconsin. As expected, all were directly connected to Ellen, her children and their children, and their mutual friends. We were there for several days before returning home.

Why am I telling you about this now in May, well after the event? Because Lois, Ellen and I had an unusual experience at a Cuban restaurant in Marathon, midway on the various islands that make up the Keys. We went out for lunch, just the three of us. By sheer accident, this random brief experience with a large group of strangers with whom we met, spoke, and interacted with civility and generosity, and then parted, knowing it would be unlikely we'll ever meet again.

Based on an ad we'd seen on the Internet, we selected a Cuban restaurant on Route 1, the road that extends from northern Maine to its end in Key West. We turned into it. As we pulled into it, we noticed about 15-20 motorcycles spread out in the parking lot, with more behind the restaurant; and with them a group of men and women hanging around and chatting with one another. All the motorcycles lined up were massive, fully outfitted, shiny Harley Davidsons; no Hondas; no Kawaskis; and no BMWs or Ducatis, just those high end, bulky polished Harleys with all sorts of communication equipment and dials on them.

At first glance the people look like most biker groups, dressed heavily in black leather outfits, somewhat older, about 45-65 age bracket, and with a variety of insignias on their jackets; with one exception, a young man of about 20 or so who he had a striking resemblance to one of the older bikers. Many of the men wore distinctive caps with Harley Davidson insignias on them, some even wore Harley T-shirts. The women with them, those with their own motorcycles or the ones who'd be riding with their male partners also were dressed similarly, some in tight jeans and with high heels. (Lois noted these high heels were "6 inch spikes" but we never measured them.) They had scarves around their necks and their hair was pulled back away from their faces. Some of the men and a few women were smoking what seemed to be Cuban cigars as they stood around. Near these motorcycles and accompanying them was a Jeep station wagon with the backdoor wide open and a metal cage; there were two women standing near it with a leashed, healthy and heavy bulldog. I'll come back to the bulldog later.

As we looked over this crowded parking lot, it was suggested perhaps I should go into the restaurant and check it out. Ellen, who'd worked in the Florida Vehicular Registry for many years looked over the motorcyclists, and based on her experiences with similar groups felt quite comfortable in assessing their behaviors. She said: "they were fine," although this term did not necessarily clarify what she meant.

Lois and Ellen went into the restaurant, the chef held the side-door open for them. I impulsively decided to check out the bikers before going in. I noticed a biker whose black leather jacket had a United States Marine Corps symbol on it, the well-known intermeshed globe, anchor and eagle; along with the bulldog with them led to my wanting to talk with him. Lois and Ellen sat at a table directly looking out on the parking lot, the motorcycles, the riders, the Jeep and the bulldog cared for by the two women.

This tall, slender biker was now talking to several of his buddies and checked me out as I was walking towards him. I was wearing my baseball cap with the same USMC symbol on it. He turned to some of the other bikers and invited several to join him as he approached. He yelled out something about "having been in the Corps." It turned out we had all been in the USMC at different times and years. Some served in Vietnam. About 5 or 6 of us stood together in the parking lot amidst the Harleys.

When former Marines meet or recognize another Marine because most of all wear some article of clothing, a cap or a Marine emblem, there's a certain bonding that almost automatically takes place. We greet one another with "Semper Fidelis" (Always Faithful), or to call one another "Buddy." This is then followed with a series of curious questions: "When were you in?" "How Long?" "Where were you stationed?" "What was your military occupation?" We see ourselves as brothers, no matter where or when we served.

Since all Marines have gone through rigorous, often punishing boot camp, and most probably had been intense, perhaps more than that, drill instructors who specialized in chronic harassment of those in their recruit units, the commonality of these experiences promotes bonding and recollecting right then and there. (Not every recruit who starts boot camp succeeds, some "wash out" for a variety of reasons.) Stories are quickly told to provide clear evidence of just how nasty and thorough these drill instructors were to make us into hard-charging, no nonsense Marines.

In all of these bonding encounters, I've never met anyone who didn't have vivid recollections of the perpetual harassments, the demanding drill instructors, sometimes sadistic who were relentless in their vigorous efforts to shape innocent and undisciplined civilians into mentally and physically prepared Marines. These recollections never quite captured the dimensions of what had taken place, but they are striking similar and never forgotten, including their possible exaggerations and embellishments. According to the Recruitment posters, the Marine Corps statements and the recollections, "the changes are forever" and they will remain with you forever. The Marine Corps history is banking on this.

As we continued chatting, the tall, thin former Marine commented about my cap: "That's a beautiful cap you're wearing," and I responded: "Do you really like it?" I took off my cap and handed it to him, saying: "I want you to have it." He said: "Oh, no, I couldn't accept it, it's yours." I then asked him what rank was he in the Corps, and he said: "I was a lance corporeal." I blurted out to him: "Well, I was a Captain, and I'm issuing you a direct order. You will accept this cap, or I will bring you up on charges." We both laughed, and I gave him my cap. In response, he took off his Harley Davidson cap and handed it to me, saying: "Then you have to take my cap," which I did, and put it on.

After having identified myself as a USMC officer, I detected a slight change in how my new-found buddies spoke to me. One or two of them referred to me as "Sir." I suggested they didn't have to do that, and they nodded.

At the suggestion of these cyclists, they thought we should take a picture, and they decided to help me on to one of their Harleys. It was the first time I'd ever been on one. One of them called over to the two women who were with the bulldog and the Jeep and shouted to them "Bring the dog over." They did this. One of the women took our picture, me on the Harley, surrounded by the other Marines and the bulldog. When my sister-in-law Ellen saw this from the restaurant, she came out and she took several pictures, too. Here's one of the pictures taken:

As for the accompanying bulldog, its significance is it's the mascot of the USMC. The bulldog for its overall size and musculature is a fierce, persistent, powerful animal. It's so strong it can bring down a massive bull when it leaps on to the neck of the bull and digs its lower jaw deeper into the bull's neck as the bull struggles to shake it off. The bulldog never quits; just like the USMC, it never yields, never gives up. It symbolizes the history of the USMC in training and in battle. Think of the bulldog and you think of the Marine Corps.

The bikers had been at the restaurant for awhile; and it was time to go. Just before leaving, the tall person I'd given my cap to came back to me by himself. He'd noticed my name "MUZIO" had been stenciled on the lower portion of the bill of the cap. Even though I'd been long out of the Marine Corps, typically with a magic marker you stencil your last name on the lid of caps. He asked me: "Is this your name?" Of course, I said "yes." He stared at me and said: "I won't forget you." We both smiled. One of us, I can't recall which of us, said: "Semper Fidelis," and the other repeated it. Then, he went back to his friends and his bike.

Somehow, they quietly and without anybody signaling, began to mount their Harleys. The two women put the bulldog back in the cage and almost simultaneously, all of the cyclists started their bikes. It was a combined overwhelming start-up roar, as they adjusted their facial scarves, which kept the dust off their faces, zipped up their leather jackets, with some putting on their helmets, although most of them didn't wear helmets, or have them.

They were ready to go; led by an older or the oldest person the column moved ahead; in a single file each bike followed behind that individual senior. As they took off, Harley engines roared increasingly, louder than a jet plane. It looked like a ballet row of dancers, with the Jeep and the two women and the bulldog in the cage bringing up the rear. One by one, they carefully entered Route 1 heading north back to Miami from where they'd come from. They'd been on a day trip from there. I went back into the Cuban restaurant and joined Lois and Ellen; we finished our lunch, and talked about what had happened in that parking lot.

2020

THE UPCOMING PRESIDENTIAL ELECTION

W ITHIN a couple of months we will select the next President of the United States. Some believe this will be one of the more important elections in a long time. Why? Because we've just been through a presidency of chaos, hate, extremism and thousands of fact-checked lies. To date, more than 180,000 people have died from Covid19, and 6 million have had the lethal virus in our country. Millions are currently unemployed; many businesses probably will never re-open during this supposedly outstanding economic; and schools across the nation have been unable to function for learning, teaching and research without great difficulty if at all. For many months our nation has been living under great stress to its citizens. Despite false promises, preventative vaccines require time and lengthy investigative processes before being rendered safe and effective before their availability. You get the picture, we are in deep trouble and so is our country.

You must be involved in the upcoming election process, no matter how difficult this has been made in certain areas of our country, and to be informed about the issues.

Enclosed is a copy of an American History professor's recent blog. She is Heather Cox Richardson of Boston College and provides references for her statements. It relates to the just completed Republican National Convention and the current occupant in the White House's behavior.

You can obtain her blog free by requesting it. It's quite informative and balanced.

Heather Cox Richardson–Letter From An American:

Lots of folks are finally paying attention to the rise of authoritarianism here in the U.S. They are right to be concerned.

Scholars have seen worrisome signs all along. Trump has dismissed nonpartisan career officials and replaced them with loyalists. He has fired the independent inspectors general. He denies Congress's right and duty to investigate members of the Executive Branch. He has used the Department of Homeland Security and other law enforcement officers of the Executive Branch as a private army. He has packed the courts. He has used the government to advance the interests of himself and his family, which he has installed into government positions. He has solicited help from foreign governments to get reelected. And he and his cronies are trying to undermine our election by preemptively saying the Democrats are committing fraud and by slowing down mail service when voters need to be able to mail in their ballots.

Now, Trump is clearly trying to change the national narrative from his disastrous response to the coronavirus and the economic crash to the idea that he alone can protect white Americans from their dangerous Black neighbors.

Stoking violence is a key tool in the authoritarian's toolkit. The idea is to increase civil disorder. As violence increases, people will turn to a leader who promises "LAW & ORDER," as Trump keeps tweeting. Once firmly in power, an authoritarian can then put down his opponents with the argument that they are dangerous criminals.

Trump is advancing just such a strategy. He and members of his administration refuse to condemn violence, and insist that legitimate protesters are all "Antifa." They are blaming Democrats and "liberal politicians and their incompetent policies" for violent protests, although most of the injuries at the protests have been caused by police or by rightwing thugs. They are stoking white people's fear of their Black neighbors, with Trump going so far as to talk of how he will keep low-income housing from the suburbs to protect the "Suburban Lifestyle Dream."

And they are going on the offensive, demanding that Democratic presidential nominee Joe Biden condemn the violence that they insist comes from protesters, while Trump is actually inciting it from rioters on the right. It is gaslighting at its finest.

America has seen this pattern before. Secessionist leaders before the Civil War needed badly to distract southern white farmers, who were falling behind in an economic system that concentrated wealth at the top, and they howled that northerners were assaulting white southerners and wanted to stamp out their way of life, based in human enslavement. They refused to permit any alternative information to reach their voters. And in the end, they succeeded in rallying their supporters to war."

But that does not have to happen here, now. We can see exactly what Trump is doing, and refuse to embrace it. Democratic leadership is calling out Trump for "willfully fanning the flames of this violence," as Representative Adam Schiff (D-CA) put it today.

Today Biden released a statement saying "the deadly violence we saw overnight in Portland is unacceptable. Shooting in the streets of a great American city is unacceptable. I condemn this violence unequivocally. I condemn violence of every kind by anyone, whether on the left or the right. And I challenge Donald Trump to do the same.... We must not become a country at war with ourselves. A country that accepts the killing of fellow Americans who do not agree with you. A country that vows vengeance toward one another...."

"As a country," he continued, "we must condemn the incitement of hate and resentment that led to this deadly clash.... What does President Trump think will happen when he continues to insist on fanning the flames of hate and division in our society and using the politics of fear to whip up his supporters? He is recklessly encouraging violence.... The job of a President is to lower the temperature. To bring people who disagree with one another together. To make life better for all Americans, not just those who agree with us, support us, or vote for us."

In Wisconsin, still reeling from the shooting of Jacob Blake in the back by law enforcement officers, the Lt. Governor cited Trump's "incendiary remarks" and attempts to create division and said that Trump should not come to Kenosha on Tuesday as he currently plans. Governor Tony Evers (D) agreed, as did Kenosha's mayor. Evers wrote: "I, along with other community leaders who have reached out, are concerned about what your presence will mean for Kenosha and our state. I am concerned your presence will only hinder our healing. I am concerned your presence will only delay our work to overcome division and move forward together."

It is important to remember that Trump's apparent power play is a desperate move.

More than 180,000 Americans have died of Covid-19 on his watch. We have far more deaths per capita than other advanced countries, and we still have no national testing program. The White House is now apparently taking the position that we will all just have to live with the disease and that schools and businesses should simply reopen, but Americans are not happy about Trump's handling of the corona virus. Today he tried to help his numbers by retweeting a thread from a far-right website saying that, in fact, only around 9000 people have died in the U.S. of Covid-19, because the rest had co-morbidities and were going to die anyway. The argument is so far off the mark that Twitter flagged it for violating rules.

Polls show Trump continuing to lag behind Biden by significant numbers. Fifty-nine percent of Americans disapproved of the programming at the Republican National Convention, and he saw no bounce from it. Trump's overall approval rating is a dismal 31%.

And Trump remains dogged by tell-all books and lawsuits that threaten to reveal criminality. Today, The New York Times ran a story by Michael S. Schmidt, a reporter covering national security and federal elections for the paper. Schmidt has a book coming out on Tuesday. It reveals that in 2017 former deputy Attorney General Rod Rosenstein limited Special Counsel Robert Mueller's investigation. Rosenstein kept Mueller from exploring Trump's own relationship with Russia while he was investigating Russia's efforts to get Trump elected and Trump's efforts to stop the inquiry. Rosenstein limited Mueller to conducting a criminal investigation and did not permit him to expand his inquiries.

Rosenstein did not tell the acting Director of the FBI, Andrew McCabe, that he had taken an investigation of Trump himself off the table, and McCabe did not realize it had happened. McCabe said that he was "surprised and disappointed" to hear this news, and had he known, he would have had the FBI do such an investigation "because we had information that indicated a national security threat might exist, specifically a counterintelligence threat involving the president and Russia. I expected that issue and issues related to it would be fully examined by the special counsel team." McCabe noted that the issue at hand "was first and foremost a counterintelligence case.... Could the president actually be the point of coordination between the campaign and the Russian government? Could the president actually be maintaining some sort of inappropriate relationship with our most significant adversary in the world?"

Meanwhile, Senator Tammy Duckworth is keeping a tally of how many days it's been since we learned that Russia offered bounties to Taliban-linked fighters for killing U.S. or allied soldiers in Afghanistan. Trump has refused to respond to that intelligence. Russian troops appear to be trying to pick a fight with U.S. soldiers in northeastern Syria, the region from which the U.S. abruptly withdrew last fall. After smaller incidents, on Tuesday, in a Russian convoy sideswiped a U.S. vehicle and a Russian helicopter buzzed the convoy. Seven U.S. soldiers were injured, none seriously. The Pentagon blamed Russian forces for "deliberately provocative and aggressive behavior." A bipartisan group of lawmakers called on the White House to "clearly communicate to the highest levels of the Russian government and military that actions like this will not be tolerated," but so far, Trump has said nothing.

<u>Notes</u>: Here are some additional references you might want to consider, too. These authors present a grim picture of Trump. You decide if you want him to be re-elected, based on the past almost 4 years. Do you want more of the same? Please pay attention and be informed.

https://www.nytimes.com/2020/08/30/us/politics/trump-russia-justice-department.html

https://www.politico.com/news/2020/08/27/us-russia-syria-troops-403721

https://mitchell.house.gov/media/press-releases/bipartisan-member-statement-condemning-russian-aggression-toward-us-troops

https://www.nytimes.com/2020/08/26/world/middleeast/pentagon-russia-syria.html

https://www.cnbc.com/2020/07/29/trump-suburban-voters-will-no-longer-be-bothered-by-low-income-housing.html

https://www.washingtonpost.com/opinions/2020/08/30/its-time-challenge-cockeyed-reaction-violence/

https://www.nytimes.com/2020/08/27/us/politics/biden-kamala-harris-speech-trump.html

https://www.cnbc.com/2020/08/30/biden-condemns-portland-violence-goes-after-trump.html

https://www.cnn.com/2020/08/30/politics/mandela-barnes-trump-kenosha-wisconsin-visit/index.html

https://www.washingtonpost.com/politics/white-house-convention-covid-testing/2020/08/27/44b53cda-e8c4-11ea-bc79-834454439a44_story.html

https://www.nytimes.com/2020/08/30/us/politics/trump-protests-violence-coronavirus.html

Additional References Provided by Muzio:

Evil Geniuses – The Unmaking of America, Kurt Anderson, New York, Random House, 2020.

True Crimes and Misdemeanors - The Investigation of Donald Trump, Jeffrey Toobin, New York, Doubleday, 2020.

Too Much and Never Enough - How My Family Created The World's Most Dangerous Man, Mary L. Trump, New York, Simon and Schuster, 2020.

2021

THREE EVENTS FROM MID-TWENTIETH CENTURY AMERICA

T HIS essay has three unique embryonic components. All three events occurred after World War II ended in August, 1945, the war to save democracy, just as World War I and other more recent wars were supposed to do. They are separated by time and distance, each about 10 years apart, and might even initially appear to be unconnected remote experiences. Their inevitable entwining might not be quickly obvious; their relationships will be spelled out.

Then, they can be put into a context of more recent widespread demonstrations of ongoing violence, hatred and racial discrimination in our country, particularly in the past 5 years or so. Such behaviors continue to exist today.

The first incident occurred in the spring of 1946. Two early teenagers from Sunnyside Queens impulsively hitchhiked to Washington, D.C. without their parents' permission and with minimal travel money. The second was in the spring of 1956 when two dear friends drove to Florida and saw something they'd never seen before on the back roads of Georgia. The third incident is related to an obituary in The New York Times on April 5th, 2021 concerning about an artist "Winfred Rembert, 75, Who Carved His Pain in Works of Art, Dies" (page D6). A terribly cruel and life-changing event occurred to him back in 1967 and it is described in the obituary.

The hitchhiking journey to Washington, D.C. was quite an adventure. We arrived there without much knowledge about the Capital area, unsure of what to do and uncertain where we'd stay. Somehow we started out in Union Station in D.C, spoke to a helpful volunteer at the Travelers' Aid booth and were given maps and information booklets about the many federal buildings and monument sites. We were touring our Capital.

There were water fountains in the station and also public bathroom facilities. When we approached them we immediately noticed signs designating different facilities for those of us who were "White only" and those for others called "Black," "Colored" or "non-White." Coming from the New York area, this was a moment of discovery; we'd never seen such signs before and were ignorant of their existence. We looked at each other and without question followed the instructions on the signs. After using these facilities we talked about how unusual, how strange such arrangements were. Then, we left Union Station and got on a bus, but when we did, as we'd started to sit in "the wrong area" we were told by the bus driver it was only for those who were "colored." We obediently moved to the designated exclusively "white" section, without questioning this.

All of this was a major new learning experience. The nation's Capital and the surrounding areas in our supposed democratic society, its buildings, monuments, and other institutions including public facilities functioned within a rigid, accepted segregated world with strict, silent compliance to disturbing (to us) procedures and regulations. Since we were 13 years old, we followed these rules, as did everybody else.

Wasn't everybody in our country free? No. Didn't we have a Declaration of Independence and a Constitution? Yes. Then why, how and did all of these historical humiliating restrictions exist to simultaneously deny other citizens of their rights and freedom? Were there "classes" of citizenry based on color?

The second incident unfolded also in the spring of 1956. One of us had just quit attending college and was taking a job in publishing in New York City; the other was leaving for the United States Marine Corps and shortly would be reporting for duty at Quantico, Virginia. They'd been buddies at college and although neither of us said this, we knew it would be one of the last times we'd spend unencumbered time together

On their way to Florida there was a planned stop in Asheville, North Carolina for a visit to the home of Thomas E. Wolfe, an American author who'd died shortly before his 38th birthday. Both of these young men had read his books, his plays, short stories, letters to his mother, and a couple of biographies. We were students and admirers of Thomas E. Wolfe. While on the trip, there was much chatter about Wolfe and our beliefs in his writings.

As we traveled south we would periodically stop and go off onto less trafficked roads. Sometimes we would get out and do some physical exercises; since one of us was going into the Marine Corps in about a month, there was desire to work out and be sure he was well prepared for the upcoming rigorous military training. From various sources he knew this would be a difficult and physically challenging experience, unlike any other training procedures.

While moving through Georgia, we decided to take another journey off the regular highway. After traveling several miles on a back road, and after viewing many farms and open spaces, as we went around a curve we came upon a scene neither of us had ever seen. It was a group of about 8 or 9 black men working on the side of the road. They were in drab dirty perhaps stripped prison clothing. Every 2-3 feet, these men were chained to each other at the ankles. They were repairing the road, and were being watched by a heavy white guard sitting on a horse and with a double-barrel shotgun right in front of him, resting across his Western saddle. We slowed down, some of the prisoners looked up at us, as did the guard. They stared at us, we stared at them. No words were spoken, just glances between those in the field and us. As we drove away slowly the guard continued to look at us, expressionless.

We drove about a quarter mile or so around a curve and then pulled over off the road and stopped. We just sat there and looked at each other; then we both spoke simultaneously. "How could this be?" "Why are they chained together?" "Is this America?" "What's going on?" Afterwards we were quiet, we didn't talk for awhile. Sixty something years later and still this scene is with me. Once in awhile my mind wanders to this matter and I think about what happened to the lives of the then-chained men and that guard on horseback.

The third event in this sequence is the obituary mentioned above as it appeared in The New York Times. It involves a near lynching that took place in rural Georgia. If you're curious about the depth and breadth of this individual's journey covering the course of his life events, you can look them up in the obituary. Only the bare details relevant to this writing will be focused upon.

Winfred Rembert died at 75. In 1967, when Rembert was 21, he almost got lynched in Georgia by an angry white mob. He was stripped of his clothing, hoisted up by his ankles. One of the white men in this mob took a knife to him and tried to castrate him; blood was pouring from his groin area. While this was going on, another white man used the "N" word and somehow convinced the rest of the mob to get him back in the jail from where he'd escaped. Rembert then did 7 years in prison with hard labor.

After being damaged and released, he moved on with his life, marrying, moving away from the South, helping to raise a family with 8 children, and eventually settling in New Haven, Connecticut. Over time, Rembert became an accomplished and respected artist. There have been many exhibitions of his creative works throughout our nation. But his earlier near lynching experience remained with Rembert forever. His inclusive artistic themes focus on growing up in the segregated South, the persistence of untoward memories and earlier life experiences there, and his harsh and tragic prison experiences. They are clearly present in his memories and art.

Historians and other scholars have written about the many lynchings of Black men by angry stirred up white mobs. There have also been lynchings and abuses of other minority groups in American history. Paradoxically, the bulk of these earlier murders have never been investigated or prosecuted through local and federal law enforcement and judicial systems. In more recent years, lynchings and other shameful discriminatory events have been curtailed, sometimes adjudicated, although various forms of subtle and public discrimination persist throughout our nation.

In recent years, particularly the past 4-5 years, there has been a decided uptick in hate, violence and lawlessness activities. On January 6th, 2021 an out-of-control mob stormed the Capital to disrupt legal election procedures and harm others. They'd been stimulated by a defeated and bizarre president who spent 77 days subverting the national election results. So, he created and perpetuated the "big election lie" propaganda, while he simultaneously had totally ignored the international pandemic as citizens suffered and thousands died.

Gradually, these invading insurrectionist rioters are being identified and hundreds have already been brought into Federal courts and charged. If they were morally responsible citizens, and believed democratic principles, they would simply turn themselves in to the authorities and cope with the consequences regarding their illegal destructive actions. If they don't, they are just criminal cowards hiding in a mob.

We are not citizens in some banana republic; or a genetically endowed cult of exclusionary Anglo-Saxons, a code term for "Whites Only." We are a remarkably diverse population constantly changing over generations in an evolving democracy based on Constitutional laws and guided by principles and procedures. Can more recent hate and extremism activities morph into even more criminal and abusive events by individuals and incited thoughtless mobs to deny the rest of us our rights? The author E.B. White reminds us: "In doubtful, doubting days, national morality tends to slip and slide toward a condition in which the test of a man's honor is his zeal for discovering dishonor in another."

Will our democracy, this more than two centuries plus 44 years old experiment in freedom and diverse change, coupled with all its flaws and disappointments endure when distortions, lies and false tales promote more violence and hold us in their senseless grip? This will depend on delicate time and unpredictable circumstances as to whether we have the moral courage, sensitive intelligence and integrity to shape our nation's format as a sustaining viable democracy. We all need to pay attention. Otherwise, there will be no democracy.

References:

Documentary Film: "All Me: The Life and Times of Winfred Rembert" (2011).

Memoir: Chasing Me to My Grave: An Artist's Memoir of the Jim Crow South. Wilfred Rembert, collaborated with Erin I. Kelly.

The New York Times Obituaries, April 5, 2021: "Wilfred Rembert, 75, Who Carved His Pain In Works of Art, Dies," Katharine Q. Seelye, page D6.

IlanStavans (Ed.) Becoming Americans-Four Centuries of Immigrant Writing, New York, The Library of America, 2009.

Charles M. Blow, "America Is Still Racist," The New York Times Opinion, May 3, 2021, page A23.

On Democracy, Collection of Essays, edited by Martha White, New York, Harper Collins, 2019.

The Year of Hate and Extremism 2020 – A Report from the Southern Poverty Law Center, Montgomery, AL. 36104. (Earlier years on the same topic are available from this organization.)

"77 Days: Trump's Campaign to Subvert the Election". <u>The New York Times</u>, February 1, 2021.

<u>The Constitution of the United States</u>. (Readily available through the National Center for Constitutional Studies (Phone: 208-645-2625).

Amendment XV, ratified February 3, 1870: Section 1. The right of citizens of the United States to vote shall not be denied or abridged by the United States or by any State on account of race, color, or previous condition of servitude. Section 2: The Congress shall have power to enforce this article by appropriate legislation.

2021

LIFE OVER DEATH

I N the <u>November 16th 2021 Science Section</u> of T<u>he New York Times</u> there's an article titled <u>Healing Messengers</u>. It's about our combat veterans who have severe life changing injuries, pain, stress, depression and suicidal thoughts, the deleterious aftereffects of their military experiences.

At the start of this article is a large strikingly photograph of a relatively young man (33) on a beach in California. The veteran in the picture is missing an entire arm and the lower portion of his other arm. At first glance, the viewer might think his legs are buried into the sand, deeply obscured from view. But he has no legs beneath the visible surface. Along with his other bodily damages they were lost via a horrible explosion in combat.

We can only remind ourselves of the thousands of surviving lives of these military veterans and their immediate families. Through their individual and group efforts, they have expressed strong interests in having access to legal psychedelic drugs to relieve their chronic suffering. These veterans are hardly the exploratory adventuresome drug users of the 1960s and 1970s who sought exciting "trips" with LSD, psilocybin, "Ecstasy" (MDMA) and other hallucinogenic agents.

Despite everything, they choose life over death. As they continue to live out their lives, they seek relief from their mental/physical pain and agony. Some universities are researching the positive effects of hallucinogenic agents, see https://med.stanford.edu/spsg/about.html. Recently, a few cities and states (such as Oregon and Washington, D.C.) are passing legislation to provide legal psychedelic drugs to them, but it is spotty. The total number of veterans with such life-changing injuries is difficult to determine. With our continual engagements in global battles, the figure could be quite high. Again and again young men and women are sacrificed in exchange for questionable political/ military decisions as our country continues to sustain world dominance.

Since September 11, 2001 about 31,000 service veterans have committed suicide. This is about 4 times those who died in actual battles since in Iraq, Afghanistan and elsewhere. Did multiple tours in combat and their battle experiences contribute to their bodies, minds and spirits being so irreparably damaged? The existing mystery for such individuals, their families and governmental agencies along with advocacy groups concerned about them is related to why have so many chosen to end their lives?

The underlying issue is: Why can't they have legally provided psychedelic drugs? Perhaps these psychedelic drugs would positively influence them before some despairingly commit suicide. Wouldn't that be a fine gift to them? Those who served in the military went off as whole humans; some returned as portions of who they once were, and so many never came back.

Here's a concluding quote by <u>Jose Martinez, the veteran Army Ranger from California</u> cited above and whose picture is described in this essay: "Psychedelics helped me realize that my problems are small compared to the world's bigger problems like starvation and cancer. And now I understand what I'm actually here for in this world, which is to make people smile and to remind them that life can be beautiful even when it's not so easy."

Maybe you want to take a look at Jose Martinez's picture in <u>The New York Times</u> article. It's a pure manifestation of his will and commitment to stay alive. Recently, our federal legislators approved $780 billion for the military. How about more money for those military servicemen and servicewoman who served and remain forever maimed? Do you believe those who fought for us can be given medical services and research programs to offset and ease the tragic destructive outcomes of their military injuries? What can <u>we</u> as individuals do about this matter? Be informed citizens. Pay attention. Seek out clarifying information from the Department of Veteran's Affairs and various Veterans' support groups (some are cited in <u>The New York Times</u> article). Pressure our state and national legislators who ultimately decide the funding and programs for such issues; the majority of whom have not served in the military.

<u>Suggested Recent Readings:</u>

<u>Man's Search for Meaning,</u> Vikktor E. Frankl

<u>It Can't Happen Here</u>, Sinclair Lewis

Printed in the United States
by Baker & Taylor Publisher Services